Studies in Interactional Sociolinguistics 6

General Editor: John J. Gumperz

Talking voices

Repetition, dialogue, and imagery in conversational discourse

Companions to this volume

Discourse strategies John J. Gumperz
Language and social identity edited by John J. Gumperz
The social construction of literacy edited by Jenny Cook-Gumperz
Politeness: some universals in language usage by Penelope Brown
    and Stephen C. Levinson
Discourse markers by Deborah Schiffrin

Talking voices

Repetition, dialogue, and imagery in conversational discourse

DEBORAH TANNEN

Department of Linguistics
Georgetown University

CAMBRIDGE
UNIVERSITY PRESS

Published by the Press Syndicate of the University of Cambridge
The Pitt Building, Trumpington Street, Cambridge CB2 1RP
40 West 20th Street, New York, NY 10011–4211, USA
10 Stamford Road, Oakleigh, Melbourne 3166, Australia

First published 1989
Reprinted 1991, 1992, 1994, 1996, 1999

British Library cataloguing in publication data
Tannen, Deborah
Talking voices: repetition, dialogue,
and imagery in conversational discourse. –
(Studies in interactional sociolinguistics)
1. Sociolinguistics
I. Title   II. Series
401',9

Library of Congress cataloguing in publication data
Tannen, Deborah
Talking voices: repetition, dialogue,
and imagery in conversational discourse / Deborah Tannen.
    p.   cm. – (Studies in interactional sociolinguistics; 6)
Bibliography.
Includes index.
ISBN 0 521 37001 9. – ISBN 0 521 37900 8 (pbk).
1. Conversation.   I. Title   II. Series
P95.45.T3635   1989
001.54'2 – dc19   89–510   CIP

ISBN 0 521 37001 9 hardback
ISBN 0 521 37900 8 paperback

Transferred to digital printing 2000

For Michael
now and from now on

Contents

Acknowledgments

To A. L. Becker and Paul Friedrich I owe an immense debt. They read and commented on many drafts as this work changed shape, and they and Ed Finegan read and commented on the entire pre-final manuscript. David Bleich, Wallace Chafe, Ralph Fasold, Barbara Johnstone, Michael Macovski, and Deborah Schiffrin read and commented on drafts of parts. This book is improved by all these gifts of time and attention, though it doubtless includes much with which each of these colleagues would disagree.

I am grateful, now as always, to my teachers at the University of California, Berkeley: Wallace Chafe, John Gumperz, and Robin Lakoff. No finer program, no richer environment for studying linguistics could I have been lucky enough to find.

I thank the friends and strangers who offered me their talk, letting me tape and analyze them. (Their various discourses are named and explained, along with other sources of examples, in Appendix I.) Some of those who have been helpful in other ways are Diane Hunter Bickers, Nils Erik Enkvist, Tom Fox, Hartmut Haberland, Paul Hopper, Christina Kakava, Fileni Kalou, X. J. Kennedy, Sharon March, John Ohala, Ilana Papele, Dan Read, Maria Spanos, and Jackie Tanner. I have benefited from discussions of Bakhtin with Ray McDermott and Mirna Velčić.

I began work on this project with the support of a Rockefeller Humanities Fellowship and continued and completed it with support from the National Endowment for the Humanities. I remain deeply grateful for these invaluable periods of uninterrupted research time. At the National Endowment for the Humanities, I owe special thanks to my unusually dedicated and able project officer, David Wise. A significant part of the writing was done while I was on sabbatical leave from Georgetown University and a Visiting Researcher at Teachers College, Columbia University. I thank Georgetown for the sabbatical leave and Lambros Comitas and the Teachers College Joint Program in Applied Anthropology for affiliation during that leave.

The author and publisher gratefully acknowledge permission to reproduce extracts from the following:

Stardust memories by Woody Allen. © 1980, United Artists Corporation, all rights reserved. Reprinted by permission of the author and United Artists Corporation.

Our own metaphor by Mary Catherine Bateson. Reprinted by permission of the author.

"Animals and us" by S. J. Gould. Reprinted with permission from *The New York Review of Books* Copyright © 1988 Nyrev, Inc.

Fly away home by Marge Piercy (Fawcett). Reprinted by permission of Simon and Schuster.

The birthday party by Harold Pinter. Copyright © 1959, 1987 by Harold Pinter. Used by permission of Methuen, London, and Grove Press, a division of Wheatland Corporation.

The journals of Sylvia Plath by Sylvia Plath. Copyright © 1982 by Ted Hughes as Executor of the estate of Sylvia Plath. Reprinted by permission of Doubleday, a division of Bantam, Doubleday, Dell Publishing Group, Inc.

Awakenings (E. P. Dutton), *The man who mistook his wife for a hat* (Simon and Schuster), and 'Tics', *The New York Review of Books*, by Oliver Sacks. Reprinted by permission of the author.

Household words by Joan Silber. Copyright © 1976, 1980 by Joan Silber. All rights reserved. Reprinted by permission of Viking Penguin Inc. and the author.

One writer's beginnings by Eudora Welty. Reprinted by permission of Harvard University Press.

1

Introduction

The central idea of this book is that ordinary conversation is made up of linguistic strategies that have been thought quintessentially literary. These strategies, which are shaped and elaborated in literary discourse, are pervasive, spontaneous, and functional in ordinary conversation. I call them "involvement strategies" because, I argue, they reflect and simultaneously create interpersonal involvement.

The field of literary scholarship has examined in depth the language of literary discourse. An understanding of the language of everyday conversation is needed as a basis for that, as well as for linguistic scholarship. Although the analysis of conversation is a burgeoning field, for the most part it has been carried out by sociologists and anthropologists more interested in social and cultural processes than in language *per se*. Without devaluing this rich and enriching body of research, much of which is cited in this book, I believe there is plenty of room in the field of conversation analysis for linguists to join in, and a need for the special attention to and knowledge about language which linguists are trained to bring to their subject.

Overview of chapters

The core of analysis in this book is to be found in chapters 3 through 5. Each of these chapters is devoted to exploring a single involvement strategy. Chapter 3 is about repetition, with particular emphasis on the repetition of words and phrases in multi-party casual conversation. Chapter 4 is about "constructed dialogue": the animation of speech framed as a voice other than the speaker's, with emphasis on stories told in conversation. Chapter 5 explores imagery, in particular the images that are evoked by graphic detail, in conversation and a number of other genres. The concluding chapter 6 shows the elaborated interplay of the involvement strategies examined here, plus others, in two artful genres: a novelistic report of a scholarly conference and a political speech modeled on the African-American sermon.

In a sense, repetition underlies all the strategies explored here. That is why chapter 3, entitled "Repetition," is the first and longest of the chapters exploring particular involvement strategies. Whereas chapter 3 concerns synchronic repetition: the recurrence of words and collocations of words in the same discourse, chapter 4 concerns diachronic repetition: the recurrence (or, as I argue, the appearance of recurrence) of words in discourse which occurs at a later time. If dialogue is verbal repetition, then imagery, discussed in chapter 5, is visual repetition: the depiction in current discourse of previously experienced visual impressions, things and people seen rather than heard.[1]

The three central chapters, and the book, move from conversational to more deliberately composed genres. This reflects the progression I posit: that conversational discourse provides the source for strategies which are taken up by other, including literary, genres, both spoken and written. Analysis of conversational discourse is the basis of the book and constitutes by far the largest part of it. But briefly at the ends of chapters 3 and 4, at length in chapter 5, and exclusively in chapter 6 I analyze examples of artfully elaborated speaking and writing that use involvement strategies basic to conversation.

Chapter 2, "Involvement in discourse," discusses the concept of involvement and the sources of my understanding and use of it. I then turn to discussing two ways that involvement is created in language: sound and sense. By means of the sound or music of language, hearers and readers are rhythmically involved; at the same time, they are involved by participating in the making of meaning. Then I list and briefly illustrate a range of involvement strategies that work in these two ways. Following this, to specify how linguistic strategies create involvement in discourse, I explore the essentially scenic and musical nature of thought, experience, and discourse. This discussion also emphasizes the association of scenes and music with emotion.

The ordering of the three chapters examining particular involvement strategies, from repetition, to dialogue, to imagery and details, is in a way a movement from relative focus on the music of
language to relative focus on meaning, from sound to sense. Repetition is powerfully musical in effect, as repeated forms establish
rhythmic patterns. Dialogue palpably embodies both; the meaning
expressed is inseparable from the sounds of voices animated, the
sounds and rhythms of speech. Imagery and details are primarily a
matter of meaning, as words create visual representations of objects, people, and scenes in which they interact, although they are
expressed in verbal forms which have sound and shape.

Chapter 3, "Repetition in conversation," focuses on repetition
and variation of words, phrases and clauses, with briefer reference
to phonological and prosodic repetition, in conversation. It begins
with a discussion of the implications of the analysis of repetition for
linguistic theory, suggesting that repetition is at the heart not only
of how a particular discourse is created, but how discourse itself is
created. I discuss what has been called "prepatterning," "formulaicity," or "idiomaticity": the many ways that any current utterance
can be seen as repeating prior utterances. I begin analysis of repetition by reference to prior research. I then suggest that syntactic
repetition functions in conversation in production, comprehension,
connection, and interaction, and that the congruence of these functions contributes to a fifth, overriding function in conversational
coherence. I consider the conventional wisdom by which repetition
in conversation is viewed as undesirable. Preparatory to more extensive illustration of repetition in numerous short conversational
excerpts, I illustrate the pervasiveness of repetition in conversation
and give a sense of the range of forms it can take. I then systemati-
cally survey types and functions of repetition by adducing numerous short examples from an extended dinner table conversation. In
the next section, I demonstrate a range of forms of repetition operating simultaneously in a single short segment from this conversation and then briefly consider how uses of repetition reflect
individual and cultural differences. I next present examples of repetition in excerpts from other discourse types: public speaking (a
scholarly talk compared with the published version of the same
talk), oratory, and drama. Finally, I demonstrate the automaticity
of repetition and discuss neurological evidence for a basic human

drive to imitate and repeat. I explore the purpose served by this
drive and the significance of automaticity for an understanding of
involvement in discourse and of language.

In chapter 4, "Constructing dialogue in conversation," I question the term "reported speech" and claim instead that language
framed as dialogue is always constructed dialogue, a creation for
which the speaker bears full responsibility and credit. To demonstrate this, I begin by considering examples of reported criticism in
everyday conversation. I then discuss the significance of dialogue in
discourse in general and in storytelling in particular. Next I present
examples of constructed dialogue from a collection of tape
recorded, transcribed conversational narratives in order to demonstrate that what is framed as dialogue is not a "report" at all because it was never spoken by anyone. If constructed dialogue does
not report speech, what then does it do? To answer this question,
I look closely at three different types of narratives which make use
of constructed dialogue: a conversational story spontaneously told
in a group of American friends, a collection of conversational
stories told by Greek women, and a Brazilian man's retelling of the
traditional fairy tale, "Little Red Riding Hood." Based on these
analyses, I suggest that speakers use constructed dialogue to create
scenes peopled by characters in relation to each other, scenes which
hearers and readers recreate upon hearing, resulting in both understanding and involvement.

Chapter 5 concerns images and details. After an opening intended to demonstrate at the same time that it discusses the emotional power of specific, concrete, imageable details in discourse, I
begin analysis by recounting examples of details told in conversation which were effective in communicating the points of stories.
Then I discuss the function and placement of details and images in
conversational narratives: first, stories told by women in modern
Greek about having been molested by men, and then narratives
spontaneously told by Americans in conversation. This section
ends with examples from two somewhat exotic sources: writing in
a small magazine by a local storyteller and columnist, and a
fictionalized account of an Australian Aboriginal storytelling. I
move then to examining details and images in nonnarrative and
quasinarrative conversational discourse. I consider details within
the strategy of listing. In the next section I discuss the role of telling

creating interpersonal rapport in conversation. I then discuss the related idea that the telling of details establishes (romantic) intimacy. After this, I shift to examining an image in a more formal conversational genre, radio talk show talk. This relatively literary example is a blend of speaking and writing in that its key image is recited from memory from a piece that the speaker had written for oral presentation on the radio. It thus serves as a bridge to examining details and images in written literary discourse, including examples from comments by book reviewers, from the novel *Household words*, and from other works of fiction and film. Having presented an example of literary speaking, I next present an example of high-involvement writing, and then discuss a recent trend in journalism toward reporting details which do not contribute significant information to the news report. I consider briefly cultural variability in valuing and using details, and also negative and unsuccessful uses. The concluding discussion recapitulates the significance of details in creating images which contribute to imagining scenes associated with emotion and enabling understanding.

In chapter 6, the concluding chapter, I show how these and other involvement strategies work together in examples of artful discourse. The chapter begins with analysis of a short segment from Mary Catherine Bateson's *Our own metaphor*, a novelistic account of a scholarly conference. I then briefly analyze an excerpt from a journalistic account of Lubavitcher Hasidim, an orthodox Jewish sect living in Brooklyn, New York. In this connection, I discuss the essential nature of interpersonal interaction for understanding all written as well as spoken texts. I then turn to political oratory. To show how the involvement strategies analyzed separately in chapters 3 through 5 work together with each other and with other strategies in another genre, I examine a speech by the Reverend Jesse Jackson. My analysis thus ends with a view toward the continuing investigation of how strategies that are pervasive and spontaneous in conversation are intertwined and elaborated in a range of types of private and public discourse.

The book ends with an Afterword in which I comment on an enterprise to which I intend it to be a contribution: humanistic linguistics.

By way of transition from this introduction to my discussion of involvement in discourse, I comment now on the subfield of linguistics to which this study belongs: discourse analysis.

Discourse analysis

Discourse analysis is uniquely heterogeneous among the many subdisciplines of linguistics. In comparison to other subdisciplines of the field, it may seem almost dismayingly diverse. Thus, the term "variation theory" refers to a particular combination of theory and method employed in studying a particular kind of data. The term "conversation analysis," as it is used to refer exclusively to work in the paradigm pioneered by ethnomethodologists Harvey Sacks and Emanuel Schegloff, refers to a particular combination of theory and method employed in studying a particular kind of data. The same could be said of the terms "transformational grammar" and "ethnography of communication." Those who do traditional studies in sociolinguistic variation, ethnomethodological conversation analysis, extended standard theory, and ethnography of communication, share assumptions and practices regarding their theories, methods, and data, as well as, perhaps most importantly, disciplinary backgrounds and training. But the term "discourse analysis" does not refer to a particular method of analysis. It does not entail a single theory or coherent set of theories. Moreover, the term does not describe a theoretical perspective or methodological framework at all. It simply describes the object of study: language beyond the sentence.

Furthermore, language in sequence beyond the sentence is not a particular, homogeneous kind of data, but an all-inclusive category. Discourse – language beyond the sentence – is simply *language* – as it occurs, in any context (including the context of linguistic analysis), in any form (including two made-up sentences in sequence; a tape recorded conversation, meeting, or interview; a novel or play). The name for the field "discourse analysis," then, says nothing more or other than the term "linguistics": the study of language. Why then does the field have a separate name? The term developed, I suspect, to make legitimate types of analysis of types of language that do not fit into the established subfields of linguistics, more narrowly focused, which had come to be regarded by many as synonymous with the name of the discipline, and to encompass work in other disciplines that also study language. Some of the work of Jakobson, Sapir, and Whorf, were they working today, would be considered discourse analysis. The term was not needed in their time because then linguistics did not exclude any of the kinds of linguistic analysis they did.[2]

A recent collection of representative articles in discourse analysis (van Dijk 1985) has been criticized by some reviewers for its heterogeneity: for not reflecting a monolithic theory and a consistent method of analysis. Some critics indulgently shake their heads and suggest that discourse analysis is not "mature" enough to be theoretically and methodologically monolithic. This strikes my ear as similar to the conversational nose-thumbing by which many have learned to apply the psychologically sophisticated epithet "immature" to behavior that does not mesh well with their expectations, or is not to their liking. Discourse analysis will never be monolithic because it does not grow out of a single discipline.

If "discourse" is nothing less than language itself, and "discourse analysis" attempts to admit a broad range of research to the analysis of language, then it is by nature interdisciplinary. Criticisms to which it has been subjected are then the inevitable fate of all interdisciplinary endeavors, as Widdowson (1988:185–6) eloquently describes and explains:

> The conventions of the paradigm not only determine which topics are relevant. They determine too the approved manner of dealing with them: what counts as data, evidence and the inference of fact; what can be allowed as axiomatic, what needs to be substantiated by argument or empirical proof. The paradigm, therefore, is a sort of cultural construct. So it is that the disciplines which concern themselves with language, from their different epistemological perspectives, constitute different cultures, different ways of conceiving of language phenomena and different ways of using language to convey their conceptions.
> ... This means that those who try to promote cross-cultural relations by being inter-disciplinary are likely to be ostracized by both sides and to be stigmatized twice over as amateur and mountebank.

Since discourse analysis embraces not just two disciplines but at least nine: linguistics, anthropology, sociology, psychology, literature, rhetoric, philology, speech communication, and philosophy, and there are culturally different subdisciplines within each of these disciplines, the goal of a homogeneous "discipline" with a unified theory, an agreed upon method, and comparable types of data, is

not only hopeless but pointless. To achieve such uniformity, were
it possible (which it obviously is not; as with Esperanto, uniformity
could only mean privileging one linguistic/cultural system and
banishing the rest), would defeat the purpose of discourse analysis:
to open up the field of language study to make welcome a variety
of theories, methods, and types of language to be studied.

To say that discourse analysis is not monolithic is not, however,
to exempt individual works (or individuals' work) from having and
having to make clear theoretical, methodological, and, when appropriate, empirical frameworks. My own analysis of discourse
grows out of my training in linguistics, with prolonged exposure to
anthropology and an earlier background in the study of English
and modern Greek literature. From Robin Lakoff I acquired a theoretical framework of politeness phenomena and communicative
style. Compatible with and complementary to this is the theoretical
framework of conversational inference which I gleaned from John
Gumperz. From Lakoff I learned a method of systematic observation of interaction and expository argumentation from accumulated examples, from Gumperz a method of tape recording and
transcribing naturally occurring interaction which becomes the
basis for interpretive microanalytic exegesis of selected samples. To
Wallace Chafe I trace my inclination to combine the recording of
naturally occurring conversation with deliberate elicitation of extended discourse, and an abiding interest in comparing speaking
and writing. From A. L. Becker I learned to question the metaphors
and constraints of "mainstream" contemporary linguistics, and my
understanding of "coherence." Paul Friedrich has contributed
greatly to my interest in and understanding of poetic language.
With the exception of Lakoff, whose training and background were
in linguistics and classics, all the scholars I have named stand
squarely on feet planted firmly in both linguistics and anthropology. The work of these scholars and others provides the foundation
for my analysis of involvement in discourse.

2

Involvement in discourse

The radio was on and that was the first time I heard that song, the one I hate. Johnny Mathis singing "It's Not For Me To Say." When I hear it all I can think of is that very day riding in the front seat with Lucy leaning against me and the smell of Juicy Fruit gum making me feel like I was going to throw up. How can a song do that? Be like a net that catches a whole entire day, even a day whose guts you hate? You hear it and all of a sudden everything comes hanging back in front of you, all tangled up in that music.

Lynda Barry, *The good times are killing me,* pp. 42–3

This book is about how repetition, dialogue, and imagery create involvement in discourse, especially conversational discourse. In this, it tells only part of the story. Repetition, dialogue, and imagery work along with other linguistic (and nonlinguistic) strategies to create involvement. My thesis is that such strategies, shaped and elaborated in literary discourse, are spontaneous and pervasive in conversation because they reflect and create interpersonal involvement. This chapter is devoted to discussing the nature of involvement in relation to linguistic strategies.

Involvement

On the first page of the Introduction to his book *Discourse strategies*, John Gumperz (1982:1) observes:

Once involved in a conversation, both speaker and hearer must actively respond to what transpires by signalling involvement, either directly through words or indirectly through gestures or similar nonverbal signals.

Conversational involvement, for Gumperz, is the basis of all linguistic understanding:

understanding presupposes conversational involvement. A general theory of discourse strategies must therefore begin by specifying the linguistic and socio-cultural knowledge that needs to be shared if conversational involvement is to be maintained, and then go on to deal with what it is about the nature of conversational inference that makes for cultural, subcultural and situational specificity of interpretation. (2–3)

In undertaking the research agenda he articulates here, Gumperz explains and exemplifies the benefit of using cross-cultural communication as a research site. In interactions in which signalling systems differ, processes become problematic and therefore visible which are crucial but likely to be overlooked in interactions among participants from more culturally similar backgrounds:

Almost all conversational data derive from verbal interaction in socially and linguistically homogeneous groups. There is a tendency to take for granted that conversational involvement exists, that interlocutors are cooperating, and that interpretive conventions are shared. (4)

For Gumperz, then, conversational involvement is the felicitous result of conversational inference, the ability to infer, globally, what the interaction is about and what one's participation in it is expected to be, as well as, locally, what each utterance means. Moreover, Gumperz shows that participation in conversation is not merely a matter of passive understanding. It is not enough to decipher the "meaning" of a given utterance. Or rather, one *cannot* truly understand the meaning of a given utterance without having a broad grasp of conversational coherence: where the utterance came from and where it is headed, how it fits into a recognizable schema in terms of the organization of the discourse and of the interaction. As Gumperz argues in his book and elsewhere (Gumperz, Kaltman, and O'Connor 1984), conversationalists need to be able not only to decipher what has already been uttered but also to foresee how it is likely to develop, at both the sentence and the discourse level.

In Gumperz's framework conversational involvement is achieved in intracultural communication but compromised in cross cultural communication. The notion of cultural homogeneity, however, is an idealization that is never completely realized. Individuals reared in the "same culture" exhibit regional, ethnic, age, gender, class, and other social and individual differences. My most extended analysis of "cross-cultural" communication (Tannen 1984) is a study of conversation among five Americans (and one native of London), showing that their conversational styles (in Gumperz's terms, their contextualization cues) differ, and that these differences lead to numerous subtle misunderstandings and misjudgments.[1] However, as Gumperz and I jointly argue (Gumperz and Tannen 1979), the level on which differences occur, and the depth of misunderstandings, are far more extreme in the case of broadly cross-cultural communication: talk among speakers from different countries in different parts of the world who speak not only different languages but languages from vastly different families. My sense of "cross-cultural" might be distinguished from Gumperz's by the appellation "cross-sub-cultural." At this level, too, conversations are characterized by more or less successful achievement of conversational involvement.

Involvement is also central in the extensive research of Wallace Chafe on speaking and writing (for example, Chafe 1982, 1984, 1985). Comparing spoken discourse in the form of informal dinner table conversation and written discourse in the form of published academic papers, Chafe finds that the prototypical spoken genre is characterized by fragmentation and involvement, whereas the prototypical written genre is characterized by integration and detachment. Chafe (1985:116) notes three types of involvement in conversation: self-involvement of the speaker, interpersonal involvement between speaker and hearer, and involvement of the speaker with what is being talked about. (This could – perhaps should – also include the hearer's involvement with what is being talked about, but that introduces another dimension to the paradigm.) These types of involvement, though distinguishable, also overlap, as will be demonstrated in chapter 5.

The focuses of Gumperz's and Chafe's uses of the term "involvement" are slightly different though closely related. For Gumperz, involvement describes an observable, active participation in conversation. It is comparable to what Goodwin (1981) calls "conversational engagement" and Merritt (1982) calls "mutual engagement": an observable state of being in coordinated interaction, as distinguished from mere co-presence. For Chafe, it describes a more psychological, internal state which shows itself in observable linguistic phenomena. These orientations are in keeping with the general epistemological orientations of these two scholars.

My own sense of involvement is closer, I think, to that of Chafe: an internal, even emotional connection individuals feel which binds them to other people as well as to places, things, activities, ideas, memories, and words. However, my sense of involvement also encompasses Gumperz's, as I see it as not a given but an achievement in conversational interaction. •

My understanding of the term "involvement" is also an outgrowth, and a part, of a growing body of research emphasizing the interactive nature of conversational interaction. What may seem at first like the self-evident claim that it takes more than one person to have a conversation, is actually a more subtle and significant one: that conversation is not a matter of two (or more) people alternately taking the role of speaker and listener, but rather that both speaking and listening include elements and traces of the other. Listening, in this view, is an active not a passive enterprise, requiring interpretation comparable to that required in speaking, and speaking entails simultaneously projecting the act of listening: In Bakhtin's sense, all language use is dialogic.

The theoretical perspective I have in mind is referred to by some as the notion that conversation is "a joint production." The bulk of research in this vein has emphasized the active role of the listener in interpreting and shaping a speaker's discourse. This sense is captured by the title of a recent special issue of the journal *Text*: "The audience as co-author." In the introduction to that issue, Duranti (1986) gives an excellent overview of the theoretical foundations of this perspective. But the point of "joint production" or "intertextuality" (to use a phrase coined by Julia Kristeva [1974:59–60] and frequently used by literary theorists) goes further than that. Not only is the audience a co-author, but the speaker is also a co-listener. On the deepest level, Bakhtin ([1975]1981) and Voloshinov ([1929]1986)[2] argue that no utterance, no word, can be spoken without echoing how others understand and have used it. McDermott and Tylbor (1983) describe the joint production of meaning in interaction as "collusion." Scollon and Scollon (1984) show that Athabaskan storytellers shape their stories in response to their listeners. Kochman (1986) demonstrates the use of "strategic ambiguity" in certain Black speech genres, such that the receiver, not the speaker, determines meaning – and the speaker intends it to be so. Erickson (1986) gives an elegant demonstration of "the influence of listeners' communicative behavior upon the communicative behavior of speakers" (294), using the metaphor that "talking with another person . . . is like climbing a tree that climbs back" (316). The interactional nature of all meaning in conversation is demonstrated, moreover, by the entire body of work in conversation analysis by Sacks and by Schegloff (who use the term "interactional achievement") and those working in their paradigm (see especially Schegloff 1982, 1988; Goodwin 1981, 1986).

My notion of involvement also depends heavily on Becker's (1982) notion of an aesthetic response, which he defines, following Dewey, as an emergent sense of coherence: coming to see how different kinds of meaning converge in a particular utterance. "For an aesthetic response to be possible," Becker (1979:241) observes, "a text must appear to be more or less coherent." Experiencing coherence also makes possible an emotional response. Perceiving meaning through the coherence of discourse constraints (Becker 1984a), as well as perceiving oneself as coherent in interaction constituted by the discourse, creates an emotional experience of insight (understanding the text) and connectedness (to other participants, to the language, to the world). This enables both participation in the interaction and also understanding of meaning. If the ability to perceive coherence is essential to a sense of being-in-the-world, the inability to perceive coherence "drives people mad." An aesthetic response is not an extra added attraction of communication, but its essence.

Coherence and involvement are the goal – and, in frequent happy occurrences, the result – when discourse succeeds in creating meaning through familiar strategies. The familiarity of the strategies makes the discourse and its meaning seem coherent, and allows for the elaboration of meaning through the play of familiar patterns: the eternal tension between fixity and novelty that constitutes creativity. Finally, to use the term coined by Gregory Bateson (1972), it sends a metamessage of rapport between the communicators, who thereby experience that they share communicative conventions and inhabit the same world of discourse.

Although this book focuses mainly on its positive face or rapport side, involvement has potentially negative sides as well, including the one that Havelock (1963) sees as key to solving the seeming puzzle of why poets were to be banned from educational processes in Plato's Republic. Poets in classical Greece, Havelock points out, were not isolated dreamers writing primarily to be read by small, specialized audiences, as they are in the contemporary United States at least. Rather, in Plato's time, the works of the great poets were orally performed before large audiences by wandering bards who mesmerized crowds and moved them emotionally. "You were not asked to grasp their principles through rational analysis," Havelock explains. "Instead you submitted to the paideutic spell." The effect of poetic performance, then, was "total engagement" and "emotional identification" (159) – in a word, involvement.

Sound and sense in discourse

As noted at the outset, my study of involvement in discourse is part of a project exploring the relationship between conversational and literary discourse. My focused interest in this area grew out of a study comparing spoken and written narratives (Tannen 1982). I had my students record casual conversations in which they happened to take part, then choose a story that someone told as part of that conversation, and later ask the person who told the story to write it down. In comparing these spoken and written versions of the "same" story, my students found, for the most part, that the written stories evinced the features that Chafe (1982) and Ochs (1979) had found to typify written expository prose, and the spoken stories, for the most part, evinced the features that they had found to typify spoken conversation. However, one pair of stories did not fit the expected pattern at all. Quite the contrary, the written story exhibited more, rather than fewer, of many of the linguistic strategies expected in conversation. Stepping back and considering the overall impact of the atypical written narrative quickly indicated why it did not fit the pattern: Whereas the other speakers, when asked to write, had "boiled down" (to borrow a term from Scollon and Scollon 1984) their rambling oral narratives into succinct expository prose, the speaker whose written narrative was twice as long as her spoken one had "cooked up" her story (another term from Scollon and Scollon) into a piece of short fiction. She had written a short story rather than expository prose. Examining the two versions more closely, I discovered that the written short story combined the "involvement" that Chafe finds typical of conversation with the "integration" he finds typical of expository writing.

This early study suggested not only that literary writing elaborates strategies that are spontaneous in conversation, but also that considering the genre of an instance of discourse is essential to understanding its nature.[3] Biber (1988) supports this observation with a multivariate statistical analysis showing that different spoken and written discourse types vary along not one but a number of dimensions. The comparison of spoken and written narratives suggested the insight that underlies the current research: that ordinary conversation and literary discourse have more in common than has been commonly thought.

The framework for this study took form, gradually, as the result of a cumulative impression from research analyzing conversation. In reading the work of others, as well as in doing my own analyses of conversation, again and again I encountered the findings that one or another linguistic strategy was characteristic of conversation which I recalled from my past life in English literature. They were the very same strategies that, in my earlier studies of literature, I had learned to think of as quintessentially literary.

In earlier work I presented a schema by which I saw these involvement strategies as working on two levels: on the one hand, sound and rhythm, and on the other, meaning through mutual participation in sensemaking. Here I develop this schema in several ways. First, I adopt the term "strategy" to replace the term I had previously used, "feature." Prodded by Becker, I abandoned "feature" as too atomistic. "Strategy" is a term with a firm foundation in linguistic research, as in Gumperz's (1982) "discourse strategies," Lakoff's (1979) "stylistic strategies," Becker's (1984b) "repeating strategies," and my own (1982) "oral and literate strategies." However, I also introduce a note of caution about this term. If "feature" has unintended connotations of trivial, disjointed parts, then "strategy," in its conventional use, has unintended connotations of conscious planning, even plotting. The term, in its linguistic sense, is used simply to convey a systematic way of using language. Second, again prodded by Becker, I move away from the idea of "levels" to get closer to a sense of language working in a variety of ways at once. Third, I have come to see what I had been referring to as sound and rhythm as essentially musical; here I have

been influenced by Friedrich as well as Oliver Sacks. Fourth, I now
regard mutual participation in sensemaking as essentially a
response to scenes, and much of the power of scenes as coming
from images which are often made up of details. Moreover, I now
see music and scenes as triggering emotions. Scenes are crucial in
both thinking and feeling because they are composed of people in
relation to each other, doing things that are culturally and personally recognizable and meaningful.

What I refer to as sound and sense are the aspects of language
that Friedrich (1986) calls music and myth. Indeed, Friedrich
regards the fusing of these two polarities as the master trope that
gives language its poetic force:

> Language is the symbolic process that mediates between, on the one hand,
> ideas/feelings and, on the other hand, the sounds produced by the tongue,
> larynx, and so forth. Poetry, analogously, is the symbolic process by which
> the individual mediates between the music of a natural language and the
> (nuances of) mythic meaning. To create felt consubstantiality between lan-
> guage music and myth *is* the master trope of poetry – "master" because it
> is superordinate to and in control over such lesser figures as image,
> metaphor, and paradox. And this master trope is unique, that is, it is diag-
> nostic of poetry. (39)

Such poetry, Friedrich argues throughout his book, is not found
only in formal poetry; rather, it is present in all language, to varying degrees.

As Becker (1984a, 1988) shows, language works in many ways
at once; in his terms, many different kinds of context constrain languaging. Sound and sense, or music and myth, operate simultaneously in language. In making this point, Friedrich cites Saussure's
observation that

> "language can also be compared with a sheet of paper: thought is the front
> and the sound the back; one cannot cut the front without cutting the back
> at the same time; likewise in language, one can neither divide sound from
> thought nor thought from sound" (1959:113). Language connects the
> universe of sound and the universe of meaning. (106)

The inseparability of these aspects of language will be seen in the
involvement strategies listed and briefly illustrated in the next section, and also in the extended analysis of three involvement strategies that comprises the bulk of this book.

It is the central theme of my analysis that involvement strategies are the basic force in both conversational and literary discourse by means of their sound and sense patterns. The former involve the audience with the speaker or writer and the discourse by sweeping them up in what Scollon (1982) calls rhythmic ensemble, much as one is swept up by music and finds oneself moving in its rhythm. In other words, they become rhythmically involved. Sense patterns create involvement through audience participation in sense-making: By doing some of the work of making meaning, hearers or readers become participants in the discourse. In other words, they become meaningfully, mythically involved. I am suggesting, furthermore, that these two types of involvement are necessary for communication, and that they work in part by creating emotional involvement. It is a tenet of education that students understand information better, perhaps only, if they have discovered it for themselves rather than being told it. Much as one cares *for* a person, animal, place, or object that one has taken care *of*, so listeners and readers not only understand information better but care more about it – understand it *because* they care about it – if they have worked to make its meaning.

Involvement strategies

I now list and briefly illustrate the involvement strategies that researchers have identified in conversation that I recognized as those which literary analysts have independently identified as important in literary discourse. I am not suggesting that these are the only ones at work, but simply that these are the ones that I repeatedly encountered in my own and others' research.

The strategies that work primarily (but not exclusively) on sound include (1) rhythm, (2) patterns based on repetition and variation of (a) phonemes, (b) morphemes, (c) words, (d) collocations of words, and (e) longer sequences of discourse, and (3) style figures of speech (many of which are also repetitive figures). The strategies that work primarily (but never exclusively) on meaning include (1) indirectness, (2) ellipsis, (3) tropes, (4) dialogue, (5) imagery and detail, and (6) narrative. The next three chapters in this book explore in depth three of these strategies: repetition, dialogue, and imagery and detail. Here I present the larger framework in which these three strategies fit by giving brief examples (suggestive not exhaustive) of past research which has identified these strategies in conversation.

Rhythmic synchrony

A number of researchers have devoted themselves to the study of conversational synchrony: the astonishing rhythmic and iconic coordination that can be observed when people interact face to face. They have shown that rhythm is as basic to conversation as it is to musical performance. A pioneer in this field is Birdwhistell (1970). Other key researchers include Kendon (1981), McQuown et al. (1971), and Scheflen (1972). (For a collection of articles on nonverbal aspects of communication including many on conversational rhythm see Kendon, Harris, and Key 1975.)

Synchrony has been observed even at the micro level. (See Kempton 1980 for a review of relevant research.) Condon (for example, 1963) filmed interaction and then observed both the self-synchrony of speakers and the synchrony among speakers and listeners. For example, a speaker's emphasis of a word, onset of a hand gesture, and even eye blinks, all occur in the same movie frame. When cultural backgrounds are shared (but not when they are not, and not when a participant is schizophrenic), such movements of listeners are also synchronized with the movements and speech of speakers.

In a study of counselling interviews, Erickson and Shultz (1982) demonstrate that successful conversation can be set to a metronome: Movements and utterances are synchronized and carried out on the beat. This phenomenon is informally observed when, following a pause, two speakers begin speaking at precisely the same moment, or when two people suddenly move – for example, crossing their legs or shifting their weight – at the same moment and in the same direction. Parallel to Gumperz's findings for verbal interaction, a participant must share rhythm in order to take part. Finding a way into a conversation is like joining a line of dancers. It is not enough to know where other dancers have been; one must also know where they are headed: To bring one's feet into coordination with theirs, one must grasp the pattern in order to foresee where their feet will come down next. The sharedness, or lack of sharedness, of rhythm, is crucial for conversational outcome. Erickson and Shultz found that counselees were able to derive more usable information from counselling interviews when conversational rhythm was established and shared. Putting the musical basis of language into print, Erickson (1982) shows that the rhythm of a conversation can be represented as a musical score.

Scollon (1982) is also interested in the musical basis of talk. He shows that conversational rhythm is composed of tempo (the pattern of beats) and density (syllables, or silence, per beat). In conversation, as in music, Scollon suggests, the key to the operation of tempo and density in interaction is ensemble:

As musicians use the term, ensemble refers to the coming together of the performers in a way that either makes or breaks the performance. It is not just the being together, but the doing together. And so a performance of a string quartet can be faulted, no matter how impeccably the score has been followed, if a mutual agreement on tempos, tunings, fortes, and pianos has not been achieved. Ensemble in music refers to the extent to which the performers have achieved one mind, or – to favor Sudnow (1979a, 1979b), one body – in the performance of their work. Of the elements which contribute to the achievement of ensemble, tempo is the guiding element. (342–3).

Scollon claims, finally, that the concept of rhythmic ensemble accounts for Gumperz's notion of contextualization. "What learning mechanism," he asks, "drives people to pay attention not only to the message but also to the metamessage?" (344) In answer, he refers to the notions of politeness and the double bind. Caught in the conflicting demands of simultaneously serving positive face (the need to be accepted) and negative face (the need not to be imposed on), the double bind comes into play when one cannot step out of the situation. Says Scollon, "it is ensemble which holds participants together in a mutual attention to the ongoing situation." In non-real time communication such as expository prose, Scollon suggests, "it comes out of learned conventions for the production of ensemble" (345). This is analogous to what I am suggesting: that conventions, or strategies, for creating involvement in conversation are used and elaborated in literary discourse.

Repetition and variation

Literary scholars have regarded as basic to literate recurrent patterns of sound (alliteration, assonance, rhyme), words, phrases or

sentences, and larger chunks of discourse. Finnegan (1977:90) goes
so far as to say, "The most marked feature of poetry is surely repetition." Scholars studying the language of conversation have also
identified, again and again, the importance of repetition.

Phonemes

Harvey Sacks demonstrated repeatedly that spontaneous conversation uses repetition of sounds and words in a systematic way. In
analyzing a short segment of casual conversation among extended
family members, Sacks (1971) points out that a speaker named
Ethel utters the word "because" three times, pronouncing it
differently each time. The "same word" is alternately realized as
"because," "cause," and "cuz." Sacks finds that the variant chosen
in each instance is "sound coordinated with things in its environment." At one point in the conversation, Ethel and her husband
Ben are urging Max, their guest, to eat some herring. Ben has just
told Max how good the herring is, and Ethel supports him by
explaining why:

'cause it comes from cold water.

Sacks argues that the variant " 'cause" is occasioned by the environment of other /k/ sounds.

Morphemes

Still trying to urge Max to eat, Ethel uses the form "because" in the
environment of other instances of the morpheme /bi/:

You better eat something
because you're gonna be hungry before we get there.

One may also notice the initial /b/ in "better."

Phrases

That conversational narratives are characterized by a high degree
of repetition of phrases and sentences was noted by Labov (1972),
Ochs (1979), Tannen (1979) and others. For Labov (1792:379),
repetition of phrases is an evaluative strategy: It is used by a
speaker to contribute to the point of the story, to answer in advance
the "withering" question, "So what?" Labov presents a number of
examples from narratives told by inner-city adolescent boys in
Black English vernacular, as, for example, in a story about a fight:

> The rock <u>went up</u> –
> I mean <u>went up</u>.

or within dialogue in another fight narrative:

> <u>You bleedin'</u>,
> <u>you bleedin'</u>,
> Speedy, <u>you bleedin'</u>!"

Finally, from a story told by an adult man on Martha's Vineyard about a bird dog that, after returning twice without a duck he was supposed to retrieve, was sent with firm instructions to go again and get the duck:

> Well, sir, he went over there a third time.
> <u>And he didn't come back.</u>
> <u>And he didn't come back.</u>

More recently, Tannen (1987a,b) and Norrick (1987) demonstrate that repetition is also frequent in nonnarrative conversational discourse (see further chapter 3).

Longer discourse sequences

The ethnomethodological branch of conversation analysis has been particularly concerned with sequencing of parts of discourse. For example, a story or joke told in conversation is likely to be followed by another story or joke (see, for example, Sacks 1978, Ryave 1978, Jefferson 1978, and other chapters in Schenkein 1978). Early work by Schegloff ([1968]1972) investigates "Sequencing in conversational openings." Merritt (1976) examines the recurrent structures in service encounters, such that questions are likely to follow questions (such a sequence might be: "Do you carry cigarettes?" "What brand would you like?").

Evidence of the repetition of discourse sequences across time can be seen in the growing body of work in cross-cultural discourse which identifies discourse patterns repeated by members of a cultural group. Becker's (1984b) analysis of repeating strategies in Javanese is an example of this. Another is Becker's (1979) analysis of "text-building strategies" in a Javanese shadow play. Other examples include Gumperz (1982) on British English vs. Indian English discourse strategies; Kochman (1981) on black and white styles; Labov (1972) on narrative structure in general and inner-city black vs. middle-class white narrative in particular; and Tannen (1980a) on Greek vs. American narrative strategies.[4]

Style figures of speech

"In figures of speech," Levin (1982:114) explains, "one says what one is thinking but encases it in a stylish frame."[5] Many of the examples he gives involve repetition and variation:

epanaphora, the beginning of successive clauses with the same word or group of words; antistrophe, the like repetition at the end of clauses; antithesis, the juxtaposition of contraries in balanced clauses; asyndeton, the combining of clauses without conjunctions; isocolon, a sequence of clauses containing the same number of syllables.   (114)

Other figures of speech listed by Quinn (1982) include anadiplosis ("repetition of an end at the next beginning") and epanados (more commonly called "chiasmus"), in which two segments contain the same two parts with their order reversed. An example taken from a Thanksgiving dinner conversation which provides one of the major sources of data for this study (see Appendix I for a list and description of sources of examples) arose when a speaker in that conversation said, with reference to having attended summer camp as a child (see Appendix II for a list and discussion of transcription conventions),

> CAMP was LIFE!
> My whole life was camp!

This is an example of chiasmus because the terms "camp" and "life" are taken from the first clause and repeated in the second, with their order reversed. A well known rhetorical example of this figure is found in John F. Kennedy's famous lines:

> Ask not what your country can do for you.
> Ask what you can do for your country.

The reason these lines have been remembered and so often repeated is a combination of the idea they convey and their "stylish frame," the aesthetic satisfaction deriving from the repetition and the reversal, and perhaps also the rhyming of "you" and "do." (I think it is this aesthetic pleasure which is commonly referred to by the colloquial word "catchy".)

Participation in sensemaking

No text of any kind would be comprehensible without considerable shared context and background. The necessity of filling in unstated information has long been regarded as a crucial part of literary discourse. For example, many critics consider poetry to be maximally effective when it conveys the most meaning in the fewest words. I am suggesting that this makes discourse effective because the more work readers or hearers do to supply meaning, the deeper their understanding and the greater their sense of involvement with both text and author.

Indirectness/ellipsis/silence

A fundamental aspect of language is what literary analysts call ellipsis and analysts of conversation call indirectness (or, in formal pragmatics, implicature): conveying unstated meaning.

Lakoff (1973, 1979) describes and explores the ways that conversationalists typically do not say exactly what they mean. Indirectness is preferred for two main reasons: to save face if a conversational contribution is not well received, and to achieve the sense of rapport that comes from being understood without saying what one means. In addition, by requiring the listener or reader to fill in unstated meaning, indirectness contributes to a sense of involvement through mutual participation in sensemaking. Brown and Levinson ([1978]1987) present a formal model for representing the systematic ways that speakers avoid making their meaning explicit.

Becker (1985, 1988, in press) discusses the importance of silence in discourse, from the silences between words and sentences to the silences representing what is not said. In this regard, Becker (in press) quotes a number of passages from Ortega y Gasset (1957):

The stupendous reality that is language cannot be understood unless we begin by observing that speech consists above all in silences ...

A being who could not renounce saying many things would be incapable of speaking ...

Each people leaves some things unsaid in order to be able to say others. Because everything would be unsayable.

For Becker (1984a:136), "silential relations," that is, "the relations of a text to the unsaid and the unsayable," comprise one of six "kinds of contextual relations," six "sources of constraints," that give discourse its character.

In a similar spirit, Tyler (1978:459) argues:

Every act of saying is a momentary intersection of the 'said' and the 'unsaid'. Because it is surrounded by an aureola of the unsaid, an utterance speaks of more than it says, mediates between past and future, transcends the speaker's conscious thought, passes beyond his manipulative control, and creates in the mind of the hearer worlds unanticipated. From within the infinity of the 'unsaid', the speaker and the hearer, by a joint act of will, bring into being what was 'said'.

Meaning, then, says Tyler, is to be found, above all, "in the resonating silence of the unsaid" (465).

Tropes

J. D. Sapir (1977) and Friedrich (1986) use the term "trope" to refer to figures of speech that operate on meaning. Sapir identifies four master tropes: metaphor (speaking of one thing in terms of another), metonymy (speaking of a thing in terms of something associated with it), synecdoche (a part for the whole), and irony (saying the opposite of what one means).

Lakoff and Johnson (1980) and the articles collected in Sapir and Crocker (1977) discuss in detail the pervasiveness and power of metaphors in everyday speech. Friedrich (1986:4) observes, "The metaphor is only one kind of analogy and part of a much larger context of analogical devices and associational thinking." He identifies a wide range of tropes, including "part-whole, parallelism, irony, outcry, proverb, and enigma," merely to "suggest the incredible richness and sheer quantity of figures that writhe within language, waiting to be exploited or working on their own." His schema includes six major categories: "imagistic, modal, analogical, contiguity tropes, formal-constructional, and expansion-condensation." The pervasiveness of these figures in language is such that "Even a single word in context involves a plurality of tropes" (29).

If Bateson (1979) is right, the working of tropes is more the norm than the exception in language: Most meaning is communicated in daily language not by the logical processes of induction and deduction but by abduction, the "lateral extension of abstract components of description" (157–8) such that, "We can look at the anatomy of a frog and then look around to find other instances of the same abstract relations recurring in other creatures, including ... ourselves" (157). According to Bateson,

> Metaphor, dream, parable, allegory, the whole of art, the whole of science, the whole of religion, the whole of poetry, totemism ..., the organization of facts in comparative anatomy – all these are instances or aggregates of instances of abduction, within the human mental sphere. (158)

For an example of analogical meaning in everyday conversation, I return to Sacks's (1971) analysis of the conversation in which Ethel and Ben offer herring to Max. Sacks poses the question of why Ethel uses the oddly formal expression "good enough" in addressing her husband:

Will you be good enough to empty this in there?

He suggests that her choice of an expression that uses the measure term "enough" is conditioned by association with a number of other measure terms in the environment: "empty," in the just cited utterance, as well as "more" and "missing" in nearby sentences.

Quinn (1982), like most rhetoricians, takes his examples of figures of speech and tropes (he does not distinguish between them) from literary sources. He notes, however, that rhetoric uses for intentional effect means of expression that also occur spontaneously and involuntarily in speech. An example he gives is "aposiopesis," suddenly discontinuing speech as if one is unable or unwilling to continue (for example, rendered speechless by emotion) (34).

Constructed dialogue

Numerous linguists (for example, Chafe 1982, Labov 1972, Schiffrin 1981, and contributors to Coulmas 1986) observe that conversational discourse frequently represents what others have said ("reported speech") as dialogue ("direct speech" or "direct quotation") rather than third-person report ("indirect speech"), and that "direct speech" is more vivid, more effective. But why is dialogue more vivid? I believe it is because the creation of voices

occasions the imagination of a scene in which characters speak in
those voices, and that these scenes occasion the imagination of alternative, distant, or familiar worlds, much as does artistic creation. Finally, the casting of ideas as the speech of others is an
important source of emotion in discourse. Recent work by ethno-
graphers of communication on affect has come hand in hand with
studies of evidentiality: How speakers frame the information they
express, what authority they claim for it (Hill and Irvine, in press).
For example, Besnier (in press) observes, "The rhetorical style of a
quote is a tool exploited by the reporter to communicate affect."

In previous research (Tannen 1986b) I found conversational dialogue to be closer to literary dialogue in an unexpected way. In
comparing how dialogue is introduced in conversational stories and
in novels, both in English and modern Greek, I expected to find
that the conversational stories employed verbs of saying to introduce dialogue, that is, speech being represented as the voices of
others, whereas novels, having at their disposal the written convention of quotation marks and indentation, would frequently omit
verbs of saying. What I found instead was that in both genres, variants of the verb "to say" were used to introduce dialogue just about
half the time in American English.[6] Introducing dialogue with no
verb of saying was more frequent in the conversational than the
literary stories: 26% as compared to 16% for the American English
samples and 22% as compared to 19% for the modern Greek samples. Whereas the writers used print conventions to identify dialogue, speakers had even more effective inexplicit means to do so:
changes in voice quality and prosody which marked entire utterances as representing, literally, a different voice.

Imagery and detail

Along with use of dialogue, use of detail and imagery is frequently
discussed and analyzed by those who comment on literary discourse, including reviewers of fiction. For example, in praising her
work, Crews (1988) comments on a novelist's use of detail (and dialogue): "Her eye for telling detail is good, and her ear for the way
people talk is tone-perfect." In the study of poetry, of course, the
creation of images with words is of primary concern. But some of
those studying everyday language have also noted its use of im-

agery. Tyler (1978) devotes a chapter to discussion of imagery, and Friedrich (1986:18) "emphasizes the emotions, imagery and image use, sensuous imagery above all (dreams)."

Chafe (1984:1099), in comparing spoken conversational and written expository discourse, found that his conversational samples were characterized by "a tendency toward concreteness and imageability." Concreteness and imageability are associated with particularity. Chafe compared two tellings of the same story by the same speaker, once in conversation and once in a scholarly article. In the article, the teller represented the key event as a series:

at dinner every evening

In speaking, she represented it as a particular event:

we were sitting around the dinner table

Chafe notes this example, among others, to illustrate that the conversational telling exhibited more involvement.

Importantly, the particular event is also represented as a scene. In response to specific details, hearers and readers imagine a scene in which the described characters, objects, and actions figure, and their ideas and feelings associated with such scenes are thereby triggered.

Narrative

Narrative has long been of central concern to literary theorists, for whom the term is synonymous with literary narrative. Recently, however, there has been increasing recognition that literary storytelling is simply an elaboration of conversational storytelling. Eudora Welty is not alone among fiction writers in locating her beginnings as a writer in the gossipy stories she heard as a child. Rosen (n.d., 1988) suggests that the emotional and meaning-making power in all discourse derives from personal narrative.

Scholars in other disciplines have come to similar conclusions. I discuss at some length below the observation by natural scientist Stephen Jay Gould (1987) that "the sciences of history," including natural history, are essentially a storytelling enterprise. Psychologist Jerome Bruner (1986) devotes a book to the thesis that cognitive science has mistakenly privileged only one mode of thinking,

"the paradigmatic or logical-scientific one" (12), to the exclusion of
the equally important narrative mode of thinking, a mode that
"deals in human or human-like intention and action" which "strives
to put its timeless miracles into the particulars of experience, and
to locate the experience in time and place" (13). Neurologist and
essayist Oliver Sacks (1986), who is quoted at length below, writes
of the importance of narrative as an "organizing principle." He
describes a patient, Rebecca (introduced below as well), who appeared hopelessly incapable when tested but "was complete and
intact as 'narrative' being, in conditions which allowed her to organize herself in a narrative way" (172–3).

Stories are a different order of discourse genre than the other
strategies listed, because they make use of all the other strategies.
And yet telling a story in conversation can itself be an involvement
strategy. In my analysis of a single dinner table conversation
(Tannen 1984), I found that speakers whose styles I characterized
as "high-involvement" told more stories than their "high-
considerateness" style friends; their stories were more often about
their personal experiences; and their stories more often included accounts of their feelings in response to events recounted.

Involvement through linguistic strategies

All the strategies listed, as well no doubt as others I have not mentioned, work to communicate meaning and to persuade by creating
involvement. The use of constructed dialogue in conversation
exemplifies the simultaneous operation of sound and sense in language. Rendering meaning by framing it as the speech of another,
and animating the voice of the other, speakers create a rhythm and
sound that suggests speech at the same time that they shape the
meaning thus presented. This is equally true for conversational and
fictional discourse. In fiction, as in oral storytelling, the recreation
of rhythms of speech is of primary concern. The representation of
the *sound* of speech is considered essential to the accurate representation of characters and their worlds.[7]

All the involvement strategies are speakers' ways of shaping
what they are talking or writing about. In the terms that Labov
(1972) devised for narrative, but which I believe apply equally to
nonnarrative discourse, they are evaluative: They contribute to the

point of the discourse, presenting the subject of discourse in a way that shapes how the hearer or reader will view it. In the terms of Gregory Bateson's (1972) framework, they contribute to the metamessage, the level on which a speaker's relationships to the subject of talk and to the other participants in talk are negotiated.

Scenes and music in creating involvement

In trying to answer the question of how involvement is created in discourse, I have been helped by Friedrich's (1986) work on the individual imagination, which he defines as "the processes by which individuals integrate knowledge, perceptions, and emotions" (18). The poetic dimensions of language fire the individual imagination. And, paradoxically, it is the activation of the individual imagination that makes it possible to understand another's speech. Communication takes place because the dialogue, details, and images conjured by one's person's speech inspire others to create sounds and scenes in their minds. Thus, it is in the individual imagination that meaning is made, and there that it matters. And it is the creation of such shared meaning – communication – that makes a collection of individuals into a community, unites individuals in relationships.

Images combine with dialogue to create scenes. Dialogue combines with repetition to create rhythm. Dialogue is liminal between repetition and images: like repetition, it is strongly sonorous. It is, moreover, a form of repetition: repeating words that purportedly were said by others at another time. But even when the words were not actually said, casting ideas as dialogue echoes the form of dialogue, the speaking of words, by others at other times in other contexts. It is the familiarity of that form that makes the dialogue "ring true" – gives it resonance and meaning. Furthermore, like imagery, dialogue is particular and creates a scene. Images create a scene visually: What did things and people look like? Dialogue creates a scene auditorially: What did people say and what did they sound like?[8]

Support for the notion that the scene is central in thinking and feeling comes from a number of different sources and areas of research. In his work on frame semantics, Fillmore (1976, 1985) emphasizes the importance of the scene for an understanding of the meaning of individual words. The idea that meaning exists only in relation to a scene is, moreover, what is meant by the term frame semantics. For example, Fillmore points out that the meaning of the expressions "on land" and "on the ground," coreferential in the images they denote, can be distinguished only by reference to the sequence of scenes, the ongoing activities, of which they are a part: In one case, a person was previously at sea and in the other a person was previously in the air.

In an anthropological study of children's reading, Varenne and McDermott (1986:207) observe:

Our analysis of the external features of homework which families do not control can be summarized in a statement to the effect that "homework" is a scene in which the knowledge particular individuals have of a topic is evaluated by someone else.

Thus a noun, "homework," has meaning only by reference to a scene that involves people in relation to each other and feelings associated with those people, their relationships, and the activities they are engaged in.

The importance of the scene also emerges in Norrick's (1985) analysis of proverbs. According to Norrick, the "scenic proverb," "the completely metaphorical proverb describing a concrete scene," is both archetypal and the statistically most frequent type of figurative proverb (102). The "proverb image" is "a concrete description of a scene which can be generalized to yield an abstract truth" (107). Norrick cites Seitel's (1969) claim that proverbs transfer meaning metaphorically from the scenes they depict to the situations in which they are uttered. He illustrates with Barley's (1972) example of the proverb, "The leopard cannot change his spots," spoken in conversation about a thief. When the proverb is spoken, the relation between the leopard and his spots (an unchangeable one) is applied to the thief and his thieving nature, to suggest that the thief cannot be expected to reform. (The interpretation of one set of relations in terms of another is an instance of abduction.)

Neurological evidence

Oliver Sacks (1986), in writing about patients with neurological disorders, provides evidence for the centrality of scenes and of music in human thinking and feeling.

"Rebecca," for example, was severely mentally retarded according to standard intelligence tests, and when Sacks evaluated her in his office according to traditional neurological criteria, she appeared a bundle of deficits:

> I saw her merely, or wholly, as a casualty, a broken creature, whose neurological impairments I could pick out and dissect with precision: a multitude of apraxias and agnosias, a mass of intellectual sensorimotor impairments and breakdowns, limitations of intellectual schemata and concepts similar (by Piaget's criteria) to a child of eight.   (171)

But then Sacks encountered Rebecca in a natural rather than a clinical setting: He happened upon her outside the clinic, "sitting on a bench, gazing at the April foliage." Seeing him, she smiled and uttered a string of "poetic ejaculations" about the beauty and emotion of spring. At that moment, Sacks saw Rebecca as a whole person. Rebecca "was composed by a natural scene, a scene with an organic, aesthetic and dramatic unity and sense" (175). Sacks sees the ability to interact with the world and organize it conceptually and experientially in scenes as essential to being human.

In contrast to Rebecca is Dr. P., the patient referred to in the title essay of Sacks's collection, *The man who mistook his wife for a hat*. Dr. P. made this bizarre mistake in perception because he suffered from a rare neurological disorder by which "he construed the world as a computer construes it, by means of key features and schematic relationships" (14). That is why, in reaching for his hat, he "took hold of his wife's head, tried to lift it off, to put it on" (10). Judging by key features and schematic relationships, he observed that his wife's head fit the model of a hat. By a similar process, in describing pictures in a magazine, Dr. P. was able to identify and describe features, but

> in no case did he get the scene-as-a-whole. He failed to see the world, seeing only details, which he spotted like blips on a radar screen. He never entered into relation with the picture as a whole – never faced, so to speak, *its* physiognomy. He had no sense whatever of a language or scene.   (9)

For Dr. P., "there was formal, but no trace of personal, gnosis" (12), so that, "Visually, he was lost in a world of lifeless abstractions" (13). In retelling *Anna Karenina*, parts of which he knew by heart, Dr. P. "had an undiminished grasp of the plot, but completely omitted visual characteristics, visual narrative or scenes."

Consequently, he "lacked sensorial, imaginal, or emotional reality" (14). In other words, "The visualisation of faces and scenes, of visual narrative and drama – this was profoundly impaired, almost absent. But the visualisation of *schemata* was preserved, enhanced" (15). Crucially, in losing the ability to perceive and think in scenes, Dr. P. lost his ability to feel emotions associated with people and places.

In these and other essays and books, Sacks returns repeatedly to the centrality of three dynamics: scenes, narrative, and music. In a postscript to his essay about Rebecca, Sacks observes, "The power of music, narrative and drama is of the greatest practical and theoretical importance" (176). He emphasizes "the power of music to organise ... when abstract or schematic forms of organisations fail" (177). In another book, Sacks ([1973]1983) discusses a series of patients with postencephalitic Parkinsonism, "among the few survivors of the great sleeping-sickness epidemic (*encephalitis lethargica*) fifty years ago" (1). The book describes their lifelong frozen, sleeping states and sudden, amazing *Awakenings* upon administration of a newfound drug, L-DOPA. In their pre-drug states, many of these patients were quite unable to move but would do so spontaneously and fluently when hearing music.[9]

The centrality of scenes and music in cognition is also at the heart of Sacks's discussion of two patients in an essay entitled "Reminiscence." Both Mrs. O'M. and Mrs. O'C. began suddenly to hear music – specific, vivid songs that they at first believed to be coming from a radio someone had left blaring. Mrs. O'C., a woman in her nineties, realized the songs she was hearing could not be coming from a radio, first because there were no commercials, and then because she realized she knew them from an era vastly distant in time and space: They were songs from her long-forgotten early childhood in Ireland, a country she had left when she was five years old. And with the songs came also-forgotten scenes of happiness from a time when she had been loved, as a small child, before she was orphaned and shipped to America to live with a stern aunt. Sacks discovered, through an EEG, that Mrs. O'C.'s sudden hearing of songs, like the same phenomenon in another old woman, Mrs. O'M., was caused by temporal-lobe seizures, which, as earlier neurologists had determined, "are the invariable basis of 'reminiscence' and experiential hallucinations" (127).

In discussing these patients, Sacks refers to the work of Wilder Penfield, who discovered that he could evoke "experiential hallucinations" by electrical stimulation of particular points in the cerebral cortex in conscious patients. "Such stimulations would instantly call forth intensely vivid hallucinations of tunes – people, scenes, which would be experienced, lived, as compellingly real." Furthermore, "Such epileptic hallucinations or dreams, Penfield showed, are ... accompanied by the emotions which accompanied the original experience" (130). So too for Sacks's patient, Mrs. O'C., "there was an overwhelming *emotion* associated with the seizures" (135).

Mrs. O'C. and Mrs. O'M. "suffered from 'reminiscence,' a convulsive upsurge of melodies and scenes ... Both alike testify to the essentially 'melodic' and 'scenic' nature of inner life, the 'Proustian' nature of memory and mind." Sacks concludes,

Experience is not *possible* until it is organised iconically; action is not *possible* unless it is organised iconically. 'The brain's record' of everything – everything alive – must be iconic. This is the *final* form of the brain's record, even though the preliminary form may be computational or programmatic. The final form of cerebral representation must be, or allow, 'art' – the artful scenery and melody of experience and action.   (141)

Involvement and emotion

In his description and discussion of these and other strange neurological cases, Sacks dramatizes that music and scenes are basic to human cognition – and also to human emotion. Recall, in losing the ability to perceive and think in scenes, Dr. P. lost his ability to feel emotions associated with people and places. When Mrs. O'M. and Mrs. O'C. were unwittingly visited by scenes and tunes from their past, they simultaneously re-experienced the emotions associated with them. This provides evidence for the association of the musical and scenic aspects of language and experience with emotion.

Part of the effect of participating in sense-making and of being swept up by the sound and rhythm of language is emotional. The similarity between conversational and literary discourse exists because both seek not merely to convince audiences (a purportedly logical process), but also to move them (an emotional one).[10] Emotion and cognition (following Becker 1979, M. C. Bateson

1984, Friedrich 1986, Tyler 1978) are inseparable. Understanding is facilitated, even enabled, by an emotional experience of interpersonal involvement.

Friedrich (1986:128) notes,

The emotive or expressive function has a strong connection with the poetic one, with which it should not be confused or identified. The main content of this relation is that the emotions are the *main* source or driving force for the poetic ... and hence are more powerful, or "deeper."

In other words, although emotion is not synonymous with the poetic force in language, it is a significant source of the language's power – its ability to fire the individual imagination.

Particularity

As noted above, Chafe (1984:1099) includes particularity as an aspect of involvement. Part of the impact of dialogue, and of details and images, is their particularity. Becker (1984b, 1988) emphasizes the need for "a linguistics of particularity," that is, the close analysis of particular instances of discourse. The study of discourse, he observes (1984b:435), "is of necessity the study of particularity." His analysis of repetition (1984b), discussed in more detail below, demonstrates the power of examining lexical repetition in creating a topic chain in the written version of a scene from a Javanese shadow play: "a particular thread in the texture of a particular tale." In a lecture discussing the need for a humanistic linguistics, Becker (1988:30) demonstrates that the constraints which account for coherence in discourse come together only in particular utterances produced in context.

Stephen Jay Gould, in praising Jane Goodall's *The chimpanzees of Gombe*, describes a kind of science that is close to Becker's humanism, the branch of science in which anthropologist Gregory Bateson worked: natural history. In this science, Gould (1987:23–4) emphasizes, the particular and the personal are not ignored; they are paramount:

Individuality does more than matter; it is of the essence. You must learn to recognize individual chimps and follow them for years, recording their peculiarities, their differences, and their interactions ... It may seem quaint to some people who fail to grasp the power of natural history that this great work of science largely tells stories about individual creatures with funny names like Jomeo, Passion, and David Greybeard. When you understand why nature's complexity can only be unraveled this way, why individuality matters so crucially, then you are in a position to understand what the sciences of history are all about. I treasure this book most of all for its quiet and unobtrusive proof, by iterated example rather than theoretical bombast, that close observation of individual differences can be as powerful a method in science as the quantification of predictable behavior in a zillion identical atoms ...

In discussing the need for close observation, Gould emphasizes the crucial nature of "true historical particulars that can only be appreciated by watching, not predicted from theory."

Identifying and tracking individual animals is the method of many studies of animal behavior. A whale researcher, for example, learned to identify individual whales by the pattern of lip grooves below their mouths (Glockner-Ferrari 1986). Cynthia Moss (1988) learned to identify individual elephants initially by their ears. In thanking those who worked with her, Moss notes, "No one who gets to know the Amboseli elephants as individuals is untouched by that knowledge and it has bound us irrevocably" (9). Getting to know the elephants *as individuals* created a sense of involvement not only between researcher and elephants but also among the researchers who shared that involvement. Like Goodall, Moss creates that sense of involvement in readers by telling the stories of named individuals.

Alberoni (1983) suggests that falling in love is always a matter of particularity: of acute perception and appreciation of the beloved's specificity, of associations with particular places and times that "produces a sacred geography of the world" (38). I believe that this parallel is not by chance, but rather that the particular is central to the emotional, which is the key to inspiration of all types: cognitive, intellectual, and creative as well as romantic. This idea is also echoed in Mary Catherine Bateson's (1984) recollection that Margaret Mead likened successful academic conferences to falling in love.

Scenes and music, then, and emotion associated with them, are the dynamics by which linguistic strategies create meaning and involvement in discourse.

Repetition in conversation: toward a poetics of talk

Repeating then is in every one, in every one their being and their feeling and their way of realizing everything and every one comes out of them in repeating.
Gertrude Stein, *The gradual making of "The Making of Americans"*
Lectures in America, p. 214[1]

Apparently there has been no other subject during my entire scholarly life that has captured me as persistently as have the questions of parallelism.
Roman Jakobson, *Dialogues* by Roman Jakobson and
Krystyna Pomorska, p. 100

Theoretical implications of repetition

According to Hymes (1981), the patterning of repetitions and contrasts is no less than a definition of structure itself. Hymes discusses the inadequacy of an early translation of a Chippewa (Ojibway) poem which changes what he calls its "structure": "its points of constancy and variation, repetition and contrast," as well as its literal content (41). Hymes explains:

The term "structure" is used here because of my belief that the true structure of the original poem is essential to knowledge of it, both ethnological and aesthetic. *By structure, I mean here particularly the form of repetition and variation, of constants and contrasts, in verbal organization.* Such structure is manifest in linguistic form. It does not exhaust the structuring of poems ... But such structure is the matrix of the meaning and effect of the poem. (42, italics in original)

Becker (1984b) examines reduplication and repetition as variants of a repetitive strategy at different levels in an episode from a wayang (Javanese shadow play), in which a boy escaping from a demon breaks a taboo by upsetting a steamer of rice. Javanese grammatical constraints preclude the use of pronouns (there is no "it" in Javanese) or of ellipsis (in Becker's terms, "zeroing") in sub-

sequent reference to inanimate topics. Instead, various forms of
dang "to steam" are repeated, resulting in a dense discourse texture
which, according to Becker, is characteristically Javanese.

Becker sees such discourse strategies as constituting the grammar
of a language: not abstract patterns but actual bits of text which
are remembered, more or less, and then retrieved to be reshaped to
new contexts. And so, by a process of repetition, "The actual
a-priori of any language event – the real deep structure – is an
accumulation of remembered prior texts"; thus, "our real language
competence is access, via memory, to this accumulation of prior
text" (435).

Becker's account of linguistic competence is similar in spirit to
that of Bolinger (1961:381), who observed:

At present we have no way of telling the extent to which a sentence like
I went home is a result of invention, and the extent to which it is a result
of repetition, countless speakers before us having already said it and transmitted it to us in toto. Is grammar something where speakers "produce"
(i.e. originate) constructions, or where they "reach for" them, from a pre-
established inventory . . .?

Thus Hymes, Becker and Bolinger all suggest that repetition is at
the heart not only of how a particular discourse is created, but how
discourse itself is created.

Prepatterning

Analysis of repetition thus sheds light on our conception of language production, or, as Becker would say, "languaging." In short,
it suggests that language is less freely generated, more prepatterned,
than most current linguistic theory acknowledges. This is not,
however, to say that speakers are automatons, cranking out language by rote. Rather, prepatterning (or idiomaticity, or formulaicity) is a resource for creativity. It is the play between fixity and
novelty that makes possible the creation of meaning. Because of
these implications for an understanding of the nature of language,
I discuss the ways language can be seen as prepatterned.

Prepatterning in language

Bolinger (1976:3) observes:

Many scholars – for example, Bugarski 1968, Chafe 1968, and especially

Makkai 1972 – have pointed out that idioms are where reductionist theories of language break down. But what we are now in a position to recognize is that idiomaticity is a vastly more pervasive phenomenon than we ever imagined, and vastly harder to separate from the pure freedom of syntax, if indeed any such fiery zone as pure syntax exists.

There has been increasing attention paid recently to idiomaticity, or prepatterning, in both the narrow and the broad senses that Bolinger describes. In the narrow sense, scholars are recognizing the ubiquity of prepatterned expressions *per se*. These have been variously named; Fillmore (1982) notes the terms "formulaic expressions, phraseological units, idiomatic expressions, set expressions." Other terms that have been used include "conversational routine," "routine formulae," "linguistic routines" and "routinized speech" (Coulmas 1981); "prepatterned speech" and "prefabs" (Bolinger 1976); "formulas, set expressions, collocations" (Matisoff 1979); and "lexicalized sentence stems" (Pawley and Syder 1983). Considerable attention has focused on the role of fixed or formulaic expressions in first and second language acquisition (for example, Corsaro 1979, Wong Fillmore 1979).

In order to move toward the broader sense of prepatterning, I will consider the range of prepatterning by which one may say that language in discourse is not either prepatterned or novel but more or less prepatterned.

A scale of fixity

Maximally prepatterned are instances of what Zimmer (1958) calls situational formulas: fixed form expressions that are always uttered in certain situations, the omission of which in those situations is perceived as a violation of appropriate behavior. Many languages, such as Arabic (Ferguson 1976), Turkish (Zimmer 1958, Tannen and Öztek 1981), and modern Greek (Tannen and Öztek 1981) contain numerous such situational formulas, many of which come in pairs.

For example, in Greek, one who is leaving for a trip will certainly be told the formula, "Kalo taxidhi" ("Good trip"). This is not unlike the American expression, "Have a good trip." But a departing American might also be told, "Have a nice trip," or a "great" one (obviously prepatterned but not as rigidly so) or something

reflecting a different paradigm, like "I hope you enjoy your trip."
Moreover, a Greek who is told "Kalo taxidhi" is likely to respond,
"Kali andamosi" ("Good reunion"), making symmetrical the in-
stitutionalized expression of feeling: One wishes the other a good
trip; the other expresses anticipation of meeting again upon return.

A similar routine in Greek with a similarly less routinized and
less reciprocal counterpart in English is "Kalos orises" ("[it is] Well
[that] you came"), parallel to the English "Welcome home." But
whereas the English "Welcome home" has no ritualized rejoinder,
the invariable response of a Greek to "Kalos orises" is "Kalos se
[sas] vrika" ("[it is] Well [that] I found you" [sing. or pl.]). Thus
an arrival event is marked in modern Greek by symmetrical routinized expressions of the sentiment, "I am happy to see you again."

As these examples and the need for this explanation testify, rigid
situational formulas are less common in American English than in
some other languages and cultures. Such expressions are always uttered in exactly the same way and are associated with – indeed, expected in – certain situations. Their omission would be noticed and
disapproved. For speakers who have become accustomed to using
such formulas in their everyday interactions, not being able to use
them (which happens when such a speaker moves to a country
where they are not used) results in an uncomfortable feeling of
being linguistically hamstrung, unable to say what one feels is appropriate or even necessary to say. (See Tannen 1980b for further
discussion of this cross-cultural phenomenon.)

Highly fixed in form but less so in association with particular
contexts are proverbs and sayings such as "It takes one to know
one," which all native speakers of English would recognize and
some would utter, if at all, in this form, although their occurrence
could not be predicted, and their omission would not be remarked.
There are cultural and individual differences with respect to how
frequently such collocations are used and how they are evaluated.

A type of expression that is highly fixed in form though less
predictable in situational association is proverbs. (See Norrick
1985 for an overview of this genre.) A good sense of the frequency
with which proverbs can be expected and used in conversation in
some cultures can be gained by reading the novels of the Nigerian
novelist Chinua Achebe. For example, in *Things fall apart* (1958:
5–6), proverbs play a crucial role when a speaker, visiting a neigh-

bor, is ready to get to the point of asking for the return of borrowed
money:

> Having spoken plainly so far, Okoye said the next half dozen sentences in
> proverbs. Among the Ibo the art of conversation is regarded very highly,
> and proverbs are the palm-oil with which words are eaten.

This excerpt illustrates the high regard in which proverbs, as fixed
formulas, are held in this culture, as in many others. Americans, in
contrast, are inclined to regard relatively fixed expressions with
suspicion and are likely to speak with scorn of cliches, assuming
that sincerity is associated with novelty of expression and fixity
with insincerity.

Although many proverbs and sayings are known to English
speakers, they are less likely to introduce them nonironically in
everyday speech. Undertaking a study of proverbs in English, Norrick (1985: 6) ended up using the Oxford Dictionary of English
Proverbs for his corpus, because he

> worked through the entire *A Corpus of English Conversation* (Svartvik and
> Quirk 1980) looking for proverbs and found only one true example and
> one marginal one in its 43,165 lines and 891 pages ... A perusal of the
> 1028 lines of transcribed conversation in Crystal and Davy (1975) for the
> sake of comparison turned up no examples whatsoever.

Although proverbs may not be routinely uttered in English conversation, idioms and other prepatterned expressions are pervasive in
American speech, although their form in utterance is often only
highly not absolutely fixed.

For English speakers, at least, it is common to use fixed expressions with some items in their canonical form altered, with no apparent loss of communicative effectiveness. This in itself is evidence
that meaning is not being derived from the expressions directly, by
a process of deconstruction according to definitions and rules, but
rather is being arrived at in a leap of association, in keeping with
Bolinger's observation that prefabs "have the magical property of
persisting even when we knock some of them apart and put them
together in unpredictable ways."

For example, I heard a politician on the radio asserting that the
investigation he was spearheading would not stop "until every
stone is unturned." There is no reason to doubt that hearers knew
what he meant, by reference to the expression "leave no stone

unturned," and no reason to believe that many hearers noticed that what he actually said, if grammatically decomposed, amounted to a promise that he would turn over no stones in his investigation. Another example is the metamorphosis of the expression "I couldn't care less" to "I could care less," with preservation rather than reversal of meaning.[2]

In addition to slightly altering formulas, it is common for speakers to fuse formulas – that is, utter a phrase that contains parts of two different though semantically and/or phonologically related set expressions. For example, some years ago, I told a number of friends and colleagues, on different occasions, that I was "up against the wire" in completing a project.[3] It took a linguist who was studying prepatterned expressions, James Matisoff, to notice (or at least to remark, by whipping out his little notebook) that I had fused two different formulas: "up against the wall" and "down to the wire" (or perhaps "in under the wire").

Since this experience, and thanks to it (and to Matisoff), I have observed innumerable fused formulas. Only a few chosen from many I have heard (or unwittingly uttered), and the originals which I believe they fused, are as follows:

It's no sweat off our backs
  – It's no sweat
  – no skin off one's nose
  – [the shirt off one's back?]
You can make that decision on the snap of the moment
  – on the spur of the moment
  – a snap decision
at the drop of a pin
  – at the drop of a hat
  – hear a pin drop
something along those veins
  – along those lines
  – in that vein
How would you like to eat humble crow?
  – eat crow
  – eat humble pie
He was off the deep
  – off the wall
  – off the deep end
If you have any changes just pipe in
  – pipe up
  – chime in

My point here is emphatically not that these speakers made mistakes (although, strictly speaking, they did), but that the altered forms of the set expressions communicated meaning as well as the canonical forms would have. In other words, the language is mistake-proof, to this extent. Meaning is gleaned by association with the familiar sayings, not by structural decomposition.

It is possible, if not likely, for the altered form to be enhanced rather than handicapped, enriched by association with more than one word or formula. For example, "eat humble crow" adds the lexicalized humiliation of "humble" from "humble pie" to the implied humiliation of "eat crow." "Pipe in" combines the enthusiasm of "pipe up" with the participation of "chime in." In another example, a speaker put her hand on her chest and said, "I felt so chestfallen."[4] One could well see this as a form of linguistic creativity rather than an error or misfire in the reaching for the word "crestfallen." Thus fixity in expression can be a source of rather than an impediment to creativity.

Fixity of form can characterize chunks of smaller as well as larger size. English includes innumerable expressions and collocations such as "salt and pepper" or "thick and thin". These are shorter collocations whose form is fixed and whose meaning may be tied to that form, so that the expression "pepper and salt" is not likely to occur, and the expression "thin and thick" is not likely to be understood, except by reference to the original formula.

Cases of fixed expressions and collocations are the clearest examples of prepatterning. All discourse, however, is more or less prepatterned, in the sense that Friedrich (1986:23) notes, citing Leech (1969): "Almost all conversation is, at the surface, literally formulaic in the sense of conjoining and interlocking prefabricated words, phrases, and other units." As the sources cited by Bolinger attest, prefabrications also exist at the level of phonology and morphology.

Wittgenstein and Heidegger have shown that all meaning is derived from words by means of associations. According to Heidegger (1962:191), "The ready-to-hand is always understood in terms of a totality of involvements," and "Any assertion requires a forehaving" (199).[5] In Wittgenstein's (1958:15) words, "Only someone who already knows how to do something with it can significantly ask a name." In other words, semantics too is a matter

prior text, in Becker's terms. Another way to express this, following C. J. Fillmore (1976, 1985), is that all semantics is frame
semantics: meaning can be gleaned only by reference to a set of culturally familiar scenarios (scripts or frames).

Pawley (1986:116), in discussing his concept of "lexicalization,"
notes that "it is important to separate those form-meaning pairings
that have institutional status in this culture from those that do not,
as well as to denote particular kinds and degrees of institutionaliza-
tion." In a similar spirit, Hopper (1988a) identifies two types of
grammar that he calls the "a priori grammar attitude" and the
"emergence of grammar attitude." These two philosophical approaches to grammar are distinguished, in part, by their differential
treatment of prepatterning. The a priori grammar attitude is
"indifferent to prior texts," not distinguishing between repetitive utterances such as idioms and proverbs, on the one hand, and "bizarre fictional utterances" on the other (121). In the emergent
grammar view (the one Hopper supports), the fact that some sentences are frequently said and others not is crucial, not incidental.
Finally, fixed expressions play a significant role in the construction
grammar of Fillmore and Kay (Kay 1984, Fillmore, Kay and
O'Connor 1988).

Bakhtin (1981:276) describes one sense in which meaning
cannot be the sole work of an individual:

Indeed, any concrete discourse (utterance) finds the object at which it was
directed already as it were overlain with qualifications, open to dispute,
charged with value, already enveloped in an obscuring mist – or, on the
contrary, by the "light" of a line of words that have already been spoken
about it. It is entangled, shot through with shared thoughts, points of view,
alien value judgments and accents . . .

The living utterance . . . cannot fail to brush up against thousands of
living dialogic threads . . .; it cannot fail to become an active participant in
social dialogue. After all, the utterance arises out of this dialogue as a con-
tinuation of it and as a rejoinder to it – it does not approach the object
from the sidelines.

Moving to larger units of text, the organization of discourse follows recognizable patterns, as discussed in chapter 2 under the involvement strategy, repetition of longer discourse sequences.

Another type of prepatterning, perhaps the most disquieting to
some, is what to say. People feel, when they speak, that they are

expressing personal opinions, experiences, and feelings in their own way. But there is wide cultural and subcultural diversity in what seems self-evidently appropriate to say, indeed, to think, feel, or opine. There is an enormous literature to draw upon in support of this argument. All the scholars cited for work showing differing discourse strategies include observations about what can be said. Some further sources include Tyler (1978), Polanyi (1985), Schieffelin (1979), and all the work of Becker.

Mills ([1940] 1967) observes that individuals decide what is logical and reasonable based on experience of what others give and accept as logical and reasonable motives. And these "vocabularies of motives" differ from culture to culture. Referring to personal experience, everyone notices, upon going to a foreign country or talking to someone of different cultural background, that things are said and asked which take one by surprise, seeming unexpected or even uninterpretable.[6]

The unexpected, like a starred sentence in syntax, is noticed. Speakers rarely notice the extent to which their own utterances are routinized, repetitious of what they have heard. For example, during the 1984 American presidential election, I heard from several individuals, as the expression of their personal opinions, that Mondale was boring. Never before or since has this seemed an appropriate and logical observation to make about a presidential candidate, a basis on which to judge his qualifications for office. Yet it seemed so in 1984, repeated back and forth in newspaper opinions, private opinions, and newspaper reports of private opinions in the form of ubiquitous polls. As Becker (ms.: 4) notes, much of "apparently free conversation is a replay of remembered texts – from T.V. news, radio talk, the New York Times . . ."

Dimensions of fixity

Given this sense in which all language is a repetition of previous language, and all expressions are relatively fixed in form, one cannot help but notice that some instances of language are more fixed than others. This may be conceived as a number of continua reflecting these dimensions. There is, first, a continuum of relative fixity in form, another of relative fixity with respect to context, and a third with respect to time.

The first two dimensions, fixity vs. novelty in form and by as-sociation with context, have already been illustrated with reference to rigid situational formulas. The dimension of relative longevity or wide-spreadness of prepatterning across time is represented, at one pole, by instant, ephemeral language which is picked up and repeated verbatim in a given conversation and then forgotten. Many examples of this are presented in this chapter. A question is repeated word for word and then answered; a listener repeats the end of a speaker's utterance by way of showing listenership, and so on. Inasmuch as the second speaker repeated the utterance of another, the second speaker found the utterance ready-made and used it as found. For that speaker in that context, the utterance was prepatterned, formulaic, if fleetingly so.

Again as illustrated by many of the examples in this chapter, some phrases are picked up and repeated in extended play of more than a single repetition, repeated by more than one speaker in a multi-party conversation. Moving along the continuum of fixity in time (in contrast to fixity in form and situation), we find expres-sions which are re-used throughout an extended interchange, but only that one. For example, during her oral examination boards, a graduate student coined the term "vanilla linguistics" to distin-guish it from the hyphenated disciplines such as socio-, psycho- and applied linguistics. Once she had done this, the phrase was picked up and used, repeated by the examiners and the student throughout that oral exam. However, it was not, so far as I know, ever used again by any of those speakers. The life of the expression was fixed, or formulaic, in, but did not outlive, that interaction.[7]

Had the student or the examiners used this term in future en-counters with each other, that term might have become formulaic for them – a kind of "private language" such as individuals and groups of individuals develop, so that collocations have for them associations and ramifications accumulated in past interactions. It is the embellishment of such a private language that gives a recog-nizable character to communication among long-time associates, and is one of the reasons that it is sad when such extended interac-tion (for example, a relationship) ends: a language has died; one is left with ways of meaning that no one one speaks to can un-derstand.

If, hypothetically, the phrase "vanilla linguistics" had been picked up by the faculty members on that examination board and used by them in professional interactions such as teaching, public lectures, or publications, or had it been subsequently repeated by the student to other students and repeatedly used by them, the phrase could have become a prepatterned expression for a larger group. Thus terms, phrases, and expressions diffuse through the language of small or large groups and become part of the language for a short or long time. Anyone returning to a home country after residence abroad notices phrases in common use that gained currency during their absence. The introduction of new terms and phrases can sometimes be perceived even when one has not been away. I recall the first time I heard someone refer to another's behavior as "off the wall": I had to ask what that meant. The phrase eventually came to sound very "natural" to me; for a time, I believe, I used it a lot; now, I believe, it has a circumscribed place in my repertoire.

In summary, then, repetition is at the heart of language: in Hymes's terms, language structure, in Bolinger's, language production, in Becker's, all languaging. Considered in this light, it raises fundamental questions about the nature of language, and the degree to which language is freely "generated" or repeated from language previously experienced.

Repetition in discourse

Friedrich (1986:154) remarks on the "intensely poetic" nature of the child's learning experience, "involving sound play, complex figures of speech, and various experiments." If repetition is an essentially poetic aspect of language (as others have argued and I will argue it is), then it is not surprising that, as Keenan (1977:125) notes, "One of the most commonplace observations in the psycholinguistic literature is that many young children often repeat utterances addressed to them," and that studies of children's discourse are the richest source of research on repetition. (The work of Bennett-Kastor [for example, 1978, 1986] is devoted to the study of repetition in first language acquisition.) Moreover, a glance at the child discourse literature reveals that nearly every study makes some reference to children's use of repetition.[8]

Grammatical parallelism – the whole network of equivalence

and contrast relations – was an abiding concern of Jakobson. Waugh and Monville-Burston (in preparation) point out that much of Jakobson's intellectual energy in the 1960s and 1970s was devoted to analyzing these relations in poems. Best known perhaps is his discussion of "Grammatical parallelism and its Russian facet," showing grammatical parallelism to be the "basic mode of concatenating successive verses" (1966:405) in Russian folk poetry. Levin (1973:30) proposes that poetry is characterized by "coupling": putting "into combination, on the syntagmatic axis, elements which, on the basis of their natural equivalences, constitute equivalence classes or paradigms." Kiparsky (1973) examines both syntactic and phonological parallelism in poetry.

Johnstone (1987a), briefly surveying research on repetition, notes that repetition is especially frequent in highly formal or ritualized discourse and in speech by and to children. It is a way, she suggests, of creating categories and of giving meaning to new forms in terms of old. Research on ritual language has tended to be carried out by anthropologists and to focus on non-English languages. In contrast, research on or noting repetition in children's language has frequently concentrated on English.

Few studies have focused on repetition in conversation or other non-formal texts. (Exceptions are Schiffrin 1982, Norrick 1987, and of course Tannen 1987a,b, the articles on which parts of this chapter are based.) Goodwin and Goodwin (1987) observe repetition in conversation as "format tying," and use this observation to critique a speech-act approach to discourse. They remark that reducing conversation to underlying actions, intentions, or moves is like studying what a musician does but ignoring the music played. They point out that the coherence of a participant's move to a preceding one may lie in the "particularities of its wording."

That "particularities of wording" play a key role in creating coherence in conversation is a premise of this study to be illustrated at length here.

Functions of repetition in conversation

Why is there repetition in conversation? Why do we waste our breath saying the same thing over and over? (Why, for example, did I write the preceding sentence, which paraphrases the one before?) The varied purposes simultaneously served by repetition can be subsumed under the categories of production, comprehension, connection, and interaction. The congruence of these functions of discourse provides a fourth and over-arching function in the establishment of coherence and interpersonal involvement.

Production

Repetition enables a speaker to produce language in a more efficient, less energy-draining way. It facilitates the production of more language, more fluently. For individuals and cultures that value verbosity and wish to avoid silences in casual conversation (for example, those I have characterized as having "high-involvement styles"), repetition is a resource for producing ample talk, both by providing material for talk and by enabling talk through automaticity. (Evidence that repetitions can be produced automatically is presented in a later section of this chapter.)

Repetition allows a speaker to set up a paradigm and slot in new information – where the frame for the new information stands ready, rather than having to be newly formulated. An example is seen in a narrative elsewhere analyzed at length (Tannen 1982), in which a woman talked about a man who worked in her office (see Appendix II for transcription conventions):

> <u>And he knows</u> Spanish,
> <u>and he knows</u> French,
> <u>and he knows</u> English,
> <u>and he knows</u> German,
> <u>and HE</u> is a GENtleman.

The establishment of the pattern allowed the speaker to utter whole new sentences while adding only the names of languages as new information.

Repetition, finally, enables a speaker to produce fluent speech while formulating what to say next. I have used the term "linking repetition" for a phenomenon found in narratives told about a film (the much-analyzed "pear stories" [Chafe 1980]), by which some speakers repeated clauses at episode boundaries. An example presented in that study (Tannen 1979:167) was taken from a narrative told about the film in Greek. I reproduce that example here,

with the lines immediately following the repetition added to
demonstrate the role of the repetition as a transition.

1 kai ta paidhakia <u>synechisane to dhromo.</u>
2 ... <u>synechisane:</u> ... <u>to dhromo,</u>
3 Kai to: n:
4 ... kai afta ... e:m kai pigainane:
5 pros tin fora pou 'tane to dhendro,

1 and the little children <u>continued (going down) the road.</u>
2 ... (they) <u>continue:d</u> ... <u>(going down) the road,</u>
3 and the: mmm
4 ... and they/these ... u:m and (they) were goi:ng
5 toward the direction where the tree was,

The speaker repeats in line 2 the final clause of the episode (line 1)
in which three children are walking down the road eating pears, as
she devises a transition to the next episode, in which they will come
upon the tree from which (unbeknownst to them) the pears had
been stolen.[9]

To the extent, then, that repetitions and variations are automatic, they enable speakers to carry on conversation with relatively
less effort, to find all or part of the utterance ready-made, so they
can proceed with verbalization before deciding exactly what to say
next.

Comprehension

The comprehension benefit of repetition mirrors that of production. Repetition and variations facilitate comprehension by providing semantically less dense discourse. If some of the words are
repetitious, comparatively less new information is communicated
than if all words uttered carried new information. This redundancy
in spoken discourse allows a hearer to receive information at
roughly the rate the speaker is producing it. That is, just as the
speaker benefits from some relatively dead space while thinking of
the next thing to say, the hearer benefits from the same dead space
and from the redundancy while absorbing what is said. This contrasts with the situation that obtains when a written document is
read aloud, and it may account for the difficulty of trying to com-
prehend such discourse – for example, the frequent inability of
listeners at scholarly conferences to follow fully (or at all) most
papers read aloud. The hearer, deprived of redundancy in such

cases, must pay attention to every word, taking in information at
a rate much faster than that at which the author compiled it.

Connection

Halliday and Hasan (1976) include repetition in their taxonomy of
cohesive devices: it serves a referential and tying function. Repetition of sentences, phrases, and words shows how new utterances
are linked to earlier discourse, and how ideas presented in the discourse are related to each other. But this is only the most apparent
and straightforward way in which repetition allows a speaker to
shape the material.

In a more pervasive and subtle way, repetition evidences a
speaker's attitude, showing how it contributes to the meaning of
the discourse. In terms of theme and rheme (Halliday 1967) or of
topic and comment, repetition is a way of contributing to the rheme
or comment. As Labov (1972) points out in introducing and
defining "evaluation," repetition is evaluative: It contributes to the
point. Here falls the function of repetition which is commonly
referred to as emphasis, as well as a range of other evaluations of
a proposition, or relationships among propositions.

For a brief illustration, consider again the excerpt about the man
who knows languages:

1 <u>And he knows</u> Spanish,
2 <u>and he knows</u> French,
3 <u>and he knows</u> English,
4 <u>and he knows</u> German,
5 <u>and HE</u> is a GENtleman.

Repetition of "and he" in the final line ("and HE is a GENtleman.")
ties the last line to the first four, indicating that the person referred
to is the same throughout. Repetition of "and he knows" in lines
1–4 also serves a tying function, indicating that all the languages
named are known by the same person. Beyond this simple tying
function, however, the repetition of the phrases establishes a list-
like rhythm, giving the impression that the languages which this
person knows constitute a long list, longer even than the one given.
Furthermore, and crucially, the evaluative effect of the list is to
communicate that the speaker finds the length of the list

impressive – and so should the listener. Moreover, the impact of the last line, "and HE is a GENtleman," is greater by virtue of its suddenly varying the frame. It carries over and reinforces the sense of admiration in the repetition of the rhythmic pattern which stresses "he."

Paradoxically, repeating the frame foregrounds and intensifies the part repeated, and also foregrounds and intensifies the part that is different. To quote Jakobson (Jakobson and Pomorska 1983: 103), "By focusing on parallelisms and similarities in pairs of lines, one is led to pay more attention to every similarity and every difference." In a passage which is especially interesting because it indicates that her fascination with repetition was inspired by her observation of conversation, Gertrude Stein (1935:213, cited in Law 1985: 26) also notes that repetition sets both similarities and differences into relief:

I began to get enormously interested in hearing how everybody said the same thing over and over again with infinite variations but over and over again until finally if you listened with great intensity you could hear it rise and fall and tell all that there was inside them, not so much by the actual words they said or the thoughts they had but the movement of their thoughts and words endlessly the same and endlessly different.

Interaction

The functions of repetition discussed under the headings of production, comprehension, and connection all refer to the creation of meaning in conversation. But repetition also functions on the interactional level of talk: accomplishing social goals, or simply managing the business of conversation. Some functions observed in transcripts I have studied (which are not mutually exclusive, and may overlap with previously discussed functions) include: getting or keeping the floor, showing listenership, providing back-channel response, stalling, gearing up to answer or speak, humor and play, savoring and showing appreciation of a good line or a good joke, persuasion (what Koch 1983a calls "presentation as proof"), linking one speaker's ideas to another's, ratifying another's contributions (including another's ratification), and including in an interaction a person who did not hear a previous utterance.[10] In other words, repetition not only ties parts of discourse to other parts, but it bonds participants to the discourse and to each other, linking individual speakers in a conversation and in relationships.

Coherence as interpersonal involvement

By facilitating production, comprehension, connection, and interaction in these and other ways, repetition serves an over-arching purpose of creating interpersonal involvement. Repeating the words, phrases, or sentences of other speakers (a) accomplishes a conversation, (b) shows one's response to another's utterance, (c) shows acceptance of others' utterances, their participation, and them, and (d) gives evidence of one's own participation. It provides a resource to keep talk going, where talk itself is a show of involvement, of willingness to interact, to serve positive face. All of this sends a metamessage of involvement. This may be the highest-level function of repetition – in the sense in which Gregory Bateson (1972) adapts Bertrand Russell's notion of logical types to describe the metamessage level of interaction: the level at which messages about relationships are communicated.

In a closely related way, repetition also serves the purpose served by all conventionalized discourse strategies at every level of language: giving talk a character of familiarity, making the discourse sound right. This is a verbal analogue to the pleasure associated with familiar physical surroundings: the comfort of home, of a favorite chair. It is the trust in a speaker one knows, or one who seems – by virtue of appearance, dress, kinesics, and ways of speaking – like one to be trusted. The pattern of repeated and varied sounds, words, phrases, sentences, and longer discourse sequences gives the impression, indeed the reality, of a shared universe of discourse.

But how, linguistically, is interpersonal involvement accomplished? In terms of the musical aspect of language, repeating a word, phrase, or longer syntactic unit – exactly or with variation – results in a rhythmic pattern that creates ensemble. In terms of mutual participation in sensemaking, each time a word or phrase is repeated, its meaning is altered. The audience reinterprets the meaning of the word or phrase in light of the accretion, juxtaposition, or expansion. In the words of Jefferson (1972:303), "a repeat" is "an object that has as its product-item a prior occurrence of the same thing, which performs some operation upon that product-item." In other words, seeing the same item a second time, listeners re-interpret its meaning. An extreme representation of listeners supplying meaning in repetitions is in Jerzy Kosinski's novel *Being there*: A simple-minded gardener is thought brilliant by those whose words he repeats. The deep meaning they glean from his utterances is entirely the result of their own work.

Repetition and variation in conversation

Conventional wisdom: the negative view

"History repeats itself," a radio announcer quipped. "That's one of the things wrong with history." This witticism reflects conventional wisdom by which repetition is considered undesirable in conversation. "You're repeating yourself" can only be heard as a criticism. One cannot say, "Wait a minute, I haven't repeated myself yet," as one can say, "Wait a minute, I haven't finished what I started to say."

Evidence of negative associations with repetition abounds. The stereotypical popular image of repetition in conversation is represented by Woody Allen (1982:363) in the screenplay of *Stardust memories*:

And Jones and Smith, the two studio executives who are always seen together, Smith always yessing Jones, repeating what he says, appear on the screen next. . . .

JONES   And what about the cancer foundation . . .
SMITH   And what about the cancer foundation . . .
JONES   . . . and the leukemia victims . . .
SMITH   . . . and those leukemia victims . . .
JONES   . . . and the political prisoners all over the world?
SMITH   . . . and the political prisoners . . .
JONES   What about the Jews?
SMITH   The Jews!

The italicized description of the action, provided by the publisher, suggests a negative Tweedledee/Tweedledum interpretation of the repetition in the dialogue. Moreover, the repetition in the dialogue seems intended to belie the verbalized concern for the victims.

Repetition here is synonymous with "yessing": buttering someone up by hypocritically displaying continual automatic agreement.

A reviewer (Prescott 1983:82) criticizes an author by saying, "Her numbing repetition of perhaps a dozen significant sentences quickly becomes irritating." The poet W. H. Auden ([1956] 1986: 3) observed that "the notion of repetition is associated in people's minds with all that is most boring and lifeless – punching time clocks, road drills, etc." He lamented that this makes "an obstacle" of "the rhythmical character of poetry" because "rhythm involves repetition." Auden's observation of the necessity of repetition for poetry highlights the contrast that repetition has been taken seriously and highly valued in literary texts (Law 1985 notes a number of studies of repetition in literature), in contrast to its devaluation in conventional wisdom applied to conversation.

This chapter demonstrates, with reference to examples from conversational transcripts, that repetition is pervasive, functional, and often automatic in ordinary conversation.

Forms of repetition

Forms of repetition and variation in conversation can be identified according to several criteria. First, one may distinguish self-repetition and allo-repetition (repetition of others). Second, instances of repetition may be placed along a scale of fixity in form, ranging from exact repetition (the same words uttered in the same rhythmic pattern) to paraphrase (similar ideas in different words). Midway on the scale, and most common, is repetition with variation, such as questions transformed into statements, statements changed into questions, repetition with a single word or phrase changed, and repetition with change of person or tense. I also include patterned rhythm, in which completely different words are uttered in the same syntactic and rhythmic paradigm as a preceding utterance. There is also a temporal scale ranging from immediate to delayed repetition, where "delayed" can refer to delay within a discourse or delay across days, weeks, months, and years. Formulaic language (or fixed expressions) is language repeated by multiple speakers over time.

All these boundaries are fuzzy. Although some expressions are readily recognizable as formulaic (for example, "A stitch in time saves nine"), many others have a familiar ring but are difficult to categorize with certainty as formulaic. Similarly, in identifying repetitions in a discourse, some cases are clearcut (such as most of those I present here), but in others, one must make what is ultimately an arbitrary decision about how far away in the transcript two occurrences may be in order for the second to be counted as a repetition of the first. Always, moreover, there is at least a theoretical possibility that both instances of the same string, or any instances of any string, are repetitions of a string which the speaker previously heard or uttered.

It would be hubris (and hopeless) to attempt to illustrate every form and function of repetition. I will try simply to indicate the pervasiveness of repetition in conversation by exemplifying many of its forms and functions, to show evidence that repetition can be automatic, and to discuss how it contributes to interpersonal involvement.

Repetition across discourses and time

My main focus in this chapter is syntactic repetition in casual conversation. To indicate, however, that repetition occurs across discourses and across time as well as within a discourse, I begin with an example of a narrative which seems to be structured around a remembered kernel sentence.

Elsewhere (Tannen 1978) I analyze a conversational story told by a woman in a small group as part of a story round that I sparked by asking if anyone had had any interesting experiences on the subway. In telling of the time she fainted on the New York subway, this speaker uttered a single sentence, with variation, three times. Near the beginning she said it twice in quick succession:

> ... a:nd ... I remember saying to myself ... [chuckling]
> "There is a person over there
> that's falling to the ground."
> ... And that person was me.
> ... And I couldn't ... put together the fact that
> there was someone fainting
> and that someone was me.

After the speaker tells the story and the group discusses it briefly, the speaker reiterates the sentence by way of closing off that story and moving on to another:

A:nd uh: ... it was funny
because in my head I said
... my awareness was such .. that I said to myself
... "Gee well there's a person over there,
falling down."
... And that person was me.
[Listener: It's weird ... mm]
Okay that was ... that experience.
... And another experience

This sentence, in its three forms, encapsulates what was interesting about having fainted on the subway, or at least what the speaker is making the point of her telling: that she had an out-of-body experience, by which she saw herself as if from the outside. The sentences share a syntagmatic frame which includes slots that are filled with slightly different items. See Table 1 for a representation of the three sentences in this framework.

Table 1.

There is	a person over there that's	falling	to the ground	and that person	was me.
There was	someone		fainting	and that someone	was me.
There's	a person over there		falling down	and that person	was me.

Insofar as this speaker repeated the sentence, slightly varied, twice after its first utterance, she could be said to have found the second and third utterances relatively ready-made in her own prior speech. I am convinced, although I cannot prove it on the basis of this example alone, that she had told this story before, and would tell it again, and that when she did so, she would use a variation of the same sentence because it encapsulated for her what was memorable and reportable about this experience. In this sense, at the time she told this story, she was repeating the sentence from her own prior discourse at earlier times.

The pervasiveness of repetition in conversation

At the beginning of each semester, I ask students in my classes to record spontaneous conversations in which they participate; they then choose segments to transcribe and analyze throughout the semester. Each term, the assignment everyone finds easiest is the one that requires them to identify lexical and syntactic repetitions in their transcripts. For example, the following segment came from a recorded conversation among four undergraduate housemates at home:[11]

(1) 1 MARGE   Can I have one of these <u>Tabs</u>?
     2   <u>Do you want to split it?</u>
     3   <u>Do you want to split a Tab?</u>
     4 KATE   <u>Do you want to split MY Tab?</u> [laughter]
     5 VIVIAN No.
     6 MARGE   Kate, <u>do you want to split my Tab!</u>?
     7 KATE   No, <u>I don't want to split your Tab.</u>

Of these seven lines, five are repetitions and variations of the paradigm established by a combination of Marge's question in line 2 ("<u>Do you want to split</u> it?") with the last word of line 1 ("Can I have one of these <u>Tabs</u>?"). Forms of repetition in this example include self-repetition:

     2 MARGE   <u>Do you want to split it?</u>
     3   <u>Do you want to split a Tab?</u>

allo-repetition:

     3 MARGE   <u>Do you want to split a Tab?</u>
     4 KATE   <u>Do you want to split MY Tab?</u> [laughter]

and repetition with slight variation, as seen in the two previous pairs. The functions of these repetitions include humor, seen in lines 3 and 4, where "a Tab" is reinterpreted as "MY Tab" (note the accompanying laughter).

This example is not unusual. In another segment of the same conversation, Vivian told about an amusing event involving her and Marge, who occupied different bedrooms in the house. Vivian had been lying in bed when she heard "this- pounding upstairs, upon the ceiling in our room." Vivian checked with Marge, who said she didn't hear it; they returned to their respective rooms. Back in her room, however, Vivian continued to hear the pounding on her ceiling, so:

(2) 1 VIVIAN So I stood on my bed →
     2 MARGE   <u>She pounded on the ceiling</u>, →
     3 VIVIAN and <u>I pounded on the ceiling</u>, →
     4 MARGE   <u>she was pounding</u> . . .
     5 VIVIAN and I hear Marge

```
6              and I hear Marge dash out of her room,
7              come downstairs and open the door,
8              and I was like ┌"No Marge...
9  MARGE                     └ She said "Marge, it's me."
               I'm like, "What is..."
10 VIVIAN      I was pounding on my ceiling.
11 MARGE       Bizarre!
```

This narrative, like the Tab interchange, is structured around a
kernel phrase, "pounding on the ceiling." The irony and point of
the story lie in the repetition: When Vivian uses the phrase "pounding on the ceiling" to describe her own retaliatory action, she
dramatizes that she created a noise similar to that created by the
original "pounding on the ceiling," making it more plausible that
Marge mistook Vivian's own "pounding" to be the externally-
produced pounding she had previously not heard. In this way, the
repetition of the phrase represents iconically the similarity of the
two sounds.[12] As in the previous example, this kernel phrase is
made up of two prior contiguous phrases from which the paradigm
is drawn: Vivian had begun the story by saying "there was this
pounding upstairs, upon the ceiling in our room."

The next example is also typical of transcripts prepared, year
after year, by students in my classes. In the dyadic conversation
from which the excerpt is taken, Frank complains that he has nothing to do because he is unemployed. His friend Terry takes the opportunity to encourage him to be more contemplative: She suggests
he take advantage of his free time "to daydream." To illustrate
what she has in mind, she recommends that he stand on a bridge
and watch the water go under it.[13] He counters that he will finish
the book he is reading. This frustrates Terry:

```
(3)  TERRY   THAT'S NOT DAYDREAMING! ... darn it!
             [laughter]
     FRANK   Well, daydreaming is something that comes natural!
             You don't don't PLAN daydreaming.
     TERRY   You don't even
             you're not even hearing what I'm SAYING! What?
     FRANK   You can't PLAN daydreaming ...
             "I'm going to go daydream for a couple hours guys, so"
     TERRY   Yes you CAN plan it!
             You can plan daydreaming.
```

Thus speakers weave the words of others into the fabric of their own discourse, the thread of which is, in turn, picked up and re-woven into the pattern. Repetitions and variations make individual utterances into a unified discourse, even as they are used for evalua-tion: to contribute to the point of the discourse.

Examples of functions of repetition

Not all transcripts show a high percentage of repeated words but many do, and all show some. In this section I exemplify a range of functions served by repetition of words, phrases, and clauses in conversation: as participatory listenership, ratifying listenership, humor, savoring, stalling, expanding, participating, evaluating through patterned rhythm, and bounding episodes. Examples come from a Thanksgiving dinner table conversation in which I partici-pated. (See Appendix I for information on this and other sources of examples.)

Repetition as participatory listenership

Examples (1)–(3) show repetition of a kernel sentence in a story or conversational segment. In these uses, each time the utterance is repeated, the theme of the story or interchange is developed, slightly changed in meaning as well as form. Another extremely common type of repetition, in a sense the most puzzling but also the most basic, is the exact or slightly varied repetition of a previ-ous speaker's utterance. Person is varied if required by the change in speaker, but no information is added, and no perceptible contri-bution is made to the development of a story, theme, or idea. (4) and (5) come from a discussion of the Whorfian Hypothesis.

(4) `1 DEBORAH   You know who else talks about that?
     2   Did you ever read R. D. Laing?
     3   The Divided Self?
     4 CHAD   Yeah. But I don't /??/.
     5 DEBORAH   He talks about that too.
     6 CHAD   He talks about it too.

Chad's repetition in line 6 ("He talks about it too."), echoing my utterance in line 5 ("He talks about that too.") seems to be simply a way for Chad to participate in the interchange by showing listenership and acceptance of my utterance. (His partially in-

audible line 4 ["Yeah. But I don't /??/."] is probably a statement
that he has read but does not remember the book. If so, his repetition could also be a claim to credit for having read it, and perhaps
for now recalling it.)

The next example comes from the same discussion:

```
(5)  1  DEBORAH   Like he says that
     2            he says that Americans ... →
     3                     CHAD ⌐Yeah
     4            or Westerners tend to uh: ...
     5            think of the body and the soul
     6            as two different things, →
     7                     CHAD ⌐Right.
     8            because there's no word
     9            that expresses body and soul together.
    10  CHAD                       ⌐Body and soul together.
    11            Right.
```

Again, Chad repeated in line 10 words in line 9, "body and soul
together," as a show of listenership and perhaps shared expertise.

At various times during the dinner conversation, each participant's career furnished a topic of talk. The preceding topic, the
Whorfian Hypothesis, grew out of a combination of the work of
one participant, David, as an American Sign Language interpreter,
and mine as a linguist. The following segment of conversation occurred when participants were discussing violence in children's cartoons, relevant to Chad's job at an animation studio. Sally and I
(not coincidentally, I suspect, the two women) claimed that, as children, we had been disturbed by violence in cartoons; three of the
four men taking part in the conversation claimed they had not:

```
(6)  1  STEVE     I never saw anything wrong with those things.
     2            ⌐I thought they were funny.
     3  CHAD      ⌐Yeah.
     4  DEBORAH   I hated them.
     5  CHAD      I agree. [i.e. with Steve]
     6  PETER     What. The cartoons?
     7  STEVE     I never took them seriously.
     8            I never ⌐thought anyone was
     9  DEBORAH          ⌐I couldn't sta:nd it.
                  [One page of transcript intervenes.]
    10  STEVE     I never ... took that seriously
    11  PETER                 ⌐I never could take it seriously.
```

In lines 7 and 10, separated by a page of transcript, Steve repeats almost the same phrase, "I never took them/that seriously." By restating his contribution, Steve continues to participate in the conversation, even though he has nothing new to add.

In line 11, Peter repeats what Steve said in lines 7 and 10, with slight variation ("I never could take it seriously."). Although line 11 adds no new information to the conversation, it nonetheless contributes something crucial: Peter's participation. Moreover, it is not only what Peter says that shows that he agrees with Steve, but also the way he says it. By repeating not only Steve's idea, but also his words and syntactic pattern, Peter's contribution is a ratification of Steve's. At the same time, the three instances of a similar statement help to constitute the discourse and give it its texture.

Such immediate repetition of others' utterances is extremely frequent in the transcript. Indeed, ratifying repetitions often result in triplets. When Steve is serving wine, Sally declines, and her refusal is immediately repeated by David and Steve, speaking almost in unison:

(7) SALLY I don't drink wine.
    DAVID She ⌈ doesn't drink wine
    STEVE   ⌊ Sally doesn't drink wine.

These immediate allo-repetitions are shows of participation and familiarity. By transforming Sally's statement of her drinking habits into a third-person statement, David shows familiarity with Sally. By shadowing (speaking along with another speaker, with only split-second delay) the same observations, Steve both ratifies David's participation and displays his familiarity with Sally too. (Steve knows Sally better; he lived with her for six years.)

Another triplet occurred in the Whorfian Hypothesis discussion. I commented that differences in ways of talking may be less cognitive than cultural. Chad and David both repeated my statement to show listenership:

(8) 1 DEBORAH like you all see the same thing
     2   but people in one culture
     3   might notice and talk about one aspect
     4   while people in another culture
     5   might notice and talk about another one.
     6 DAVID   Yeah and which would have ...
     7   nothing to do with language.

8 DEBORAH   It's EXPRESSED in language.
9 CHAD   It's e<u>xpress</u>ed in language.
10 DAVID   └ It's e<u>xpress</u>ed in language.

There is a striking parallelism in my proposition in lines 2–5. However, I am focusing here on the triplet in lines 8–10: Chad's and David's nearly simultaneous repetition of my phrase (line 8, "It's e<u>xpress</u>ed in language"), showing understanding of my idea and also ratification and acceptance of my wording.

Ratifying listenership

In (9), Chad was telling about a promotional whistle-stop train tour he had participated in. He described a scene in which the train pulled into a station, and pandemonium resulted as a crowd rushed the train to approach the character being promoted: a man dressed as a large mouse.

(9) 1 CHAD   they all want to touch this . . . silly little mouse
     2 STEVE   At five o'clock in the MORNING on the TRAIN station.
     3 CHAD   Yeah.
     4 DAVID   <u>In New Mexico.</u>
     5 CHAD   <u>In New Mexico.</u>
     6   With ice on the . . . ICE hanging down from things . . .

The main speaker, Chad, ratifies Steve's contribution (line 2: "At five o'clock in the MORNING on the TRAIN station.") by saying (line 3) "Yeah." But he ratifies David's contribution "In New Mexico" (line 4) by repeating it (line 5), incorporating it into his nar-rative.[14]

In another example, Chad remarked on his observation of the way a deaf friend of David manipulates space when he signs. Chad responded to my request for clarification by incorporating my word into his discourse. (Note too how the repetition of "room" grounds his discourse and gives substance to its main point.)

(10) CHAD   Y'know, and he'd set up a room,
                 and he'd describe the room,
                 and people in the room
                 and where they were placed,⌉
      DEBORAH   ⌊spatially?
      CHAD   and <u>spatially</u>,

Rather than answering my question "yes" or "no," Chad continues speaking, implicitly answering affirmatively by incorporating my word ("spatially") into his discourse.[15]

Humor

Humor is a common function of repetition with slight variation. Peter used repetition as a resource for humor when I commented on how well-behaved his dog Rover was. Steve simply agreed, but Peter converted my statement into an agrammatical wry one:

(11) 1 DEBORAH   Rover is being so good.
      2 STEVE   I know.
      3 PETER   He's being hungry.

When Peter echoes my line 1, "Rover is being so good," substituting "hungry" for "good," the resulting line 3, "He's being hungry," is humorous because he used the same grammatical frame to convert a common construction into an odd one.

A triplet that uses a prior syntactic frame to generate a humorous locution arose following my request for permission to tape record the conversation:

(12) 1 PETER   Just to see if we say anything interesting?
      2 DEBORAH   No. Just to see how you say nothing interesting.
      3 PETER   Oh. Well I- I hardly ever say nothing interesting.

In line 2, I used the wording of Peter's question, "say anything interesting," to create the reversal, "say nothing interesting." Peter made further use of the oddness of this locution in line 3, heightening the humor with a double negative, "I hardly ever say nothing interesting."[16]

In a final example of humorous repetition, the guests were sitting down to dinner as Steve, the host, was moving between the dining room and the adjoining kitchen. In the following excerpt, Steve repeated his own words because he was not heard the first time. (He began speaking when he was in the kitchen.) Then I picked up his phrase and repeated it in an exaggerated chanting manner, playing on the fact that the phrase "white before red" reminded me, rhythmically, of "i before e" in the children's spelling mnemonic "i before e except after c." I did not finish the paradigm because David

did so for me, introducing yet another joke by substituting a sala-
cious word, "bed," in the final slot:

(13)   STEVE   The only trouble about red and white wine
       DEBORAH   No, I'm not going to be doing any work /??/
       STEVE   The only trouble about red and white wine is
                  you should have <u>white before red</u>.
       DEBORAH   <u>White before red</u> except <u>after</u>
       DAVID   ⌐ <u>after</u> bed.

The humor of David's building on my humor by inserting "bed" in
my chanting paradigm is enhanced (and occasioned) by its rhyme,
that is, repetition of the vowel sound in "red."

Savoring

Not only can humor be created by repeating, but its appreciation
can be displayed by repeating. For example, in the discussion of
why Sally and I were disturbed by cartoon violence, Steve suggested
it was because we "took them literally." Then David followed up:

(14)   1 DAVID   That because you have a-
                    /arcane/ view of reality. [laughter]
       2 DEBORAH   Cause we're sensitive. [laughing]
                    [laughter]
       3 SALLY   Cause we're <u>ladies</u>.
                    [laughter]
       4 STEVE   <u>Ladies ... Ladies.</u> [laughing]

I built on the paradigm established by David (line 1, "That's because you have a- /arcane/ view of reality") by slotting in a mock-
ingly self-congratulatory adjective (line 2, "Cause we're sensitive").
Sally followed up by repeating the same paradigm, slotting in a
word that is ironic because of its association with women of
another era (line 3, "Cause we're ladies"). The word "ladies," uttered with Sally's British accent and applied to us, tickled Steve,
who repeated it twice while chuckling and laughing (line 4). He
seemed to be repeating her word in order to savor it, thereby also
showing his appreciation of her irony.[17]

Stalling

Repeating a preceding utterance with slight variation is used in
many other ways as well. One such way is to repeat a question,

transforming second to first person. This allows the responding speaker to fill the response slot without giving a substantive response. At one point in the conversation, David was talking about American Sign Language. Peter asked him a question, and David responded by echoing the question with rising intonation:

(15)   PETER But <u>how do you learn a new sign.</u>
       DAVID . . . <u>How do I learn a new sign?</u>

During playback, I learned that David had been uncomfortable with the speed of Peter's speaking turns. This, combined with the pause preceding his response ("How do I learn a new sign?"), led me to conclude that David repeated the question to slow down the conversation – an additional, related function of the repetition.

Expanding

Here I began a dyadic interchange with Peter by asking a question:

(16)   1 DEBORAH   <u>Do you read?</u>
       2 PETER   <u>Do I read?</u>
       3 DEBORAH   <u>Do you read</u> things just for fun?
       4 PETER   Yeah.
       5   Right now <u>I'm reading</u>
       6   Norma Jean the Termite Queen.

Peter transforms my second person question (line 1, "Do you read?") into the first person (line 2, "<u>Do I read?</u>") as a stalling repetition. I repeated my initial question with elaboration (line 3, "Do you read things just for fun?"). Peter answered (line 4, "Yeah."), then grounded an expansion in the repetition with transformation of the question ("I'm reading" + name of book). Thus the reformulation of the question is the first step in the process of expansion; the question is then used as a scaffold on which to construct on-going talk.

Repetition as participation

(17) occurred in the context of talk about the composer Schumann. (Sally and Steve are professional musicians.) Sally had said that Schumann destroyed his fingers for piano-playing with a "contraption" that he designed to stretch them. This led me to recall a newspaper article about a case of mutilation involving a finger:

(17) 1 DEBORAH   I read something in the newspaper,
      2   I won't tell you.
      3 DAVID   What contraption?
      4 STEVE   <u>I don't want to hear about it.</u>
      5 DEBORAH   <u>You don't want to hear about it.</u>
      6 SALLY   Tell it. Tell it.
      7 DAVID   <u>We want to hear about it.</u>
      8 SALLY   /?/
      9 DAVID   Steve can go in the other room.
     10 STEVE   <u>I don't want to hear about it.</u>

Sally's self-repetition in line 6 ("Tell it. Tell it.") displays her eager-
ness to hear the (presumably gruesome) story. Steve repeats in line
10 exactly what he said in line 4 ("I don't want to hear about it").
In line 5, I ratified what Steve said in line 4 by transforming his first
person statement into the second person ("You don't want to hear
about it."). David uses the same syntactic frame in line 7 to distin-
guish himself and the others from Steve ("We want to hear about
it."). The result is a lot of talk resulting from a few words and
ideas, linked together and distinguished by repetition.

The following example shows how repetition makes a fabric of
conversation. Here Steve and his brother Peter recall the quonset
huts in which they lived as children. (Quonset huts were odd-
looking temporary structures built by the United States government
to house returning veterans and their families following the Second
World War.)

(18) 1 STEVE   Cause they were built <u>near the swamp</u>.
      2   We used to go ... hunting frogs ⌐ <u>in the swamps</u>,
      3 DEBORAH   ⌐ Where was it.
      4   Where were yours?
      5 STEVE   <u>In the Bronx.</u>
      6 PETER   └ <u>In the Bronx.</u>
      7   <u>In the East Bronx?</u>
      8 DEBORAH   How long did you live in it?⌉
      9 STEVE   │ Near the swamps?
     10   .... Now there's a big cooperative building.
     11 PETER   └Three years.
     12 DEBORAH   <u>THREE YEARS?</u>

Steve is preoccupied with his recollection that the quonset huts
were near the swamps where he remembers playing as a child, and
he repeats this three times:

```
 1 STEVE   Cause they were built near the swamp.
 2         We used to go ... hunting frogs in the in the swamps,
 9 STEVE                              └Near the swamps?
```

In lines 6 and 7, Peter utters "In the Bronx," shadowing Steve's line 5, and also offering information that was as much his as Steve's, since they are brothers:

```
 5 STEVE   In the Bronx.
 6 PETER        └In the Bronx.
 7         In the East Bronx?
```

Peter's utterance in line 7 ("In the East Bronx?") is both a repetition of Steve's words in line 5 and an immediate self-repetition with expansion, adding "east" and introducing rising intonation. (The intonation seems to orient the answer to me, the questioner, to imply, "Do you know where the East Bronx is?"). Steve then echoes Peter's intonation (though not his words) when he utters line 9 with rising intonation, "Near the swamps?" Finally, Peter answers my question in line 8 "How long did you live in it?" with line 11 "Three years," and in line 12 I respond by repeating Peter's answer with emphasis ("THREE YEARS?").[18]

Evaluation through patterned rhythm

A type of repetition that does not involve repeating words at all is patterned rhythm. In a segment immediately preceding the lines cited in (9) describing pandemonium in a railroad station, Chad said:

```
(19)  1 CHAD   Because everyone ... was ... they were so INSANE.
      2         They'd come in and run in ...
      3         and "I want to touch him."
      4         Well, when you have six thousand, five thousand,
      5         six thousand ten thousand people come in,
      6         they all want to touch this ... silly little mouse
```

Why does Chad say that the people "come in and run in"? The second verb rephrases, with slight intensification, the idea of the first. (Koch 1984 examines such instant self-paraphrases as lexical couplets.) But it is not the case that the repetition with variation adds nothing: On the contrary, it creates the vivid impression of many people in great movement, through its intensifying, list-like intonation.

Another instance of list-like intonation occurs when Chad says lines 4 and 5 ("six thousand, five thousand, six thousand ten thousand people come in"). In addition to the repetition of "come in" from line 2, there are four items in the list which describe how many people were involved. Such a list might be expected to follow an order of increasing number. Instead, the order six, five, six, ten seems to be random; what is crucial is the rhythm established by the list. Furthermore, the violation of expected sequence contributes to the impression of confusion and disorder.

Chad again achieves a listing effect in the following comment, spoken in the discussion about cartoons. He defends violence in cartoons by explaining that the cartoon producer wanted his cartoons to include a variety of scenes:

(20) 1 CHAD   you have to run the gamut of everything.
      2   /You get/ scary parts, good parts, this things,
      3   and everything else.

Rather than giving a list of the specific parts that a cartoon should have, Chad provides a relatively contentless list. Of the four kinds of parts he named, only one is specific: "scary parts." "Good parts" is not specific; all parts of a work should be good. "This things" is a kind of filler (also a speech error), and "everything else" is a filler which sums up. Yet the effect of Chad's comment is clear: Cartoons should include a variety of types of scenes. The meaning of the statement lies not in the meaning of the words, but in the patterned rhythm: the listing intonation.

The intonational pattern of a speaker's utterance also provides a resource for the participation and play of others. This was seen in (13), where David fit the word "bed" into the rhythm of my mock chant. Throughout the dinner table conversation, Steve, the host, engaged in self-mockery by simultaneously displaying and parodying hosting behavior – in Goffman's (1974) terms, "guying" so as to perform the behavior and distance himself from it at the same time. (The model for his parody, according to Steve, was his grandmother.) Picking up on Steve's pattern, I urged Peter to stop carving the turkey and start eating by saying, "Sit, sit." David immediately played on this repetitive pattern by saying, "No, carve, carve."

The reduplication of "Sit, sit" signifies intensity ("Sit immediately," or "I insist that you sit"). By contrast, the reduplication in "Carve, carve" signifies repeated aspect: "Keep carving," or "Carve away." Thus David used a repetition of my rhythmic pattern to echo but also to transform the meaning of the pattern: By repeating, he used it as a resource for his own creativity.

Repetition also shows repetitive aspect in an explanation by Chad of a certain method of learning. In a discussion of learning theories, he described the behavior of a learner by saying, "and you miss and you miss and you miss and you miss and you miss." The repetition communicates iconically, "You repeatedly miss."

A final example of listing intonation, and also an exact repetition for repeated aspect, comes from my study of modern Greek conversational stories told by women about being molested (see Appendix I for the background to this corpus of stories). The speaker is telling a group of women about an experience in which a man threw her down and tried to rape her. She dramatizes what she said to him:

(21)   1 Ton evriza, "Dhen drepese, palianthrope?"
        2 Toupa, toupa, toupa ekei...
        3 "Satyre, yero, aïdhestate, saliari,"
        4 Toupa, toupa, toupa.

        1 I cursed him, "Aren't you ashamed, scoundrel?"
        2 I-told-him, I-told-him, I-told-him there...
        3 "Satyr, (dirty) old man, repulsive (creature), slobberer,"
        4 I-told-him, I-told-him, I-told-him.

In line 3, the four epithets with which the speaker addresses her attacker seem to represent a longer list of names that she called him. Furthermore, the two sets of triple "toupa" (/tupa/) have the rhythmic effect of machine-gun fire. (The staccato effect of the plosive stops in /t/ and /p/ is hardly communicated by the English paraphrase, "I-told-him".) It gives the impression that she kept yelling at the man, emitting a stream of abuse.

Bounding episodes

Episodes within a larger conversation are often bounded by repetitions at the beginning, which operate as a kind of theme-setting, and at the end, forming a kind of coda. This is not surprising, since openings and closings are often the most ritualized parts of any discourse. In (22), a short duet between Peter and me, repetition both launches and terminates an episode of a discussion of how, upon first getting divorced, one wants to date many people (Peter and I were both divorced, he very recently and I long since); but then:

(22) 1 DEBORAH   Then you get bored.
      2 PETER   We:ll, I think I got bored.
                   [Deborah laughs]

      3   Well I- I mean basically what I feel is
      4   what I really LIKE, ... is people.
      5   And getting to know them really well.
      6   And you just CAN'T get to know
      7   ... TEN people REALLY WELL.
      8   You can't do it.

      9 DEBORAH   Yeah right.
     10   You have to- there's no-
     11   Yeah there's no time.
     12 PETER   └There's not time.
     13 DEBORAH   Yeah ... it's true.

Lines 1–2 set the theme and launch the episode when Peter transforms my statement from line 1 ("Then you get bored") into line 2 ("We:ll, I think I got bored.") His comeback is amusing (note my laughter) partly because of its rhythm: He draws out "well" and then utters "I think I got bored" in a quick, sardonic manner. The humor derives from the fact that it is a repetition, the quickness of his utterance conveying, iconically, that the boredom I predicted he would eventually experience has already, quickly, overtaken him.

In lines 3–8, Peter explains his statement in line 2. His argument is then structured by a series of self-repetitions, as each utterance picks up a word or phrase from a previous one. This is best illustrated by reproducing the transcript with repeated words circled and linked:

3 Well I- I mean basically (what I) feel is

4 (what I) really like   is (people)

5 And (getting to know) them (really well.)

6 And (you just CAN'T) (get to know)

7 ... TEN (people) (REALLY WELL.)

8 (You can't) do it.

Though repetition is pervasive in this middle section of the episode, it is not as monolithic as the repetition in which I join Peter to provide the episode's closing boundary. In lines 9–13, Peter and I wove each other's words together into a coda comparable to that of a musical composition, through the picking up and repeating of "Yeah," "there's no(t)," and "time."

The preceding discussion demonstrates some of the functions of repetition in conversation. The functions illustrated are not exhaustive, but they give a sense of the kind of work repeating does.

The range of repetition in a segment of conversation

Thus far I have demonstrated different types and functions of repetition by reference to a large number of short conversational excerpts. Furthermore I have concentrated on the repetition of phrases and clauses, including the repetition of rhythmic patterns thereby created. To see how a variety of levels of repetition work together to create involvement, in the next section I show a range of types of repetition in a single short segment from the Thanksgiving conversation.

First I present the segment, a short interchange on the topic of eating, as I had originally transcribed it, and invite readers to examine it for instances of repetition:

(23) CHAD   I go out a lot.
     DEBORAH   I go out and eat.
     PETER   You go out? The trouble with ME is if I don't prepare and eat well, I eat a LOT. ... Because it's not satisfying. And so if I'm just eating like cheese and crackers, I'll just STUFF myself on cheese and crackers. But if I fix myself something nice, I don't have to eat that much.
     DEBORAH   Oh yeah?
     PETER   I've noticed that, yeah.
     DEBORAH   Hmmm ... Well then it works, then it's a good idea.
     PETER   It's a good idea in terms of eating, it's not a good idea in terms of time.

To facilitate identification of repetition, I later laid the segment out in lines and moved bits of the lines around. I present the same segment in that form below:

```
1  CHAD        I go out    a lot.
2  DEBORAH     I go out    and eat.
3  PETER    You go out?

4                    The trouble with ME is
5          if   I don't prepare
6          and    eat   well,
7               I eat   a LOT. ...
8     Because   it's      not satisfying.
9  And so if   I'm just eating like        cheese and crackers,
10              I'll   just STUFF myself on cheese and crackers.
11      But if   I           fix myself something nice,
12               I don't have to eat that much.
13 DEBORAH                                Oh yeah?
14 PETER    I've noticed that,              yeah.

15 DEBORAH     Hmmm...
16      Well   then it works,
17             then it's    a good idea.
18 PETER              It's    a good idea in terms of eating,
19                    it's not a good idea in terms of time.
```

Verse structure

The fertile field of ethnopoetics has identified "poetic" structure in American Indian narrative (Tedlock 1972) and, more recently, conversation (Woodbury 1985). Hymes (1981), working in this tradition, calls attention to verse structure created by patterns of repetition and variation, which he sees as having been neglected for the more readily salient line structure. In this segment, I initially saw only the patterns of lines: phrases and clauses bounded by intonational contours and verbal particles which Chafe (1986) shows characterize all spoken discourse. Hymes (p.c.) pointed out that the segment has a verse structure as well. The segment can be seen as having three verses, separated by line spaces in the transcript, which are strikingly similar in structure to the pattern seen in (22), also a duet between Peter and me. Lines 1–3 of the current example constitute an opening, and lines 15–19 a closing or coda. As in (22), these bounding sections are characterized by the most striking repetition. The center verse constitutes the meat of the interchange, like the filling in a sandwich, made up of an if/then proposition that Peter creates and elaborates (i.e. If I don't take the time to prepare good food, I eat a lot; if I do prepare good food, I eat less).

Lexical repetition

Perhaps the first thing one notices about this segment is the repetition of the word "eat." The best way to represent visually the cohesive function of these (and other) repetitions is to highlight them on the transcript itself. Therefore I present the segment again, with the highlighting of the repetition under discussion superimposed on it:

```
 1   CHAD      I go out a lot.
 2   DEBORAH   I go out and eat.
 3   PETER     You go out?

 4        The trouble with ME is
 5          if  I don't prepare
 6         and    eat  well,
 7                I eat  a LOT. ...
 8    Because  it's         not satisfying.
 9  And so if  I'm just eating like        cheese and crackers,
10             I'll just STUFF  myself on cheese and crackers.
11      But if  I          fix  myself something nice,
12             I don't have to eat that much.
13   DEBORAH                                       Oh yeah?
14   PETER     I've noticed that,                  yeah.

15   DEBORAH   Hmmm...
16        Well  then it works,
17              then it's     a good idea.
18   PETER           It's     a good idea in terms of eating,
19                   it's not a good idea in terms of time.
```

A number of other repetitions are quickly perceived when the transcript is studied briefly. First is the repetition of the two-word verb "go out" found in the triplet uttered by all three speakers in the opening verse:

```
 1   CHAD         I   go out   a lot.
 2   DEBORAH      I   go out   and eat.
 3   PETER      You   go out?
```

In addition to setting the topic of talk, eating, these lines establish a sense of rapport among the three speakers by their echoes of each other's use of the phrase "go out."

In the middle verse, a solo by Peter, there is a highly noticeable repetition of the phrase "cheese and crackers" as well as of the words "just," "myself," and "yeah":

```
 9  And so if  I'm  just  eating like        cheese and crackers,
10              I'll  just  STUFF myself  on  cheese and crackers.
11  But if   I            fix  myself  something nice,
12           I don't have to eat that much.
13  DEBORAH                               Oh  yeah?
14  PETER    I've noticed that,               yeah.
```

When Peter utters "cheese and crackers" for the second time (line 10), he does so more quickly than the first, and his intonation remains steady and low across the phrase. The effect of this intonation is to mark the self-reference to his earlier utterance of the same phrase.

The meanings of the two instances of "just" are somewhat different. In the first instance, line 9 "And so if I'm just eating like cheese and crackers," "just" is a mitigator, meaning "only": "if I'm eating only cheese and crackers." But in the second instance, line 10, "I'll just STUFF myself on cheese and crackers," it is an intensifier: "I'll absolutely stuff myself with cheese and crackers." This difference in the meanings of the repeated word "just" under-lines the significance of its repetition. In other words, he didn't just (!) repeat the word because he meant the same thing. It also illus-trates again that repetition is a resource by which the same word or phrase can be used in a different way.

When Peter says line 14, "I've noticed that, yeah," his "yeah" repeats mine in the preceding line, ratifying my listener response to his talk and giving a sense of coda to that verse of the segment. Like the first three lines, the last four are highly repetitive:

```
15  DEBORAH  Hmmm...
16       Well  then it works,
17             then it's     a good idea.
18  PETER        It's     a good idea in terms of  eating,
19             it's  not  a good idea in terms of  time.
```

The words and phrases "then," "it's a good idea," and "in terms

of," which make up the bulk of this part of the discourse, are all
repeated. The repetition of these words serves to highlight the
words that are not repeated: "eating" and "time," the key points of
contrast. They are highlighted by their newness in contrast to the
sameness of the repeated words.

Another example of repetition involves items somewhat farther
from each other which nonetheless seem to cohere through their
rhyming:

```
1   CHAD         I go out  a lot.
2   DEBORAH      I go out and eat.
3   PETER        You go out?

4                    The trouble with ME is
5           if   I don't prepare
6          and      eat   well,
7                I eat   a LOT. ...
8   Because    it's       not  satisfying.
9   And so if  I'm just eating like        cheese and crackers,
10             I'll   just STUFF myself on cheese and crackers.
11        But if  I            fix myself something nice,
12             I don't have to eat that much.
13  DEBORAH                              Oh yeah?
14  PETER      I've noticed that,            yeah.

15  DEBORAH   Hmmm ...
16      Well   then it works,
17             then  it's      a good idea.
18  PETER        It's       a good idea in terms of eating,
19              it's not  a good idea in terms of time.
```

I have drawn the connection between lines 8 and 19 as a broken
rather than a solid line because it strikes me that the argument to
be made for the repetition of "it's not" is a bit weaker than that to
be made for the repetition of "a lot." This is both because the lines
in which "it's not" appears are further apart, and also because "it's
not" is a structure occasioned by grammatical conventions for negation in English. Nonetheless, there are other grammatically correct ways to effect negation, such as "it isn't." The choice of "it's
not" rather than other alternatives echoes the earlier use of "a lot."

Another kind of patterning which is also closely linked to the
grammar of the language is that of pronouns and discourse
markers:

```
 1  CHAD       I│ go out a lot.
 2  DEBORAH    I│ go out (and) eat.
 3  PETER      You  go out?
 4                 ┌  The trouble with ME is
 5          (if) I│   don't prepare
 6         (and)│    eat (well),
 7              I│  eat / a LOT. . . .
 8     Because  i│t's /    not satisfying.
 9  (And) so (if) I│'m /just eating like      cheese and crackers,
10             I│'ll/ just STUFF myself on cheese and crackers.
11     But (if) I│ /       fix myself   something nice,
12             I│/don't have to eat (that) much.
13  DEBORAH   /                            Oh yeah?
14  PETER     /I│'ve noticed (that)              yeah.
15  DEBORAH/  Hmmm . . .
16     (Well)  then it works,
17             then it's    a good idea.
18  PETER         It's    a good idea in terms of eating,
19                it's not a good idea in terms of time.
```

Although these function words are likely or even required to occur frequently in any English discourse, nonetheless their frequent occurrence plays a part in giving the discourse its characteristic shape and sound. In this sense, their repetition plays a significant role in establishing the shared universe of discourse created by conversational interaction in that language. As Becker (1984b: 435) demonstrates for Javanese textbuilding strategies, "This kind of non-rational homology is one of the things that binds a culture." Such conventionalized figures both grow out of and contribute to the textual and noetic aesthetic of a language and culture. Perceiving and using them is part of what makes an individual a member of the culture.

A particularly intriguing repetition in this segment occurs when Peter says line 7 "I eat a LOT." This utterance is a blend of the ends of Chad's and my utterances in lines 1–2:

```
1  CHAD      I go out │ a lot.
2  DEBORAH   I go out │ and eat.
7  PETER     I eat a LOT.  ⤶
```

In this way, the idea that Peter expresses is a response to what Chad and I said, at the same time that the form of his response – its repetition – is a ratification of our preceding contributions. Ongoing discourse is thus woven of the threads of prior talk. When fishing for words, speakers cast a net in the immediately surrounding waters of conversation.

I now return briefly to a repetition mentioned earlier, found in lines 10 and 11:

```
10          I'll just | STUFF myself | on cheese and crackers
11   But if  I          | fix myself  | something nice,
```

Here the choice of "fix myself" seems to be occasioned by the pattern of the preceding "stuff myself." This becomes even more compelling when the choice of "fix myself" is considered in contrast to the use of "prepare" in lines 5–6: "If I don't prepare and eat well." The unmarked case, one might surmise, would have been for Peter to repeat the same word he used to introduce the idea: "prepare."

Phonological repetition

An example of repetition of sounds in this segment is the repetition of initial /t/ in line 19:

19   it's not a good idea in terms of time.

Repetition of medial vowels was seen in the "lot/not" pattern discussed above. It is also seen in the repetition of the vowels in "just," "stuff," and "much":

```
 9   And so if  I'm just eating like       cheese and crackers,
10                I'll just STUFF myself on cheese and crackers.
11   But if  I            fix myself something nice,
12                I don't have to eat that much.
```

One wonders whether the vowel sound / ʌ / in "trouble" (line 4, "The trouble with ME is") should also be included in this constellation. In order to know how much attention to pay to such patterns of sound, it might help to know if it is statistically significant or random for vowel sounds to recur in such close proximity. In the absence of such evidence, however, it can nonetheless be observed that repetition of sounds contributes to the musical effect of the discourse. One need only listen to a language with recurrent vowel or consonant sounds not used in one's own language, to experience the impressions they make – for example, for Americans, the recurrent nasals in Portuguese, pharyngeals in Arabic, or velar fricatives in Hebrew.

Repetition as rapport

The end of the segment under analysis provides an example of how the form of the discourse can serve to create rapport and ratify an interlocutor's contribution. In lines 18 and 19, Peter disagrees with my comment that taking time to prepare food is a good idea, but he does so by casting his disagreement in the paradigm of my utterance:

```
15  DEBORAH  Hmmm...
16          Well then it works,
17               then it's    a good idea.
18  PETER        ┌─────────────────────────────────────┐
                 │ It's    a good idea in terms of eating, │
19               │ it's not a good idea in terms of time.  │
                 └─────────────────────────────────────┘
```

Thus the form of the discourse, repetition, sends a metamessage of rapport by ratifying my contribution, even as its message disagrees with what I said.

Individual and cultural differences

I believe it is by means of such metamessages of rapport that apparently contentious conversational styles may be based on highly affiliative motives, as found in what I call the high-involvement style of the New York Jewish speakers in my original study of the Thanksgiving conversation (Tannen 1984), of whom Peter is one, and the Philadelphia Jewish speakers among whom Schiffrin (1984) observed "Jewish argument as sociability." I believe it is not coincidental that this style is characterized by much repetition, as Schiffrin's examples demonstrate (though her own interests in the examples lie elsewhere). It is found as well in the repetition of formulas to create rapport while disagreeing in the highly ritualized modern Greek verbal art of "mantinades" as described by Herzfeld (1985).

   This raises the question of the extent to which frequency of repetition is culturally variable. My research documents the pervasiveness of repetition for conversation in modern Greek and in several varieties of American English. Conversations recorded by my students indicate that all conversations exhibit some, but some exhibit a lot. The conversation of adolescents is particularly rich in repetition, not only among Americans but also, according to Nordberg (1985), among Swedes. I expect, however, that degree and type of repetition differ with cultural and individual style.

Since repetition of sentences and ideas is a means of keeping talk going in interaction, the relative frequency of this type of repetition should be correlated with the cultural value placed on the presence of talk in interaction. This is supported by the relative infrequency of repetition as well as formulaic expressions as reported by Scollon (p.c.) among Athabaskan Indians, who place relative positive value on silence in interaction (Scollon 1985). In striking contrast are the talk-valuing cultures of East European Jewish-Americans mentioned above, and of Black Americans (Erickson 1984), among those who have been observed to use a lot of syntactic repetition.

Becker 1984b suggests that the repeating strategies which he describes in a wayang drama are characteristic of a Javanese aesthetic of density. Moreover, he observes repeating strategies in other Southeast Asian cultures, including characteristic pathologies: A common way of displaying madness in Java is echolalia (p.c.). Another practice that Becker (1984c:109) describes fits this pattern as well. When East Javanese audiences enjoy a lecture, they repeat phrases which they appreciate to their neighbors (a practice reminiscent of what I have described in American conversation as "savoring repetition"). At least one American guest lecturer was unnerved by the buzz of voices in the audience, mistaking the show of appreciation for lack of attention. This misunderstanding results from divergent, culturally patterned strategies of repetition.

The most extensive analysis of repetition as a culturally and linguistically favored strategy is found in the work of Johnstone on modern Arabic prose (Koch 1983a,b, Johnstone 1987b). Johnstone (1987a) argues that the grammatical structure of Arabic makes repetition strategies especially available to Arabic speakers.

Although no scholar, so far as I know, has focused exclusively or intensively on repeating strategies in Black American rhetorical style, analyses of Black American discourse indicate that it makes use of self- and allo-repetition in characteristic ways. Erickson (1984) finds in a conversation among Black American adolescents the allo-repetition of call/response that typifies audience participation in Black worship (a response pattern described by Heath 1983 as well).[19] Self-repetition is also found in Black English conversation. For example, Hansell and Ajirotutu (1982:92) note, in discourse among a white researcher, a black assistant, and two black teenagers recorded by John Gumperz, one of the teenagers adopts a "'public address' style similar to that used by black preachers and politicians." Although the authors are concerned with other aspects of this discourse, the transcript shows that it includes both exact repetition ("Now you know I'm right about it/you know I'm right about it") and parallelism built on the construction "X is a dog":[20]

(24)   Now they make it look like <u>Wallace is a dog</u>
       and <u>Nixon is</u> the next <u>dog</u>
       and <u>Humphrey is</u>
       well . . [laughter] you know
       a little bit higher than the other two <u>dogs</u> . .
       [laughter] but <u>he's</u> still <u>a dog</u>.   (91)

Cultural patterns do not prescribe the form that a speaker's discourse will take but provide a range from which individuals choose strategies that they habitually use in expressing their individual styles. In examples from the Thanksgiving dinner conversation, preliminary impressions suggest that Steve often repeated his own words, as in (6) "I never took that seriously" and (17) "I don't want to hear about it". Peter frequently shadowed others' utterances, as seen also in (6) "I never could take it seriously" and (18) "In the Bronx", and will be seen in (34). Chad frequently used relatively contentless listing intonation, as in (19), "come in and run in" and (20), "scary parts, good parts, this things, and everything else". And I frequently immediately paraphrase myself, as in (23), "Then it works, then it's a good idea." Documenting individual and cultural repeating strategies, like other aspects of individual and cultural styles, remains a relatively unexplored and promising area of research.

Other genres

It is a premise of this study that literary (in the sense of artfully developed) genres elaborate and manipulate strategies that are spontaneous in conversation. Having demonstrated that repetition is pervasive and functional in conversation, I now turn briefly to examples of nonconversational discourse types to show that they use repetition strategies such as those observed in conversation. As mentioned at the outset, Johnstone (1987) notes that formal or ritualized discourse is often particularly rich in repetition. In this section I give brief examples of three formal discourse types: public speaking, oratory, and drama, to show that they make artful use of the same repetitive strategies that I have shown in conversation.

Public speaking

The following excerpt is from an address given by John Fanselow, an unusually gifted public speaker, at the 1983 Georgetown University Round Table on Languages and Linguistics. In his "paper" (which was actually an extemporaneously composed but nonetheless polished and fluent talk), Fanselow was explaining what he calls "the tape recording syndrome": the pattern of behavior by which teachers who are ostensibly attempting to record their classes for analysis and self-evaluation keep turning up without having made the recording, blaming their failure on one or another tape recorder malfunction.[21]

(25) The point is, I think,
      (I've done this in many countries incidentally
      even Japan, where, you know, electronics is no problem.)
      Same syndrome.
      Same syndrome.
      Both with American teachers,
      and teachers from other lands.
      I think we're fearful of looking.
      I think we're fearful of looking.
      I think teachers are fearful of looking,
      and we're fearful of looking.

The repetition that characterizes this excerpt is set in relief by contrast with the same comment as it appears in Fanselow's (1983: 171) written version of his paper:

(26) One reason I think many teachers fail to tape for a long time is
      that they are fearful of listening to themselves. And, I think that
      a central reason why we who prepare teachers avoid evaluations
      is that we, like those we prepare, are fearful of listening and
      looking as well. The tape recording syndrome is widespread.

There is parallelism in the written version, too, but it is less rigid. Furthermore, the "fearful of looking" construction appears twice in the written version, compared to four times in the spoken one.

Contrasting the printed version makes clear some of the functions of repetition in the spoken version. The point that "The tape recording syndrome is widespread," which is lexicalized in the written version (i.e. conveyed by external evaluation), is conveyed in the spoken version by internal evaluation accomplished by repetition:

Same syndrome.
Same syndrome.

The repetition of the phrase "same syndrome" implies that the syndrome is widespread; repetition, in other words, is working to communicate repeated aspect. Similarly, the exact repetition:

I think we're fearful of looking.
I think we're fearful of looking.

gives the impression that many people are "fearful of looking."

The observation that teacher trainers are "like those we prepare" in being fearful is also lexicalized in the written version but implied in the spoken version by parallelism:

I think TEACHErs are fearful of looking,
    and   WE 're fearful of looking.

Placing "teachers" and "we" in the same paradigmatic slot in the same syntactic string, implies that the two groups are in the same semantic class and foregrounds their similarity. In this instance, emphatic stress is placed on "teachers" and "we" to bring this contrast into focus.

Oratory

Oratory is a kind of public oral poetry. In her analysis of oral poetry, Finnegan (1977:90) stresses the importance of repetition to a definition of poetry:

The most marked feature of poetry is surely repetition. Forms and genres are recognised because they are repeated. The collocations of line or stanza or refrain are based on their repeated recurrence; metre, rhythm or stylistic features like alliteration or parallelism are also based on repeated patterns of sound, syntax or meaning. In its widest sense, repetition is part of all poetry. This is the general background against which the prosodic and other features of oral poetry must be seen.

The Reverend Martin Luther King, Jr. was a master of poetic oratory. Consider, for example, the most famous of his speeches, delivered at a march on Washington on August 23, 1963, which is known by one of its recurring phrases.[22]

King's speech begins eloquently but prosaically compared to the rhythmic and rhetorical crescendo that it builds to. The rhetorical

crescendo begins, toward the end, with a series of repeated phrases
of the type that Davis (1985) describes as "the narrative formulaic
unit" of the "performed African-American sermon."[23] The first
such formulaic unit is the one that has come to be regarded as the
"title" of the address: "I Have a Dream":

(27)   I say to you today, my friends,
       even though we face
       the difficulties of today and tomorrow,
       I still have a dream.
       It is a dream deeply rooted in the American dream.
       I have a dream that one day this nation will rise up
       and live out the true meaning of its creed:
       "We hold these truths to be self-evident
       that all men are created equal."
       I have a dream that one day
       on the red hills of Georgia
       the sons of former slaves
       and the sons of former slave-owners
       will be able to sit down together
       at the table of brotherhood.

The phrase "I have a dream" is repeated six more times, introducing four more expansions that described hoped-for equality in
image-rich and sound-rich language.

Especially interesting are pairs of parallel constructions embedded within the repetitions of the formula:

(28)   I have a dream
       that my four little children
       will one day live in a nation
       where they will not be judged
           by the color   of their skin
       but by the content of their character.
       I have a dream today.

The substitution of character for skin color as the basis by which
people will be judged is made effective by the parallel syntactic constructions and similarity in initial consonants: the /k/ sound of
"color," "content," and "character."

The last section of this speech reverberates with another quotation and repetition. King recites the words of the American patriotic song that ends, "From every mountain-side, let freedom ring."
The last line of this song then becomes another repeated formula:

(29)   And if America is to be a great nation,
       this must become true.
       So <u>let freedom ring</u>
       from the prodigious hill tops of New Hampshire.
       <u>Let freedom ring</u>
       from the mighty mountains of New York.
       <u>Let freedom ring</u>
       from the heightening Alleghenies of Pennsylvania.
       <u>Let freedom ring</u>
       from the snowcapped Rockies of Colorado.
       <u>Let freedom ring</u>
       from the curvaceous slopes of California.
       But not only that.
       <u>Let freedom ring</u> from Stone Mountain of Georgia.
       <u>Let freedom ring</u> from Lookout Mountain of Tennessee.
       <u>Let freedom ring</u> from every hill and molehill of Mississippi.
       "From every mountainside,
       <u>let freedom ring</u>."

King repeats and elaborates on the lines from the song. The repetition of "Let freedom ring," tolling like a bell, is interspersed with
parallel references to mountains and hills by a variety of names in
a range of states.

The repetitions of "Let freedom ring" are separated into two
groups. Each syntactic string in the first group of five is characterized by the pattern:

   from the X (adjective) Y (noun naming a hill or mountain) of Z (state
   name).

Individual strings are made more coherent by sound repetitions:

   from the prodigious <u>h</u>ill tops of New <u>H</u>ampshire.
   from the <u>m</u>ighty <u>m</u>ountains of <u>N</u>ew York.
   from the <u>c</u>urvaceous slopes of <u>C</u>alifornia.

Having swept across the United States from New England (New
Hampshire), across the Northeast (Pennsylvania), the West
(Colorado), to the Western coast (California), King moves, with
the phrase "but more than that," to the second group of three
parallel constructions and to the Southern part of the United States
(Georgia, Tennessee, and Mississippi), where he concentrated his
nonviolent organizing efforts toward desegregation and voting
rights. King thus encompassed the entire country with a list that
names a few of its states.

The speech ends with a triple repetition of a third clause, this one repeated from what he identifies as "the old Negro spiritual":

(30)   <u>Free at last!</u>
       <u>Free at last!</u>
       Thank God almighty,
       we are <u>free at last!</u>

The speeches of the Reverend Jesse Jackson make use of similar linguistic strategies: repetition of sounds, words, and clauses, echoing of well-known quotations and phrases (including those of King), surprising juxtapositions and reversals, and parallel constructions. The concluding chapter of this book contains a close analysis of these and other involvement strategies in Jackson's 1988 speech to the Democratic National Convention. For the present, I note simply that repetition works both to communicate ideas and to move audiences in oratorical discourse.

Literary discourse: drama

In comparing the dinner table conversation with the play written about it, Glen Merzer's *Taking comfort* (see Appendix I for explanation), I examined instances of sound and word repetition in 10,000 word segments of each. Repetition of word-initial sounds is twice as frequent in the play, whereas word or phrase repetition is twice as frequent in the conversation. This is shown in Table 2.

Table 2. *Repetition in 10,000-word segments of conversation and drama*

	Conversation	Drama
Sound	48	91
Word or longer	575	229

To illustrate, I present a short segment from the play, rearranged in intonation units. The speaker is a woman named Nancy who is about to see Larry, her former lover, after a long separation.

(31)   1 When I talk to myself,
       2   I talk to Larry.
       3 We have terrific fights in my head

4 that he always wins.
5 Now he'll be speaking for himself.
6 I wonder if he'll do as well.

The repetition in lines 1 and 2 sets up a syntagmatic paradigm to highlight the relationship between "myself" and "Larry" – the identity that Nancy feels between herself and the man she lived with and loved for many years. But in line 5 ("Now he'll be speaking for himself."), the verb "talk" changes to "speak." Line 5 invokes the common expression "speak for oneself." This enhances the significance of varying the verb.

This type of variation seems to be felt as necessary when discourse is written, to avoid the impression of monotony. (A similar finding is reported by Chafe 1985.) When repetition of words is found in drama, it seems to be deliberate, intended to play up and play on the repetition of exact words which characterizes conversation. Pinter is a master of this. Consider, for example, this segment from his play, *The birthday party*:[24]

(32) STANLEY Meg. Do you know what?
      MEG   What?
      STANLEY Have you heard the latest?
      MEG   No.
      STANLEY I'll bet you have.
      MEG   I haven't.
      STANLEY Shall I tell you?
      MEG   What latest?
      STANLEY You haven't heard it?
      MEG   No.
      STANLEY (advancing).   They're coming today.
      MEG   Who?
      STANLEY They're coming in a van.
      MEG   Who?
      STANLEY And do you know what they've got in that van?
      MEG   What?
      STANLEY They've got a wheelbarrow in that van.
      MEG   (breathlessly).   They haven't.
      STANLEY Oh yes they have.
      MEG   You're a liar.
      STANLEY (advancing upon her).   A big wheelbarrow. And
               when the van stops they wheel it out, and they wheel
               it up the garden path, and then they knock at the
               front door.
      MEG   They don't.

STANLEY   They're looking for someone.
MEG   They're not.
STANLEY   They're looking for someone. A certain person.
MEG   (hoarsely).   No, they're not!
STANLEY   Shall I tell you who they're looking for?
MEG   No!
STANLEY   You don't want me to tell you?
MEG   You're a liar!
(pp. 23–4)

By repeating words and phrases, Pinter plays on the effect of repetition in ordinary conversation, highlighting its absurdity and using it to create a sense of ominousness and threat.

The automaticity of repetition

The discussion and analysis so far have been intended to demonstrate that repetition is a fundamental, pervasive, and infinitely useful linguistic strategy. At the outset I also claimed that it can be automatic. I would like now to support that claim and then explain why I believe it is important.

Neurolinguistic research demonstrates the automaticity of certain kinds of language production. Whitaker (1982) describes aphasic patients who suffered complete destruction of the language-producing areas of the brain and consequently lost their spontaneous language-producing capacity. Nevertheless, they retained the ability to repeat exactly; to shadow (i.e. repeat with a split-second delay); and to repeat with simple transformations, such as changes in tense, person, and sentence type. They were able to do this because this type of language production is performed in a different part of the brain: a part devoted to automatic functioning. Whitaker's examples of automatic language production by brain-damaged aphasic patients are strikingly similar to repetitions and variations found in samples of ordinary conversation. Obviously, there is a crucial difference between the use of repeating strategies by aphasics and nonaphasics in that the former are limited to such automatic language production, whereas the latter use repetition in addition to and in conjunction with deliberate language production. Nonetheless, the research on aphasics provides evidence of the automaticity of these repeating strategies. (Research on language comprehension demonstrates that prepatterned speech is also

processed more efficiently by the brain. See, for example, Gibbs
1980, 1986; Gibbs and Gonzales 1985; Van Lancker 1987.)

Whitaker's (1982) survey of neurolinguistic research shows that
repeating, varying, and shadowing prior utterances can be automatic language capacities. I have presented examples of these
phenomena in conversation; it remains to show evidence of their
automaticity. Is it coincidental that these types of language production can be automatic and are pervasive in conversation, or are they
pervasive because they can be automatic? Bolinger (1961:381) observes: "How much actual invention ... really occurs in speech we
shall know only when we have the means to discover how much
originality there is in utterance." If it can be shown that repetition
in conversation is evidence of automaticity, rather than of "originality" in utterance, then this study may contribute in a modest way
to answering Bolinger's question.

Shadowing

The type of repetition in conversation that is most demonstrably
automatic is shadowing: repeating what is being heard with a split-
second delay. A number of segments previously cited include this
phenomenon, for instance from (6):

10   STEVE   I never ... took that seriously
11   PETER   └ I never could take it seriously.

Peter began to utter line 11 a split-second after Steve began line 10
and spoke along with him. In other words, Peter shadowed Steve.
He also did so in (17):

5   STEVE   In the Bronx.
6   PETER   └ In the Bronx.

Shadowing occurs frequently in the transcripts studied. For example, Chad shadowed Steve, the host, when Steve offered the
guests a choice of port or brandy after dinner. (Talk about the
dinner, its food and rituals, interspersed the conversation.)

(33)   1   DAVID   I don't know what ... uh ... port tastes like.
       2   STEVE   Port is very sweet. Port is very rich. →
       3   CHAD   └ Port is very sweet. Very rich. →
       4   STEVE   Syrupy red wine.
       5   CHAD   And brandy's very alcoholic.

Chad's line 3 ("Port is very sweet. Very rich,") repeats, with slight variation (deletion of the second "Port is"), Steve's self-repetition (with variation) in line 2 ("Port is very sweet. Port is very rich.") Chad began saying line 3 before Steve began the second part of line 2, in which he says that port is "very rich"; yet Chad repeated that part of Steve's utterance as well. This indicates that Chad was shadowing Steve: repeating what he heard, as he heard it, with a split-second delay.

(34) is a segment of talk which I have previously analyzed in detail (Tannen 1983b, 1984) to demonstrate that overlapping talk can be cooperative and rapport-building rather than interruptive. I cite the segment here to demonstrate that the overlap and consequent metamessage of rapport are accomplished, in large part, by repetition, and furthermore that at least some of that repetition is automatic.

In this segment, Steve is identifying a building in New York City that was significant to him in his childhood:

(34)   1 STEVE   Remember where W I N S used to be?
       2 DEBORAH   No.⌉
       3 STEVE   ⌊Then they built a big huge skyscraper there?
       4 DEBORAH   No. Where was that.
       5 STEVE   Right where Central Park West met Broadway.
       6   That building shaped like that. [shows with hands]
       7 PETER   ⌊ Did I give you too much? [serving turkey]
       8 DEBORAH   ⌊ By Columbus Circuit? ... That-
                    Columbus Circle?   ⌊
       9 STEVE   ⌊ Right on Columbus
                    Circle.
      10   Here's Columbus Circle,
      11   here's Central Park West,
      12 DEBORAH   Now it's the Huntington Hartford Museum.
      13 PETER   ⌊ That's the Huntington Hartford, right?
      14 STEVE   Nuhnuhno.
      15   Here's Central Park West,
      16 DEBORAH   ⌊ Yeah.
      17 STEVE   here's Broadway.
      18   We're going North, this way?
      19 DEBORAH   ⌊ uhuh
      20 STEVE   And here's this building here.
      21   The Huntington Hartford is ⌈on the South side.
      22 DEBORAH   ⌊On the other- across.

```
23                  Yeah, rightrightrightrightright.
24                  ┌And now that's a new building with a:┐
25   STEVE          └And there was ...      └ and        │ there was
26                  uh- STORES here,
27                  and the upper- SECOND floor was W I N S̈.
28   DEBORAH                                         └ oh:
29   STEVE          And we listened to:┐
30   DEBORAH                           │Now it's a round place
31                  with a: movie theater.
32   STEVE          Now- there's a round- No.
33                  The next .. next block is
34                  but ... but .. THIS is a huge skyscraper  →
35   DEBORAH        └oh
36   STEVE          right there.
37   DEBORAH                 └ Oh yeah
```

This segment exhibits numerous instances of self- and allo-repetition.[25] I will focus only on two that provide evidence for automaticity.

First consider lines 12 and 13:

```
12   DEBORAH   Now it's the Huntington Hartford Museum.
13   PETER              └ That's the Huntington Hartford, right?
```

In line 13, Peter said roughly the same thing that I said in line 12, even though Peter began to say line 13 before I had gotten very far into line 12. One might surmise that Peter said the same thing because he simply happened to think of the same thing to say, a split second after I thought of it. When one considers, however, that Steve's response in line 14 "nuhnuhno" (a triple "no") indicates that Peter and I were both wrong, it seems unlikely that we both happened to make exactly the same mistake about the building Steve had in mind.

The evidence for the automaticity of Peter's shadowing is even stronger when supplemented by playback. When I replayed this segment for Peter, he commented that he did not really know the areas that were being discussed because he had not lived in New York City as an adult, as Steve and I had. It is clear, then, that he decided to say something before he knew just what he would say, trusting that he would find what to say, ready-made, in what I said. This strategy would have worked perfectly if I had been right: It would have appeared that we both knew the location Steve had in mind. Even as things turned out, the strategy worked well. Everyone present had the impression that Peter was a full participant in the interaction; no one noticed anything odd, or suspected that Peter did not know what was being talked about. It was the dual strategy of repetition and overlap, i.e. shadowing, given the appropriateness of its use among these speakers, that made it possible for Peter to participate successfully. Significantly, the three conversants who were not speakers of a high-involvement style could not take part, even though Sally had lived in New York for years and Chad had just returned from a visit there. (Indeed, this segment began as an interchange with Chad about his trip to New York.) I am suggesting that it is the automaticity of such strategies that enables speakers to take part, relatively effortlessly, in conversations with just those others with whom they share conversational style.

Further evidence of the automaticity of repetition is found in lines 30–1 and 32:

30–1 DEBORAH Now it's a round place with a movie theatre.
32   STEVE   Now- there's a round- No.
33   The next .. next block is

In 30–1, I offered a description of the place that Steve was trying to identify. In line 32 Steve began to repeat what I had said as ratification of my listenership ("Now- there's a round-"). But as he spoke he realized that what I (and consequently he) had said did not match the image he had in his mind. He then cut short his repetition ("No") and explained that the building I (we) were naming is on "the next block." This is evidence that the repetition in 32 did not grow out of his mental image of the setting he was describing, but rather was an automatic repetition of my prior words, subject to subsequent checking as he spoke.

These examples provide evidence for the automaticity of allo-repetition. The automaticity of self-repetition is evidenced in the way the same words are subsequently spoken. (35) consists of a number of lines taken from a segment in which Chad voiced the opinion that sign language seems more iconic than spoken language. (This is a frequent observation by non-signers that irritates speakers and proponents of ASL.) In countering this view, David, a sign language interpreter, described a hypothetical situation in

which "a speaking person is talking about what happened," and he
explained that the speaker gets "an image of what happened." After
a brief description of a hypothetical image, David continued:

(35) 1 DAVID When you speak
      2   you use words to ... to recreate that image
      3   in the other person's mind.
      4 CHAD   Right.
      5 DAVID And in sign language,
      6   you use SIGNS to recreate the image.

In line 2, the intonation on "recreate that image" rises and falls. In
the repetition of the same phrase in line 6, David's pitch rises on
"signs" but remains monotonically low and constant throughout
"to recreate the image." This intonation signals given information
and the impression that the phrase in its second occurrence is uttered automatically. Its meaning does not have to be worked out
anew on subsequent reference, but is carried over ready-made.

    A similar example was seen in (5):

      4 DEBORAH or Westerners tend to uh: ...
      5   think of the bódy and the sóul
      6   as two different things,
      7 CHAD   └ Right.
      8 DEBORAH because there's no word
      9   that expresses body and soul together.
     10 CHAD   └Body and soul together.
                    Right.

When I uttered "body and soul together" in line 9, I ran the words
together, with monotonic intonation, in contrast to the word by
word articulation of the words "body" and "soul" in lines 5 and 6
("the bódy and the sóul as two different things").

    Finally, in (23), the phrase "cheese and crackers" was uttered
very differently in its first and second appearances:

      9 And so if I'm just eáting like   cheése and cráckers.
     10   I'll just STUFF myself on cheese and crackers.

In line 9 the phrase had standard statement intonation, with pitch
low on "cheese" and higher on "crackers." In contrast, when the
phrase was repeated in line 10, it was spoken much more quickly,
with steady low pitch, indicating that the phrase was now "given"
and therefore could be rushed through. Moreover, in both these

examples, the effect of the way the second occurrences were spoken was to make them sound automatized the second time. In the words of Pawley (1986), the entire phrase became lexicalized, that is, it behaved like a word, an indivisible unit.

The drive to imitate

In a recent essay about "Tics," Oliver Sacks (1987) gives an account of Gilles de la Tourette's syndrome, "a syndrome of multiple convulsive tics." In Sacks's description, this syndrome can take the form of the drive to imitate and repeat gone haywire. By representing an extreme form of the drive, however, it provides evidence for the existence of such a drive.

Sacks quotes extensively from a 1907 account by a ticqueur called O.:

I have always been conscious of a predilection for *imitation*. A curious gesture or bizarre attitude affected by anyone was the immediate signal for an attempt on my part at its reproduction, and is still. Similarly with words or phrases, pronunciations or intonation, I was quick to mimic any peculiarity.
When I was thirteen years old I remember seeing a man with a droll grimace of eyes and mouth, and from that moment I gave myself no respite until I could imitate it accurately. (38)

O.'s drive to imitate was not confined to imitation of others; it was an expression of a general urge to repeat, including the drive to imitate himself:

One day as I was moving my head I felt a "crack" in my neck, and forthwith concluded that I had dislocated something. It was my concern, thereafter, to twist my head in a thousand different ways, and with ever-increasing violence, until at length the rediscovery of the sensation afforded me a genuine sense of satisfaction, speedily clouded by the fear of having done myself some harm. (38)

Thus the ticqueur's characteristic compulsive motions can be understood as the urge to re-experience a particular sensation.

Elsewhere, Sacks (1986: 117–18) gives an account of a contemporary Touretter whom he chanced to observe on a New York City street displaying the same pattern of behavior, intensified, now seen from the outside:

My eye was caught by a grey-haired woman in her sixties, who was apparently the centre of a most amazing disturbance, though what was happening, what was so disturbing, was not at first clear to me. ...
   As I drew closer I saw what was happening. *She was imitating the
passers-by* – if "imitation" is not too pallid, too passive, a word. Should
we say, rather, that she was caricaturing everyone she passed? Within a
second, a split-second, she "had" them all.

Sacks ([1973] 1983) also describes a similar compulsion to repeat
words and actions in patients suffering from post-encephalitic Parkinsonism (a disease that slows them down or freezes them, as
previously noted) when they are "speeded up" by the drug L-DOPA.
   Why do humans experience a drive to imitate – a drive that is
intensified and sent haywire by the bizarre neurological maladies
described by Sacks?[26] Freud observed, in a line that Kawin (1972:
1) uses as the epigraph to a book on repetition in literature and
film, "Repetition, the re-experiencing of something identical, is
clearly in itself a source of pleasure." In a related observation, Norrick (1985:22), citing Mieder (1978), notes that "newspaper head-
lines are often modelled on proverbs and proverbial phrases in
order to attract attention and arouse emotional interest." This is
obviously true, and yet surprising. Wouldn't common sense suggest
that what is prepatterned, fixed, and repetitious should be boring
rather than attention-getting, bland rather than emotional? Why is
emotion associated with fixity? Perhaps partly because of the pleasure associated with the familiar, the repetitious.
   What purpose could be served by the drive to imitate and repeat?
None other, I think, than the fundamental human purpose of learning. Becker (1984a:138) proposes a

kind of grammar, based on a different perspective on language, one involving time and memory; or, in terms of contextual relations, a set of prior
texts that one accumulates throughout one's lifetime, from simple social
exchanges to long, semimemorized recitations. One learns these texts in
action, by repetitions and corrections, starting with the simplest utterances
of a baby. One learns to reshape these texts to new context, by imitation
and by trial and error. ... The different ways one shapes a prior text to
a new environment make up the grammar of a language. Grammar is
context-shaping (Bateson 1979:17) and context shaping is a skill we ac-
quire over a lifetime.

That imitation and repetition are ways of learning is supported by
the extensive findings of imitation and repetition in children's talk.

The drive to imitate is crucial in artistic creativity as well. Sacks (1987: 41) cites Nietzsche's ([1888] 1968:428) argument that artists experience:

The *compulsion to imitate*: an extreme irritability through which a given example becomes contagious – a state is divined on the basis of signs, and immediately enacted – An image, rising up within, immediately turns into a movement of the limbs . . .

Indeed, when I described to writer friends Sacks's account of Touretters' compulsions to imitate observed behavior, they were overcome with an awkward guilt and self-consciousness: They (like me) recognized the impulse in themselves. Actors also find art in an impulse to imitate, if Albert Finney is typical: "'As a lad, I always liked watching how people walked and acted,' he recalls. 'I used to imitate people'" (Dreifus 1987:56).

In observing that the prepatterning that characterizes idioms is not restricted to utterly fixed expressions, Bolinger (1976:7) asks, "may there not be a degree of unfreedom in every syntactic combination that is not random?" The word "unfreedom" suggests one reason that many may resist the view of language as imitative and repetitious, that is, relatively more prepatterned and less novel than previously thought. Sacks (1987:39) describes an aspect of the experience of Tourette's as an "existential conflict between automatism and autonomy (or, as Luria put it, between an 'It' and an 'I')." In this framework, seeing language as relatively imitative or prepatterned rather than freely generated seems to push us toward automatism rather than autonomy – make each of us more "it" and less "I." But a view of language as relatively prepatterned does not have to be seen this way. Rather, we may see it as making of us more interactional "I's."

We are dealing with a delicate balance between the individual and the social, the fixed and the free, the ordered and the chaotic: polarities that are of central concern to Friedrich (1986). According to Friedrich, the individual imagination manipulates, interprets, rearranges, and synthesizes – based on familiar, recognizable elements. The elements can be manipulated, interpreted, rearranged, and synthesized precisely because they are familiar and fixed. In the numerous examples presented in this chapter, speakers repeated parts of prior talk not as mindless mimics but to create new meanings.

Paradoxically, it is the *individual* imagination that makes possible the *shared* understanding of language. Linguistic prepatterning is a means by which speakers create worlds that listeners can recreate in their own imaginations, recognizing the outlines of the prepatterning. Through prepatterning, the individual speaks through the group, and the group speaks through the individual.

The examples I have given suggest that much repetition in conversation is automatic. Just as canonical formulaic expressions have been shown to be processed by automatic brain function, I suggest that speakers repeat, rephrase, and echo (or shadow) others' words in conversation without stopping to think, but rather as an automatic and spontaneous way of participating in conversation. Another book by Oliver Sacks (1984) dramatizes the paradoxical necessity of automaticity for freedom. Following a severe accidental injury, Sacks's leg was surgically repaired. But despite his surgeon's insistence that he was completely healed, he had no proprioception (that is, self-perception) of his leg: He had no sense of its being a part of him, of its even being there, or of ever having been there. Consequently, he walked as if he had no knee.

Sacks's knee did not "return," spiritually, conceptually, and pragmatically, until he was tricked into using it automatically. Caught off guard by being shoved into a pool, he automatically began to swim. When he stepped out of the pool, he walked normally for the first time following his accident. What he had not been able to accomplish with all his conscious efforts had occurred without effort, by automaticity and spontaneity. Sacks eloquently emphasizes the necessity of automatic, spontaneous use for one to sense one's body as part of one's self. The more spontaneous and automatic one's behavior, the more strongly one feels a sense of self. In other words, automaticity is essential to a sense of "I" rather than antithetical to it.

Conclusion

The view of repetition I am proposing echoes Jakobson's view of parallelism in poetry (1966:428–9):

any word or clause when entering into a poem built on pervasive parallelism is, under the constraint of this system, immediately incorporated into the tenacious array of cohesive grammatical forms and semantic values. The metaphoric image of "orphan lines" is a contrivance of a detached onlooker to whom the verbal art of continuous correspondences remains aesthetically alien. Orphan lines in poetry of pervasive parallels are a contradiction in terms, since whatever the status of a line, all its structure and functions are indissolubly interlaced with the near and distant verbal environment, and the task of linguistic analysis is to disclose the levels of this coaction. When seen from the inside of the parallelistic system, the supposed orphanhood, like any other componential status, turns into a network of multifarious compelling affinities.

If one accepts that at least some (and probably all) of conversation is also a system of pervasive parallelism – though not necessarily rigid in the same way as poetry – then Jakobson's observations apply as well to conversation. Utterances do not occur in isolation. They echo each other in a "tenacious array of cohesive grammatical forms and semantic values," and intertwine in a "network of multifarious compelling affinities." One cannot therefore understand the full meaning of any conversational utterance without considering its relation to other utterances – both synchronically, in its discourse environment, and diachronically, in prior text.

I have presented examples of repetition in ordinary conversation to illustrate its pervasiveness, and some of its forms and functions. I have suggested that repetition in conversation can be relatively automatic, and that its automaticity contributes to its functions in production, comprehension, connection, and interaction. These dimensions operate simultaneously to create coherence in discourse and interpersonal involvement in interaction. Repetition is a resource by which conversationalists together create a discourse, a relationship, and a world. It is the central linguistic meaning-making strategy, a limitless resource for individual creativity and interpersonal involvement.

4

"Oh talking voice that is so sweet": constructing dialogue in conversation

Oh talking voice that is so sweet, how hold you alive in captivity, how point you with commas, semi-colons, dashes, pauses and paragraphs?

Stevie Smith, *Novel on yellow paper*, p. 46

The previous chapter examines synchronic repetition: repeating one's own or another's words within a discourse. It also, however, says a bit about diachronic repetition: repeating words from a discourse distant in time. One way that people frequently talk about a situation in which a speaker repeats another's words at a later time is the situation generally referred to as "reported speech," generally assumed to come in two forms: "direct" and "indirect" speech, discourse, or quotation. "Direct quotation" is commonly understood to apply when another's utterance is framed as dialogue in the other's voice ("Sam said, 'I'll come'"). "Indirect quotation" (or "indirect discourse" or "speech") is commonly understood to apply when another's speech is paraphrased in the current speaker's voice ("Sam said he would come").

In this widely-accepted schema, "direct quotation" and "indirect quotation" are clearly distinguished in the abstract, but in actual discourse many equivocal cases arise. For example, Voloshinov ([1929]1986:131) describes the power of what he calls "texture-analyzing" indirect discourse in the novel which

incorporates into indirect discourse words and locutions that characterize the subjective and stylistic physiognomy of the message viewed as expression. These words and locutions are incorporated in such a way that their specificity, their subjectivity, their typicality are distinctly felt ...

The following example of this strategy is taken from the novel *Household words* (see Appendix I for information on this novel and its choice for analysis). A man is telling the novel's protagonist,

Rhoda, why he can only pay a low price for her recently deceased husband's pharmacy:

He had a lovely new wife, a baby on the way, and he could go no higher in price. (93)

On the surface, the man's words are reported indirectly; there are no quotation marks. Yet the "stylistic physiognomy" – the sound of the man's voice – is suggested by incorporating into the exposition "words and locutions" he is implied to have used ("lovely new wife," "baby on the way"). So on consideration, the line is also, in a way, direct discourse: a representation of his actual words.

Even in the traditional framework, then, the boundary between direct and indirect discourse is fuzzy. On the deepest level, moreover, as has been shown in the preceding chapter in the context of Becker's illumination of grammar as prior text, and as Kristeva (1986:37) puts it, in paraphrase of Bakhtin, "any text is constructed as a mosaic of quotations; any text is the absorption and transformation of another." Thus even what seems like indirect discourse, or discourse that does not quote at all, is, in a sense, quoting others. My concern in this chapter, however, is to demonstrate that instances in which dialogue is presented as "direct quotation" are also not clearcut. Rather, even seemingly "direct" quotation is really "constructed dialogue," that is, primarily the creation of the speaker rather than the party quoted.

Reported speech and dialogue

For Voloshinov/Bakhtin, dialogue is crucial: not dialogue *per se*, that is the exchange of turns that is of central concern to conversation analysts, but the polyphonic nature of all utterance, of every word. This polyphony derives from the multiple resonances of the people, contexts, and genres with which the utterance or word has been associated. As Bakhtin ([1952–3]1986:91) puts it, "Each utterance is filled with the echoes and reverberations of other utterances to which it is related by the communality of the sphere of speech communication."

In the terms of Becker (1984b, 1988, ms.), every utterance derives from and echoes "prior text." Recursively demonstrating what he is describing, Becker uses the Javanese term *jarwa dhosok*, pressing old language into new contexts, to characterize every act of utterance. There are no spanking new words.[1] Both the meanings of individual words (indeed, as frame semantics and the philosophy of Heidegger and Wittgenstein have made clear, words can have meaning precisely because of their associations with familiar contexts) and the combinations into which we can put them are given to us by previous speakers, traces of whose voices and contexts cling inevitably to them.

Not only is every utterance dialogic, but also hearing and understanding are dialogic acts because they require active interpretation, not passive reception. In exploring dialogue in this sense, Voloshinov ([1929]1986) devotes extensive analysis to reported speech. He introduces this focus as follows:

The productive study of dialogue presupposes, however, a more profound investigation of the forms used in reported speech, since these forms reflect basic and constant tendencies in the active reception of other speakers' speech, and it is this reception, after all, that is fundamental also for dialogue. (117)

The notion that even the simplest understanding of situated language requires active interpretation based on prior linguistic experience also underlies Gumperz's (1982) concept of conversational inference.

In his extended discussion of reported speech, Voloshinov criticizes "earlier investigators" for "divorcing the reported speech from the reporting context":

That explains why their treatment of these forms is so static and inert (a characterization applicable to the whole field of syntactic study in general). Meanwhile, the true object of inquiry ought to be precisely the dynamic interrelationship of these two factors, the speech being reported (the other person's speech) and the speech doing the reporting (the author's speech). After all, the two actually do exist, function, and take shape only in their interrelation, and not on their own, the one apart from the other. The reported speech and the reporting context are but the terms of a dynamic interrelationship. (119)

Furthermore, Bakhtin ([1975]1981:340) observes:

that the speech of another, once enclosed in a context, is – no matter how accurately transmitted – always subject to certain semantic changes. The context embracing another's word is responsible for its dialogizing background, whose influence can be very great. Given the appropriate methods for framing, one may bring about fundamental changes even in another's utterance accurately quoted.

The essence of this observation is metaphorically expressed in a Wolof proverb ("Lu nekk manees na ko toxal, mu mel na mu meloon ba mu des wax") which holds, "Everything can be moved from one place to another without being changed, except speech." [2]

My concern in this chapter incorporates Voloshinov's notion that the reported speech and the reporting context are dynamically interrelated as well as Bakhtin's that the meaning of the reported speech itself can be – indeed, I would say, is inevitably – transformed by the reporting context. Moreover, I wish to call attention to the dynamic relationship between the reported speech and the *reported* context. I am claiming that the term "reported speech" is grossly misleading in suggesting that one can speak another's words and have them remain primarily the other's words.

My reasons for claiming that one cannot, in any meaningful sense, "report" speech are as follows. First, much of what appears in discourse as dialogue, or "reported speech," was never uttered by anyone else in any form. Second, if dialogue is used to represent utterances that were spoken by someone else, when an utterance is repeated by a current speaker, it exists primarily, if not only, as an element of the reporting context, although its meaning resonates with association with its reported context, in keeping with Bakhtin's sense of polyphony. In the deepest sense, the words have ceased to be those of the speaker to whom they are attributed, having been appropriated by the speaker who is repeating them. This claim is proffered in counterpoint to Voloshinov/Bakhtin, whose chief material is the reported speech of novelistic prose, and in contradiction to American folk wisdom applied to the reporting of others' speech in daily dialogue, the language of everyday conversation. In short, I wish to question the conventional American literal conception of "reported speech" and claim instead that uttering dialogue in conversation is as much a creative act as is the creation of dialogue in fiction and drama.

Dialogue in storytelling

Rosen (1988) argues for the crucial, transforming, pervasive and persuasive power of the autobiographical mode of discourse.[3] As evidence, he cites Hymes's (1973:14–15) vivid description of a visit to Mrs. Tohet, an American Indian woman, and her rendition of a traditional Indian story. Hymes emphasizes the animation of dialogue in the woman's performance:

All this in detail, with voices for different actors, gestures for the actions, and, always, animation. For that, as people will be glad to tell you, is what makes a good narrator: the ability to make the story come alive, to involve you as in a play.

Along with details and images, the animation of voices "makes the story come alive," "involves" hearers "as in a play."

Rosen (1988:82) takes another piece of evidence not from an exotic language and culture but from a familiar one: academic discourse. He cites Gilbert and Mulkay's (1984) juxtaposition of the way a scientist told about a scientific idea in an interview and the way he wrote about the same idea in a scholarly article. In an interview, the scientist spoke about his reaction when a colleague first suggested the innovative idea:

It took him about 30 seconds to sell it to me. It was really like a bolt. I felt, "Oh my God, this must be right! Look at all the things it explains."[4]

In contrast, "In the formal paper we are told that the experimental results suggested a model which seemed an improvement on previous assumptions and which was, accordingly, put to the test." The scientist submerged the drama of the revelation, its emotional character, when writing in scholarly prose but conveyed it in conversation by casting his reaction to his colleague's innovative idea in dialogue representing his thoughts.

Rosen (n.d.) shows that storytelling in literature is a refinement of storytelling in everyday life – and that storytelling is at the heart of everyday life. He argues that storytelling is "an explicit resource in all intellectual activity," (citing Eagleton) "a disposition of the mind" (8), (citing Barbara Hardy) "a primary act of mind transferred to art from life," a "meaning-making strategy" (13) that represents the mind's "eternal rummaging in the past and its daring, scandalous rehearsal of scripts of the future". Storytelling, in other words, is a means by which humans organize and understand the world, and feel connected to each other. Giving voice to the speech of people who are depicted as taking part in events – and we shall see presently that such voice-giving can be quite concrete – creates a play peopled by characters who take on life and breath.

The involving effect of animated dialogue is at the heart of Eudora Welty's (1984) location of her beginnings as a fiction writer in the conversational stories she heard as a child in Mississippi. Welty writes that she was first exposed to vivid storytelling in the magic of dialogue when her family acquired a car and took a gossipy neighbor along on excursions:

My mother sat in the back with her friend, and I'm told that as a small child I would ask to sit in the middle, and say as we started off, "Now *talk*."
    There was dialogue throughout the lady's accounts to my mother. "I said" ... "He said" ... "And I'm told she very plainly said" ... "It was midnight before they finally heard, and what do you think it *was*?"
    What I loved about her stories was that everything happened in *scenes*. I might not catch on to what the root of the trouble was in all that happened, but my ear told me it was dramatic.   (12–13)

Note that Welty's telling is, in itself, a retelling (of which this is another), since Welty claims as the source of her account not her own recollection but what she has been told, presumably by her parents. Note too that Welty herself creates a scene (a child nestled between two adults in the back seat of a car), an inextricable part of which is dialogue:

"Now *talk*."
"I said" ...
"He said" ...
"And I'm told she very plainly said" ...
"It was midnight before they finally heard, and what do you think it *was*?"

Her concern in retelling this scene from her childhood is to capture the way the meaning and sound of dialogue created for her a sense of drama in storytelling – a drama she sought to recreate in writing as an adult (and I seek to recreate by quoting Welty's retelling).[5]

In addition, Welty points out the active nature of listenership:

Long before I wrote stories, I listened for stories. Listening *for* them is something more acute than listening *to* them. I suppose it's an early form of participation in what goes on. Listening children know stories are *there*. When their elders sit and begin, children are just waiting and hoping for one to come out, like a mouse from its hole.   (14)[6]

That listening is a form of active participation is also emphasized
by Bakhtin ([1952–3]1986:68): "The fact is that when the listener
perceives and understands the meaning . . . of speech, he simultaneously takes an active, responsive attitude toward it." This is why
storytelling is a key element in the establishment of interpersonal
involvement in conversation: It heightens the active participation of
listeners. As Welty points out, the construction of dialogue contributes powerfully to this participation.

Welty knows that narratives in ordinary conversation are artistic
creations, both in the artful telling and in the inseparable contribution of the speaker in constructing the story. This assumption is
seen again in her recollection (or, more accurately, her artful reconstruction) of Fannie, a woman who came to the Welty house to
sew. Like the gossipy neighbor, Fannie delighted Eudora with her
stories about other people, which the child did not understand but
nonetheless loved to hear:

> The gist of her tale would be lost on me, but Fannie didn't bother about
> the ear she was telling it to; she just liked telling. She was like an author.
> In fact, for a good deal of what she said, I daresay she *was* the
> author. (14)

Welty does not, by calling her the author of her tales, criticize
Fannie; rather, she places her among the ranks of talented
storytellers.

The suggestion that oral stories are created rather than reported
was made by another professional storyteller: a former medicine
show pitchman, Fred "Doc" Bloodgood (1982). When I asked him
in a letter about the accuracy of elements of his sample pitches, he
declined to answer, explaining instead, "Anyway, as my dad
always told me, 'never let a grain of truth interfere with the story'."
I doubt that Bloodgood's father ever said this, but it doesn't matter
whether or not he did. What matters is that "as my dad always told
me" is an apt, particular, and familiar way to introduce a general
maxim as dialogue.

The casting of thoughts and speech in dialogue creates particular
scenes and characters – and, as discussed in chapter 2, it is the
particular that moves readers by establishing and building on a
sense of identification between speaker or writer and hearer or
reader. As teachers of creative writing exhort neophyte writers, the

accurate representation of the particular communicates universality, whereas direct attempts to represent universality often communicate nothing – a seeming paradox that may underlie Becker's (1984b) call for the "substitution of particularity for the pursuit of generality or universality as the goal of our craft".

Reported criticism in conversation

As stated at the outset, my main point in this chapter is to argue that "reported speech" is not reported at all but is creatively constructed by a current speaker in a current situation. The bulk of this chapter is devoted to examining closely instances of dialogue in conversational stories. Before doing this, however, I want to demonstrate that taking information uttered by someone in a given situation and repeating it in another situation is an active conversational move that fundamentally transforms the nature of the utterance. This is in contrast to the folk wisdom by which the concept "reported speech" is taken literally.

The folk wisdom I have in mind can be viewed in the common attitude toward reported criticism. In addition to divorcing the reported speech from the reporting context, most Americans, at least, also divorce reported speech from the reported context: On hearing that another has spoken ill of one, most people look right through the "reporter" to encounter the reported source. Not only do they not question the teller's motive in repeating the comment, but, even more significantly, they do not ask how the reported comment grew out of, was situated in, or was triggered by the context in which it was uttered. They do not consider the possibility that the reported utterance might have been provoked by someone present at the time, including the reporter, or constructed in the service of some immediate interactional goal – for example, establishing solidarity with a present party by comparing her favorably to an absent party, or by sympathizing with a complaint that a present party has voiced about an absent one. The literal truth of the report is not questioned. Quite the opposite, opinions expressed in one's absence seem to have an enhanced reality, the incontestable truth of the overheard.

Any anger and hurt felt in response to reported criticism is, for Americans at least, typically directed toward the quoted source rather than the speaker who conveys the criticism. (In contrast, an Arab proverb has it that "The one who repeats an insult is the one who is insulting you.") For example, a man who worked in a large office invested a great deal of his own time in making signs identifying the various departments of his firm. A co-worker told him that the boss did not like the colors he chose for the signs. The man felt unappreciated by and angry at the boss for his ingratitude, but he never had a chance to say anything to the boss, who did not say anything to him, except to thank him and praise him for his efforts – praise that the man assumed to be hypocritical, taking his co-worker's report of the boss's opinion as the truer truth. He did not ask why his colleague chose to tell him something that would predictably hurt. And he did not ask why – in what context, to serve what immediate interactional goal – the boss made the remark.

The constellation of co-workers and boss is parallel to that of siblings and parents, a configuration which yields innumerable examples of hurt and resentment created by repeating to family members things said about them by other family members in their absence. Not only are family members particularly sensitive to reported criticism, but the intimacy of family bonds makes it particularly likely that information will be repeated because exchanging personal information is a means of maintaining intimacy.

Elsewhere (Tannen 1986a) I adduce and discuss many examples of repeating criticism. I will recap only two here. A recent college graduate, whom I call Vicki, made a decision not to return home to spend Christmas with her family. She knew that her sister, whom I call Jill, was not planning to go home either. Vicki wrote to her mother explaining her reasons; on receiving a reply saying that her mother understood, she considered the matter amicably settled. But in a telephone conversation, Jill "reported" that their mother understood and accepted her own decision, because she was still in college, but was upset about Vicki's. Vicki was troubled to learn that her mother was upset by her decision, and angered by what seemed like obvious illogic: a daughter in college should be more, not less, obligated to go home for the holiday.

Both sisters took the remarks made about an absent sister to a present one as the truth. When Jill repeated their mother's remark, she was, after all, repeating what she had heard. I submit, however, that the remark was not the truth, but simply an account devised by the mother in conversation with Jill to avoid criticizing her directly. The puzzle of the mother's illogic can be solved by fitting the remark into the context in which it was made. She did not want to make a direct complaint to either of her daughters. By not telling either daughter of her distress at spending a Christmas alone, she was avoiding putting obvious pressure on them. But by telling Jill that she was upset by Vicki's decision, she was communicating her feelings indirectly. By transmitting the remark to Vicki, Jill converted an indirect criticism – avoiding telling a person she is behaving unacceptably – into a direct one: exactly what the mother had chosen not to do.

A similar dynamic is at work in another example of sisters. One (whom I call Alexandra) was dating a man ten years younger than she, when the other, Lynn, was dating a man ten years older. Their mother, who was given to worrying about her daughters, was concerned about both. She feared that the younger boyfriend would not marry Alexandra, and that the older one would marry Lynn and then die and leave her a widow. Not wishing to cause her daughters pain, she did not express her concerns directly to them. But she saw no reason not to express her concerns about each to the other. When she expressed her concern about Lynn to Alexandra, Alexandra wanted to protect her sister, so she put herself in the line of fire: "But Mom, John is ten years younger than I am! What difference does age make?" This placed the mother in the position of having to include the daughter she was talking to in her criticism ("That's right: I'm worried about you too") or of finding a reason, any reason, to exclude her. This is what the mother did: "Well, that's different. You don't have to worry that he will die first." Alexandra wanted her sister to know that she had stood up for her, so she reported the conversation to her. But Lynn was impressed not by the information that her sister had stood up for her but rather by the hurtful information that her mother disapproved of her boyfriend. Moreover, she was upset by the inconsistency: Why should her mother judge her more harshly than her sister? Again, it is not that the sister who repeated the mother's words was lying or intentionally misrepresenting what she had heard. But she was taking the mother's words as true rather than as sculpted for her benefit. Indeed, the mother's remarks were provoked by Alexandra's drawing a comparison between herself and her sister.

The point of these examples is to dramatize that taking an utterance said about someone in their absence and transforming it into an utterance said in the person's presence, fundamentally changes the nature of the utterance. These anecdotal examples exemplify the common situation in which criticism of a non-present third party is uttered in conversation. Cheepen (1988) finds, in examining casual conversation among friends, that speakers frequently adopt the strategy of negatively evaluating non-present third parties to redress a disturbance in the balance of status among participants. Since such a strategy is a common one, everyone has the power to make much mischief by taking comments from situations in which they were uttered and hauling them to different ones. The point here is that doing so is not a passive act of "reporting" but rather an active one of creating an entirely new and different speech act, using the "reported" one as source material.

I refer to the phenomenon of repeating criticism to provide familiar, easily recognizable, and emotionally meaningful evidence that Americans tend to take literally the act of what is accordingly called "reported speech." They assume that when quotations are attributed to others, the words thus reported represent more or less what was said, the speaker in question being a neutral conduit of objectively real information. The conveyor of information is seen as an inert vessel, in Goffman's (1974) terms, a mere animator: a voice giving form to information for which the quoted party is the principal, the one responsible. With Bakhtin, I want to claim that there is no such thing, in conversation, as a mere animator (in contradistinction, for example, to someone who reads an academic paper written by a scholar who could not be present as scheduled at an academic meeting, a situation I examine elsewhere [Tannen 1988b]).

Goffman (1953:41, cited by Shuman 1986:23) notes,

We must also be careful to keep in mind the truism that persons who are present are treated very differently from persons who are absent. Persons who treat each other with consideration while in each other's immediate presence regularly show not the slightest consideration for each other in situations where acts of deprivation cannot be immediately and incontestably identified as to source by the person who is deprived by these acts.

In this formulation, Goffman suggests that speakers treat an absent person without consideration because they cannot easily be identified by the aggrieved person. I suggest instead that absent persons are treated without consideration *because they do not exist in that context*; in other words, in contexts in which they are absent, they are not perceived as persons, that is, not perceived as potentially affected by the acts of that context.[7] Rather, absent parties are simply resources for the facework of the immediate context. It is, furthermore, the view of oneself as not a person but simply the subject of conversation that makes some people feel uncomfortable to learn that they have been talked about. Thus the utterances that strike an aggrieved party as "acts of deprivation" when repeated often do not actually become that until they are repeated in a context in which the party at issue is present.

The folk wisdom about reported criticism in particular and reported speech in general reflects the pervasive American attitude toward language and communication that Reddy (1979) has identified as the conduit metaphor, the misconception of communication as merely a matter of exchanging information, language being a neutral conduit. Becker (1984a) points out that a similar metaphor underlies linguists' conventional reference to language as a "code." Information is thus seen as immutable, true or false, apart from its context. In direct contrast with this view, I am claiming that when a speaker represents an utterance as the words of another, what results is by no means describable as "reported speech." Rather it is constructed dialogue. And the construction of the dialogue represents an active, creative, transforming move which expresses the relationship not between the quoted party and the topic of talk but rather the quoting party and the audience to whom the quotation is delivered.

My examples have shown, however, that to say that quoted speech does not have the meaning it seems to have on report, is not to say that it was necessarily not uttered by the speaker to whom it is attributed. My claim would not be undermined even by a tape recording "proving" that the words were spoken as reported. Neither am I claiming that when the reported words were not actually uttered, the reporter is lying or intentionally misrepresenting what was said. Rather, the point is that the spirit of the utterance, its nature and force, are fundamentally transformed when the

object of the criticism is present rather than absent. This is a particular instance of the general phenomenon that changing the context
of an utterance changes its meaning. Herrnstein Smith (1978:65)
observes that a quotation is a "fictive utterance" because, in quoting
another, one presents a "facsimile" of the other's words: "The fac-
tuality of the subject does not compromise the fictiveness of the tale
for it is not the events told that are fictive but the *telling* of
them" (128).

I am suggesting, then, that what is called "reported speech,"
"direct speech," "direct discourse," or "direct quotation" (that is, a
speaker framing an account of another's words as dialogue) should
be understood not as report at all, but as constructed dialogue. It
is constructed just as surely as is the dialogue in drama or fiction.
This view does not diminish our image of the individual speaking;
rather it enhances it. Bakhtin ([1975]1981:338) observes, "Every
conversation is full of transmissions and interpretations of other
people's words." The act of transforming others' words into one's
own discourse is a creative and enlivening one.

Reported speech is constructed dialogue

I have argued above that when speech uttered in one context is
repeated in another, it is fundamentally changed even if "reported"
accurately. In many, perhaps most, cases, however, material
represented as dialogue was never spoken by anyone else in a form
resembling that constructed, if at all. Rather, casting ideas as dialogue rather than statements is a discourse strategy for framing information in a way that communicates effectively and creates
involvement. To support this claim, I present in this section brief
examples taken from narratives recorded by participants in casual
conversation with their families and friends.[8] Each example is accompanied by brief discussion demonstrating that the dialogue animated in the narrative was not actually spoken by the person to
whom it is attributed. In other words, it is not reported speech but
constructed dialogue. The following examples, in the order in
which they appear, illustrate dialogue representing what wasn't
said, dialogue as instantiation, summarizing dialogue, choral dialogue, dialogue as inner speech, the inner speech of others, dialogue
constructed by a listener, dialogue fading from indirect to direct,

dialogue including vague referents, and dialogue cast in the persona of a nonhuman speaker.

Dialogue representing what wasn't said

(1) comes from a conversation in which a young woman tells her friend that when she was a little girl, her father frequently embarrassed her by berating her in front of her peers for not having responded to his orders quickly and efficiently. She represents, in the form of dialogue, what she did *not* say to her father:

(1) You can't say, "Well Daddy I didn't HEAR you."

This is a clear example of dialogue constructed rather than reported as the speaker states explicitly that the line of dialogue was not spoken.

Dialogue as instantiation

Specific dialogue is often constructed to illustrate an utterance type that is represented as occurring repeatedly. Several examples follow.

(2) is from a conversation that took place among several women who work together, while they were having lunch in a restaurant. In this excerpt, Daisy animates a line of dialogue in order to illustrate the shared maternal experience of ceasing to accompany their children in play activities when it is no longer required.

(2)   DAISY   The minute the kids get old enough to do these things
               themselves,
             ⌐that's when
    MARY └"You do it yourself."
    DAISY   Yeah that's when I start to say . . .
→   "Well . . . I don't think I'll go in the water this time.
→   Why don't you kids go on the ferris wheel.
→   I'll wave to you."

It is clear from the general time frame established, "The minute the kids get old enough" ("the minute" is, of course, meant figuratively, not literally), that the dialogue (indicated in the example by quotation marks and arrows at the left) is offered as an instantiation of a general phenomenon. This becomes even clearer when the context suggested by the dialogue changes before our eyes from "go in the water" to "go on the ferris wheel." Although rhythmically one blends into the other in a single coherent flow of discourse, the scene changes as the general point of the story is instantiated in two different scenes: from going swimming to going on a ferris wheel.

(3) is taken from a young man's account of having been punished as a boy. As background to the story about a specific instance of punishment, he establishes that his mother set his father up as the one to fear:

(3)   whenever something happened,
→   then "Oh wait until your father comes."

As in the previous example, although this may well be the gist of what the mother said, there is no reason to believe that these are precisely the words she always spoke every time. Another level on which this dialogue could not have been spoken as it is represented here is that of language: The teller of this story is a native of a Spanish-speaking country, so anything his mother said to him when he was a boy was said in Spanish.

Finally, a teacher recounts what he says to a new class when he appears before them as a substitute teacher:

(4)   I have very strict rules,
     a:nd ... one of the first things I tell them
     after I tell them my name,
→   is ... "When you follow my rules,
→   you'll be happy,
→   when you do not follow my rules,
→   you will be-
→   Pain and consequences.
→   You will be very UNhappy."

Once more, it is highly unlikely that these precise words were uttered each time the teacher entered a new class – especially considering the abrupt cutting off of breath following "be" and preceding the highly stylized interjected phrase, "pain and consequences." But the sense of what the teacher presents himself as saying to each class is better captured by a particular instance of speech than it would be by a general summary representing the gist of what he always says (for example, "I tell them that they will be happy if they follow my rules but they will be unhappy if they don't").

Summarizing dialogue

(5) shows a line of dialogue that is explicitly identified as representing the gist rather than the wording of what was said in a single discourse. The speaker says she was part of a group having dinner at a Philippine restaurant when one of the members of her dinner party loudly criticized the restaurant, within earshot of the staff:

(5)   and this man is essentially saying
→   "We shouldn't be here
→   because Imelda Marcos owns this restaurant."

By using the present tense ("this man is essentially saying") as well as the first person pronoun ("We shouldn't be here") and proximal deixis ("We shouldn't be here because Imelda Marcos owns this restaurant."), the speaker casts her summary of the man's argument in dialogue. But she characterizes it as a summary, what he "essentially" said rather than what he specifically said.

Choral dialogue

The next example comes from a narrative that was told by a woman (who happened to be me) about an experience in the Athens airport: A Greek woman tried to go directly to the front of a line in which Americans (including the speaker) had been waiting for a number of hours. The Americans objected to her behavior and resisted her justifications for breaking into the line until she said that she had small children with her.

(6)   And then all the Americans said
→   "Oh in that case, go ahead."

In this example, the dialogue is attributed to more than one speaker: "all the Americans." This is impossible, unless one imagines the line of Americans speaking in unison like a Greek chorus, which is unlikely (despite the Hellenic setting of the story), and, as I can attest, not the case. Rather, the line of dialogue is offered as an instantiation of what many people said.

    Similar examples are frequent in the narratives collected. Just one more will be given. In (7) a woman is telling about having seen two mothers on a subway train with their children:

(7)   and the mothers were telling the kids,
→   "Hold on to that, you know, to that post there."

Since they are not likely to have spoken in unison, the wording sup-
plied instantiates rather than represents what the *two* mothers said.

Dialogue as inner speech

People often report their own thoughts as dialogue. (8) is taken
from a narrative about riding the New York subway. The speaker
describes a strange man who entered the car and:

(8)   started mumbling about ... perverts,
→   ... and I thought "Oh God,
→   if I am going to get
→   someone's slightly psychotic attitude on perverts
→   I really don't feel like riding this train."

It is unlikely that these words actually represent the words the
speaker spoke to himself at the time, if he spoke to himself in words
at all, especially since the phrase "slightly psychotic attitude" seems
stylized for performance effect.

The inner speech of others

If it is questionable that dialogue in a narrative accurately
reproduces what a speaker thought at a time past, it is unquestion-
able that when a speaker reports what someone else thought, the
words thus animated in dialogue do not correspond to words actually thought by the other person. The animation as dialogue of the
thoughts of a character other than the speaker was particularly frequent in the narratives told in conversation by Greek women. The
following example comes from a story told by a Greek woman
whom I call Marika (more will be heard from her later) about being
accosted by a man late at night in Venice. Having taken to carrying
a rock with her for self-defense, she drew the rock from her pocket
and took a step toward the man while brandishing the rock. The
man then turned and left. She (ironically) casts her interpretation
of his motivation for suddenly leaving in the words of his
(projected) thoughts:

(9)   Sou leei, "Afti dhen echei kalo skopo."

[Literally: He says to himself, "She doesn't have a good purpose."
Idiomatically: "She's up to no good."]

Presenting the thoughts of a character other than oneself is a clear
example of dialogue that must be seen as constructed, not reported.

(10) presents the thoughts of another person as dialogue, but introduces them not so much as what he actually thought but as what
he must have been thinking, judging from his behavior and facial
expression. In a story about a baseball game, the teller increases the
impact of his greatest remembered pitch by describing the batter:

(10)   And he- you could just see him just draw back like
→   "Man, I'm going to knock this thing to Kingdom Come."

By dramatizing the confidence of the batter, the speaker intensifies
the dramatic tension that will be resolved when he triumphs over
the batter by pitching his deceptive "knuckleball."

The word "like" is frequently used to introduce dialogue that, in
a sense, is just what it says: not what the person actually said but
rather what the person appeared to have felt like.[9] Thus in (11) a
woman tells of an incident in which her fifteen year old sister was
riding a bicycle with a basketball stuffed under her shirt, giving her
the appearance of being pregnant. She fell off the bike when she
was almost hit by a bus. The narrator says,

(11)   And the bus driver was like "Oh my Go::d!"

The speaker is not suggesting that the bus driver literally said "Oh
my God," but that his reaction was such that he must have been
thinking something like that. Although the speaker cannot know
what the bus driver felt (she wasn't even there), she can use the
resource of presenting what he felt like in order to make her story
dramatically effective.

(12) is taken from a story about a tourist's experience in Japan.
The teller was one of a group being led by a Japanese guide when:

(12)   and um they didn't tell us,
       first of all,
       that we were going into the bath,
       so we were standing in the room,
       and they said "Okay, take your clothes off."
→   We're like "What?!"

and um
[listener: It's prison]
they gave us these kimono
and we put the kimono on,
they brought us to this other room,
and they said, "Okay, take the kimono off."
→   And we're like "What are you talking about?"

Lines attributed to the speaker(s) who gave orders to disrobe are introduced by the word "said," whereas the reactions of the speaker
and other members of his group (represented in a single voice) are
introduced with a form of be + like. There is no suggestion,
however, that the speaker and his friends actually said, "What?"
and "What are you talking about?" but simply that they felt in a
way that would be reflected in such utterances. It is likely that they
did not actually say anything but just complied with the directions
they were given. Casting their thoughts as dialogue allows a
dramatization based on the state of their understanding of events
at the time, rather than the clarity of hindsight.

Dialogue constructed by a listener

In the conversational narratives I have examined, a listener often
supplies a line of dialogue animated in the role of a character in
someone else's story. In (2), the listener, Mary, constructed an utterance in the role of Daisy (or any parent) addressing her children:

DAISY   The minute the kids get old enough
         to do these things themselves,
         ⌈ that's when
→ MARY⌊ "You do it yourself."

The "you" in Mary's utterance refers not to the conversationalists
present but to the children in Daisy's discourse who want to do
something adventuresome. In this active form of listenership, the
listener's construction of dialogue appropriate to someone else's
narrative demonstrates how thoroughly the listener appreciates the
perspective of the speaker. When a listener utters a line of dialogue
for a story she isn't telling, that dialogue certainly cannot be considered "reported."

    Even more extreme is (13), in which a listener supplies a line of
dialogue that is intentionally absurd. This excerpt follows an amus-

ing story told by Lois about how her brother cast a fishing rod and
accidentally sunk a lure in their father's face. Lois describes her
father arriving at the hospital holding the lure in his face. Joe, a
listener, offers a line of dialogue spoken by a hypothetical nurse
that satirizes the absurdity of the situation:

(13)   LOIS   So he had the thing.
              So he's walkin' around ...
→   JOE   "Excuse me, Sir, you've got a lure on your face."

Encouraged by general laughter, Joe goes on to construct an
equally absurd response by Lois's father:

→   JOE   "Ah ... lure again?
           [laughter]
→   Boy ... gets stuck there every week."
           [laughter]

Joe uses Lois's story as material for elaboration; by constructing dialogue, he creates a dramatic scene even more absurd than the one
Lois described.

Fadeout, fadein

In (14), an excerpt from a narrative told by a woman about her experience with a dentist, an indirect quotation fades into a direct
one:

(14)   It was like he was telling everybody
→   to "have your wisdom teeth taken out."
       And I didn't see any point
       as long as they weren't bothering me.

"Telling everybody to" is the grammatical means of introducing an
indirect quotation, but it is followed instead by a direct quotation:
"have your wisdom teeth taken out." The speaker might recall what
the dentist said to her, but she can't know the precise words in
which he spoke to "everybody." Finally, she concludes as if the
reported line had been spoken to her ("I didn't see any point as long
as they weren't bothering me").

   (15) is taken from the same story as (7), about the mothers in
the subway car:

(15)   And uh finally the mother opened up the stroller
→   you know and uh told the kid to "SIT THERE."

As in (14), the mother's speech is introduced with the word "to," suggesting that indirect discourse is to follow. But by assuming the voice quality of a mother giving instructions to her child, the speaker ends by animating rather than reporting the dialogue.

Vague referents

(16) comes from the same discourse as (1), in which a young woman tells how her father embarrassed her by giving her peremptory orders in front of her peers. In (16), the use of vague referents makes it clear that the dialogue was never actually spoken as reported:

(16)   He was sending me out to get tools or whatever
→   [imitating father] "Go get this
→   and it looks like this and the other"

If her father had uttered precisely these words, not even he could have expected her to locate what he wanted.

Nonhuman speaker

The preceding examples come from conversational narratives. However, discourse need not be narrative to exploit the expressive potential of constructed dialogue. The final example comes from conversation taped at a dinner party. A guest notices the hosts' cat sitting on the window sill and addresses a question to the cat: "What do you see out there, kitty?" The host answers for the cat:

(17)   She says,
→   "I see a beautiful world just waiting for me."

The host animates the cat's response in a high-pitched, childlike voice. By animating dialogue, the two speakers create a spontaneous mini-drama with the cat as central character. The constructed dialogue becomes a resource for a fleeting but finely coordinated verbal *pas de deux* performed by a pair of speakers.

In summary, the preceding examples of dialogue found in conversational discourse have demonstrated that much of what takes the form of dialogue is by no means a "report" of what others have said but constructions by speakers to frame information in an effective and involving way. Specifically, casting ideas as dialogue establishes a drama in which characters with differing personalities, states of knowledge, and motives are placed in relation to and interaction with each other. I have argued that in these examples what appears as dialogue was never spoken by anyone. In cases where dialogue was actually spoken, what we know of human memory impels us to doubt that the exact wording could be recalled. Moreover, even if the words had been uttered as "reported," their repetition in another context changes their nature and meaning and makes them the creation of the current speaker.

Constructed dialogue in a conversational narrative

Having adduced snippets of a large number of different conversational narratives to demonstrate that dialogue animated in conversational discourse is constructed dialogue, I now present a complete narrative in order to show how such pseudo-quotations work in context. The lines of dialogue in the following story were not spoken by the characters to whom they are attributed for the reasons shown in the preceding section. What, then, are they doing in the story? The speaker uses the animation of voices to make his story into drama and involve his listeners.

The narrative was told by a young man who came home from his work as a resident in the emergency room of a hospital, to a group of his friends gathered in his home, hosted by his wife. Asked whether anything interesting had happened at the emergency room, he responded by telling this story. (The story also evidences a lot of repetition.)

(18) 1 We had three guys come in,
      2 one guy had a cut right here.
      3 On his arm? [Listener: uhuh]
      4 Bled all over the place, right? [Listener: Yeah]
      5 These three guys were hysterical.
      6 They come bustin' through the door.
      7 Yknow you're not supposed to come in to the emergency room.
      8 You're supposed to go to the registration desk, yknow?
      9 and fill out all the forms before you get called back.
     10 They come bustin' through the door,
     11 blood is everywhere.
     12 It's on the walls, on the floor, everywhere.

13 [sobbing] "Ít's okay Billy, wé're gonna make it /?/."
14 [normal voice] "What the hell's wrong with you."
15 W-we-we look at him.
16 He's covered with blood yknow?
17 All they had to do was take a washcloth at home
18 and go like this . . .
19 and there'd be no blood.
20 There'd be no blood.
21 [Listener: You put pressure on it.]
22 Three drunk guys come bustin' in,
23 all the other patients are like, "Ugh. Ugh."
24 They're bleedin' everywhere yknow.
25 People are passin' out just lookin' at this guy's blood here.
26 [Listener: Like "We're okay."]
27 "Get the hell outta here!"
28 [Listener: Yknow he's got stories like this to tell every night,
   don't you?]
29 Yeah [Listener: Mhm]
30 "Get the hell outta here!" yknow?
31 These three guys-
32 "What the hell's wrong with you guys.
33 You don't know anything about first aid?
34 Hold onto his arm."
35 [innocent voice] "We rai:sed it above his hea::d."
36 "Oh yeah." shh shh [sound of whizzing motion]
37 [Listener: So it bled up.]
38 Yknow they're whimmin' his arm around
39 [upset voice] "Come here Billy!
40 No, come here Billy!"
41 Two guys yankin' him from both sides.
42 [sobbing] "Am Í gonna die?
   [loud, sobbing ingress]
43 Am Í gonna die?"
44 He's passed out on the cot.
45 Anyway so . . . [sobbing] "Am Í gonna die?"
46 "How old are you."
47 "Nineteen."
48 "Shit. Can't call his parents."
49 [hysterically pleading voice] "Don't tell my parents.
50 Please don't tell my parents.
51 Yóu're not gonna tell my párents, are you?"
52 [Listener: /?/ "We're gonna wrap you in bandages."]
53 What happened.
54 Then the cops were there too, the cops.
55 ["bored" voice] "Whó stabbed dja."

56 "I didn't get stabbed.
57 I fell on a bottle." ...
58 "Come o::n, looks like a stab wound to mé."
59 [Listener: Well this is Alexandria, what do you think?]
60 [Listener: Really no shit.]

This story creates a drama involving a dramatic setting (a blood-spattered emergency room) and characters in tension: The young men "bursting in" without having gone through the required registration procedure and displaying emotional distress out of proportion to the seriousness of the victim's wound are at odds with the hospital staff who are trying to maintain order and keep the gravity of the wound in perspective. These dramatically interacting characters are created by the advancing of action in dialogue that is animated in distinct voices.

There are at least five different voices animated in this narrative, and each of these voices is realized in a paralinguistically distinct acoustic representation: literally, a different voice. These are the voices of Billy's friends, the speaker and other hospital staff, Billy, a policeman, and the other patients.

Billy's friends

Billy's two friends are represented by one voice, and the quality of that voice creates the persona that the speaker is developing for them. In line 13 they are presented as trying to reassure Billy, but the quality of the voice animating their dialogue shows that they are hysterical themselves. It is breathy, rushed, overly emotional, out of control:[10] (Layout reflects rise and fall of intonation.)

13 [sobbing] "It's   we're
              o
                 kay Billy,   gonna make it /?/."
   _____

39 [upset voice] "Come
                    here Billy!
40 N   come
     o,   here Billy!"

The friends protest in line 35 that:

                       rai:sed   he
35 [innocent voice] "We   it above his   a
                                      d."

The quality of the voice in which this line is uttered suggests belabored innocence that is really stupidity.

Hospital staff

Another example of more than one person animated in the story as a single voice is the speaker himself, merged with the rest of the hospital staff.[11] The quality of this voice is loud and strident, suggesting frustration and impatience but also reasonableness and calm. Dialogue uttered by this persona is the closest to the speaker's normal intonation and prosody:

```
14   [normal voice] "What              wrong
                              the hell's          with you."
     _____
```

```
30   "Get           out of
               the hell          here!"
     _____
```

```
32   "What                 wrong
                  the hell's          with you guys.
                                              aid?
33   You don't know anything about first
34   Hold         a
              onto his  rm."
     _____
```

```
36   "O   ye
          h    ah."
     _____
```

```
46   "How
              old are you."
     _____
```

```
48   "Sh   Can't          pa
          it.       call his    rents."
```

52   [Listener: /?/ "We're gonna wrap you in bandages"]

In line 52 dialogue is animated by a listener who assumes a voice quality similar to that adopted by the speaker when he is animating the voice of himself and the staff.

Billy's voice

Billy himself is animated in the most paralinguistically marked roleplay. The voice representing him is sobbing, gasping, desperate, out of control:

```
                    Í gonna die?
42  [sobbing] "Am
                          Í gonna die?"
43  [loud, sobbing ingress] Am
    _____

                             Í gonna die?"
45  Anyway so ... [sobbing] "Am
    _____

47  "Nineteen."
    _____

49  [hysterically pleading voice] "Don't
                              tell my parents.
50  Please
          don't tell my parents.
51  Yóu're                  pár          you?"
          not gonna tell my     ents, are
    _____

       did
56  "I     n't get stabbed.
                bot
57  I fell on a    tle." ...
```

The paralinguistically exaggerated role-play of Billy's voice, and the slightly less marked animation of his friends' voice, both emotion-filled, contrast sharply with the relatively ordinary quality of the voice in which the speaker/hospital staff dialogue is represented. These contrasting voices create the dramatic tension between the unreasonable behavior of "these three drunk guys" and the reasonable behavior of the speaker/staff. This contrast highlights as well the central tension in the story: that the visual display of blood and the extremity of the boys' emotional display were out of proportion to the severity of the wound.

Policeman

Marked in a different direction is the stereotypically flat voice of the policeman:

```
55  ["bored" voice] "Who
                          stabbed dja."
    _____

58  "Come      looks                       m
             o::n,      like a stab wound to   e."
```

This voice is that of a jaded detective who has seen it all, knows it all, and is just doing his job.

Other patients

Finally, the other emergency room patients are animated in a single voice:

23   all the other patients are like, "U   U

                                  gh.   gh."

_____

                        "We're
26   [Listener: Like   okay."]

Animating the grunts of disgust displayed by the other patients in the emergency room ("Ugh. Ugh.") provides internal evaluation contributing to the depiction of a dramatic scene in which "blood is everywhere."

   It is clear in all these examples, for reasons parallel to those explained for the dialogue presented in the preceding section, that the lines of dialogue in this story are not reported but rather constructed by the speaker, like lines in fiction or drama, and to the same effect. Through the animation of dialogue with paralinguistically distinct and highly marked voice quality, the speaker constructed a drama involving lifelike characters in dynamic interaction. As onlookers to the drama, the audience becomes involved by actively interpreting the significance of character and action.

Modern Greek stories

(9) was taken from the collection of stories told by Greek women about being molested. Americans, on reading translations of those stories, often commented that they found them very vivid.[12] This impression seems to reflect a phenomenon frequently observed, and supported by folk wisdom, that Greeks are good storytellers. In the original study, I identify and illustrate the linguistic features that contribute to that impression – features which I suggest contribute to the creation of involvement: both the involvement of the audience and the sense of the speaker's own involvement in the storytelling.[13] Here I will further examine and discuss one involvement strategy in the Greek women's stories: constructing dialogue.

   Fifteen of the 25 narratives told by the Greek women used constructed dialogue. The remaining 10 did not report dialogue at all. In 25 stories I collected from American women about being molested, I found only one instance of constructed dialogue. This is not to imply that the 15 Greek stories and the one American story which present dialogue do so because talk occurred during the incidents they report, whereas talk did not occur during the events described in the stories that do not include dialogue. While it is theoretically possible that molestation events in Greece are more likely to involve talk than similar events in New York City (where I recorded most of the American stories), this is information I cannot know. Furthermore, I would not claim that American storytellers never effectively use dialogue. All the preceding examples indicate that they do. All I am claiming, then, is that the construction of dialogue which I am about to illustrate in the Greek women's stories is one of a range of involvement strategies that I found to typify this collection of modern Greek conversational stories.

The representation of speech in dialogue is a narrative act, not the inevitable result of the occurrence of speech in the episode. By setting up a little play, a speaker portrays motivations and other subtle evaluations internally – from within the play – rather than externally, by stepping outside the frame of the narrative to make evaluation explicit.

(19) comes from Marika, the same speaker who told the story from which (9) was taken (about using a rock to scare off a man who accosted her in Venice at night) as well as Example (21) in chapter 3 (about emitting a stream of verbal abuse at her attacker). In (19) Marika explains why she contacted the friend of a friend during a trip to Rhodes by casting her motivation as dialogue she spoke to her travelling companion:

(19)   Tis leo tis xadhelfis mou,
→   "Kaiti, dhen pame
→   kai ston systimeno ton anthropo
→   na mi fygoume apo tin Rodho
→   kai dhen echoume patisi to podharaki mas."
     "Pame," mou leei.

     I say to my cousin,
→   "Katie, shouldn't we also go
→   to the person we were told to look up,
→   so as not to leave Rhodes
→   without having set foot [on his doorstep]."
     "Let's go," she says to me.

By casting the decision in the form of dialogue, Marika creates a scene dramatizing her motivation in contacting the man who attacked her. She shows by her phrasing (i.e. internal evaluation) that she was motivated by a sense of obligation to behave properly, not by a desire to spend time with this or any man.

Marika then tells that the man insisted on taking them for a tour of Rhodes, for which excursion he showed up with a friend. She lets us know what she feared – and builds suspense thereby with dramatic foreshadowing – by reporting her thoughts in the form of direct quotation:

(20)   Leo, "Ti thelei.
        Dhyo ekeinoi, dhyo emeis,
        ti echei skopo na mas kanei."

        I say [to myself], "What does he want.
        Two [of] them, two [of] us,
        what does he plan to do to us."

In four stories Marika represents her thoughts as direct quotations to herself, sometimes even addressing herself by name:

(21)   "Kala" leo,
        "Marika edho eimaste tora."

        "Okay" I say [to myself],
        "Marika, here we are now."

Thus Marika frames her own thoughts as a dialogue with herself.

A variation on constructed dialogue – definitely constructed but not exactly dialogue – that is prominent in the Greek spoken stories is the use of sound words, or sound non-words, to represent action. There are 13 instances of sound words in the 25 Greek narratives. A few examples follow.

In continuing her story about looking up a man on the island of Rhodes, Marika uses the sound word /bam/ to dramatize the man's physical assault that occurred after the companion he brought along diverted her cousin, leaving her alone with him:

(22)   peftei aftos apano mou
        xereis apano mou – BAM.

        he falls on top of me
        yknow on top of me – BOM.

In (23) Marika uses the sound word /plaf/ to describe another assault, this one by a famous writer to whom Marika had been sent to show him her work. He takes her into a sitting room, where:

(23) opou vlepeis ton [name]
      opos einai kontochondros
      na pesi epano mou paidhia
      etsi epese – PLAF.

      when you see [name]
      as he is short-and-fat
      falling on top of me, guys,
      like that he fell – PLAF.

The connotations of these two sound words are different, reflecting the nature of the assaults they dramatize. In (22), the attack suggested by /bam/ is a forceful one: The girl being attacked is young (16 or 17 years old), and her attacker is in his prime (about 45); she is slight and he huge:

ego tosi,
aftos ekei vouvali orthio,

I like that [idiomatically, "me, a little bit of a thing"],
he there a standing bull,

and he hurls her onto the ground from a standing position in a deserted outdoor setting. In contrast, in (23), /plaf/ gives a sense of a sloppy, undignified, absurd assault made by a man who is singularly implausible in the role of seducer; his attack is ridiculous and unpleasant but not dangerous. Marika is now a grown woman, and the man who hurls himself upon her is

kondos, chondhros, 102 eton, e, misokaraflos,
ta matia tou einai aspra,
dhiladhi otan ton vlepeis aïdhiazis

short, fat, 102 years old, uh, half bald,
his eyes are white,
in other words when you see him you are revolted

Furthermore, she is sitting down at the time of the assault; she is bigger than he, and his wife is in the next room. These very different connotations are captured by the differing sound words.

Finally, in the rock-in-Venice story from which (9) also comes, Marika uses three successive sound words to represent action which is not otherwise described:

(24)   vgazo tin petra – DAK!
       pali 'dho etsi – DOUK!
       ekane TAK!
       kai exifanisthi aftos.

       I take out the rock – DOK!
       again here like this – DOOK!
       he went TOK!
       and he disappeared.

Since I audio-taped but did not videotape the narration, I cannot reconstruct the gestures that accompanied the sound words, but I can reconstruct that Marika's "DAK"/"DOUK" (/dak/ /duk/) represented some form of attack with the rock. "Ekane TAK!" ("[It/ He] went [lit. made/did] /tak/!") would have been disambiguated by a gesture as well.

The sound words that appear in the Greek narratives are: /bam/, /gan/, /ga/, /dak/, /duk/, /tak/, /mats/-/muts/, /plaf/, /ax/, /a/, and /psit/-/psit/. The last is somewhat different, I believe; it represents literally a sound that men utter in public to get the attention of women and chase away cats. All the other sound words are intended to represent action and are composed primarily of the large-sounding back vowels /a/ and /u/; the abrupt voiceless and voiced stops /p/ /b/, /t/ /d/, and /k/ /g/; and consonant clusters /ts/ and /pl/. The sound words are phonologically graphic, patterning with similar phenomena in many other languages (Ohala 1984), and they contribute to involvement by forcing the hearer to recreate the action represented by the sound.

Thus constructed dialogue, including sound words, is a strategy that patterns with many others to make the stories told by Greek women about being molested involving.

Brazilian narrative

Constructed dialogue in the Greek stories is part of a network of discourse strategies that create involvement. It seems likely that the use of constructed dialogue is associated not only with Greek but also with other individual and ethnic styles that come across as "vivid," as Kirshenblatt-Gimblett (1974) and Tannen (1984) have shown for East European Jews and Labov (1972) and others have demonstrated for American Blacks, Besnier (in press) reports that conversational stories in Nukulaelae, a small, predominantly Polynesian society on an isolated atoll, are typically told exclusively in dialogue, whether or not the speaker personally experienced or observed the events.

There is evidence that Brazilian speech falls into this category as well, and that constructed dialogue is a dimension of that effectiveness. In a pilot study comparing how Brazilian and American speakers told the story of Little Red Riding Hood, Ott (1983) found that Brazilian speakers used far more constructed dialogue. The American man in the study used six such instances, all formulaic for this fairy tale:

"Grandma, what a big nose you have."
"All the better to smell you my dear."
"Grandma, what big ears you have."
"All the better it is to hear you my dear."
"Grandma, what a big mouth and big teeth you have."
"All the better to eat you with my dear."

The American woman in the study used 15 instances of dialogue, including the formulas found in the American man's story, but also including some improvised variations on them (for example, "What long whiskers you have"; "The better to wiggle them at you my dear") and the casting of other parts of the story in dialogue. For example, she casts the mother's instructions to Little Red Riding Hood as direct address ("Go to your grandmother's house"). The Brazilian woman who told the same fairy tale used 20 instances of dialogue, and the Brazilian man used 43!

The Brazilian man's version of the fairy tale represents almost all action in dialogue. In part through dialogue, he makes the familiar story into a unique drama through the creation of scenes. For example, at the beginning (as translated into English by Ott):

One time on a beautiful afternoon, in her city, her mother called her and said:
"Little Red Riding Hood, come here."
"What is it, mother? I am playing with my dolls, can I continue?"

The speaker first set the scene in a particular place (a city), at a particular time of day (afternoon), with particular weather (beautiful). He then depicted action between characters, including dramatic conflict: The mother calls her daughter to perform a task for her;

the daughter is engaged in a particular activity, playing with dolls, which she resists interrupting. Thus, casting the story in dialogue allows for rich particularity.

Long segments in this account are composed only of dialogue. For example, when the little girl is accosted by the wolf on her way to her grandmother's house:

> "Little Red Riding Hood, Little Red Riding Hood."
> And Little Red Riding Hood stopped and looked: "Who is there?"
> "Ah, who is talking here is the spirit of the forest."
> "Spirit? But I don't know you."
> "No, but I am invisible, you can't see me."
> [imitating child's voice] "But what do you want?"
> "Where are you going, Little Red Riding Hood?"
> "Ah, I'm going to my granny's house."
> "What are you going to do there, Little Red Riding Hood?"
> "Ah, I'm going to take some sweets that my mother prepared for her."
> "Ah, very good ... the sweets are delicious, they are, they are, they are, they are ..." [licking his lips]
> "Do you want one?"
> "No, no, no. no. [Accelerated] Spirits don't eat. Okay, okay. Then, now, yes, yes, you are going to take it to your granny ... remember me to her, okay?"
> "Okay, bye."

Through constructed dialogue and other features, this Brazilian speaker created a vivid new story out of a standard fairy tale.

Coincidentally, the fairy tale "Little Red Riding Hood" is a fictionalized, indeed mythologized, version of the same story type as the one represented by the Greek stories: a female being molested by a male. It is intriguing to note parallels between the evaluative framework of the Brazilian man's telling of the fairy tale and the conversational stories told by the Greek women. For example, as was seen in Marika's narrative about Rhodes, the Brazilian man portrays Little Red Riding Hood's innocence by indicating her reluctance to go on the excursion that made her the object of the attack: Far from looking for trouble, she wanted only to stay quietly at home playing with her dolls. Similarly, just as Marika portrayed herself as simply doing the socially proper thing (not failing to look up someone she was asked by a family friend to look up), so the Brazilian man's version of Little Red Riding Hood portrays the little girl as behaving properly in running an errand for her

mother even though she'd rather play, and politely offering sweets
to the wolf when he admired them.

Dialogue in writers' conversation

A large number of the stories I recorded in modern Greek were told
in a gathering of women who happened to be writers. This was not
intentional; it came about because I was at the time writing a book
about a modern Greek writer, and so I had made social contact
with other writers. Marika, the source of many of the examples I
chose for citation here, was a member of this group. It seems likely
that her particularly vivid storytelling style is not unrelated to the
verbal ability that she brings to bear in her creative writing.

I had a rare opportunity to observe a naturally-occurring juxtaposition of accounts of the same interaction told by two people,
one a writer and the other an editor at the publishing company that
was publishing the writer's book. It happened that I knew them
both, and in the course of conversation with me, each one, knowing I knew the other, told me about a telephone conversation that
had taken place between them. The author had been dilatory about
obtaining permission for an illustration in his book. Publication
was delayed as a result, and the publisher had spent a great deal
of time trying to track down the copyright holder himself. The
author furthermore had repeatedly failed to respond to the publisher's phone messages and letters. The author finally called the
publisher to give him the necessary information, and he apologized
at the same time.

Although both men agreed on these circumstances and on the
content of their conversation, the way they reported their conversation to me differed with respect to representation of dialogue. The
author described the interchange this way:

I said, "I'm sorry to have been so exasperating."
[pause] And there was a long silence.

The editor described it this way:

He apologized, but when the time came for me to say, "That's all right,"
I didn't say it, so there was a long silence.

The author's recounting of this conversation is, I believe, more dramatically effective. Although both accounts include constructed dialogue, they do so for different functions. The author gave a line of dialogue to represent what he actually said ("I'm sorry to have been so exasperating"). In contrast, the editor represented that utterance by naming its intention ("He apologized"). The editor used a line of dialogue to represent what he didn't say ("That's all right"). The writer left that line unstated, assuming that I could surmise what is omitted when silence follows an apology. In other words, the dialogue the author included was particular dialogue – what was said. The dialogue that the editor included was a general representation of the kind of statement that could have been said but wasn't. The author's omission of such dialogue constitutes a major involvement strategy – using ellipsis to force the hearer to supply part of the meaning. In short, the author's account created a little drama in which I as hearer was invited to participate by supplying unstated meaning myself. The editor's account has the germs of the same drama but it is realized more as a fully interpreted report than as a little play. I, as hearer, was invited to do less of the work of sensemaking and, I submit, to be less involved, less moved, by the account.

I think it is not a coincidence that the more effective story (minimal though it was) was told by the author, a writer of fiction. I don't know whether or not the words he reported are exactly the words he spoke. I don't think it matters. It may be that as a writer he has a good memory for exact wording. But it may also, or instead, be that he has a good sense of possible wording, that the words he reported were not exactly the ones he had spoken, but they had an authentic ring. He seems to have a sense that retelling his apology in the form of constructed dialogue will be vivid – a particular apology – and will occasion in the hearer the imagination of what will come next.

This example suggests that the use of constructed dialogue, like other linguistic strategies that create involvement, is differentially exploited in the conversation of different speakers. Therefore the relationship between conversational and literary discourse is variable not only with respect to different genres or discourse types but also with respect to individual abilities and predilection – in other words, individual style.

Conclusion

I have argued in this chapter that the term "reported speech" is a misnomer, an abstraction with no basis in the reality of interaction. When speakers cast the words of others in dialogue, they are not reporting so much as constructing dialogue. Constructing dialogue creates involvement by both its rhythmic, sonorous effect and its internally evaluative effect. Dialogue is not a general report; it is particular, and the particular enables listeners (or readers) to create their understanding by drawing on their own history of associations. By giving voice to characters, dialogue makes story into drama and listeners into an interpreting audience to the drama. This active participation in sensemaking contributes to the creation of involvement. Thus understanding in discourse is in part emotional.

Becker (in press:5) notes "the pervasiveness of a kind of indirect quotation in all our languaging. *Everything* anyone says has a history and hence is, in part, a quotation. *Everything* anyone says is also partly new, too . . ." The constructing of dialogue for framing as reported speech reflects the dual nature of language, like all human behavior, as repetitive and novel, fixed and free, transforming rather than transmitting what comes its way. Moreover, and perhaps paradoxically, it is a supremely social act: by appropriating each others' utterances, speakers are bound together in a community of words.

Constructing dialogue, moreover, is an example of the poetic in everyday conversation. In the terms of Friedrich (1986), it is a figure that fires the individual imagination. The creation of voices occasions the imagination of alternative, distant, and others' worlds by linking them to the sounds and scenes of one's own familiar world.

5

Imagining worlds: imagery and detail in conversation and other genres

The artist's life nourishes itself on the particular, the concrete: that came to me last night as I despaired about writing poems on the concept of the seven deadly sins and told myself to get rid of the killing idea: this must be a great work of philosophy. Start with the mat-green fungus in the pine woods yesterday: words about it, describing it, and a poem will come. Daily, simply, and then it won't lower in the distance, an untouchable object. Write about the cow, Mrs. Spaulding's heavy eyelids, the smell of vanilla flavouring in a brown bottle. That's where the magic mountains begin.

Sylvia Plath, *Journals*[1]

"I wish you were here to see the sweet peas coming up."

A line of a poem? It could become one. But as it was, it was just a fragment of conversation, words uttered by a friend on one coast to a friend on the other. But these words have something in common with a poem: They spark a flash of feeling. They make us not just think about, but feel, the distance of the American continent separating two people, the longing to be in the presence of someone loved, to report not important events, but small ones, small perceptions.

"I wish you were here to see the sweet peas coming up."

Why is this more moving than the simple, "I wish you were here"? Partly because "Wish you were here" is a fixed expression, a cliche. But mostly, I think, it is because of the sweet peas – small and ordinary and particular. The sweet peas coming up provide a detail of everyday life that brings everyday life to life. The sweet peas create an image – a picture of something, whereas "Wish you were here" suggests only the abstract idea of absence. And the sound of "sweet peas" is moving: the repeated high front vowel, /i/, suggests something small and tender, and this impression is intensified because it echoes the same sound in "here" and "see."

Similarly, the repeated, symmetrically bounding sibilants /s/ and /z/ in /switpiz/, almost adjacent to the /s/ of "see," are soothing and alluring. And semantic associations are at work as well: One is moved by the "sweet" of "sweet peas," the word "sweet" having gathered meaning associated with people, their character and their relationships. It would not have been quite as moving to say, "I wish you were here to see the geraniums coming up," or "the tomatoes," or "the asparagus."[2]

In thinking about why I had an emotional response when my friend said, "I wish you were here to see the sweet peas coming up," I was reminded of the line from a poem by T. S. Eliot: "I am moved by fancies that are curled around these images and cling." My concern in this chapter is the way and the why that fancies curl around and cling to images. More specifically (and more prosaically), I explore how details create images, images create scenes, and scenes spark emotions, making possible both understanding and involvement.

The role of details and images in creating involvement

I have argued that involvement is created by the simultaneous forces of music (sound and rhythm), on the one hand, and meaning through mutual participation in sensemaking, on the other. A major form of mutual participation in sensemaking is creating images: both by the speaker who describes or suggests an image in words, and the hearer or reader who creates an image based on that description or suggestion. Furthermore, as discussed in chapter 1, the power of images to communicate meaning and emotions resides in their ability to evoke scenes. Images, like dialogue, evoke scenes, and understanding is derived from scenes because they are composed of people in relation to each other, doing things that are culturally and personally recognizable and meaningful.

Through images created in part by details, a hearer or reader imagines a scene. I use the term "imagine" both in relation to "images" and in relation to Friedrich's (1986) sense of the individual imagination. On one hand, "imagine" refers to creating images in the mind. The particularity and familiarity of details make it possible for both speakers and hearers to refer to their memories and construct images of scenes: people in relation to each other engaged in recognizable activities. And the construction of a scene in comprehension by hearers and readers constitutes mutual participation in sensemaking. On the other hand, details, as I have argued for dialogue and repetition, are poetic, in Friedrich's sense, in that they fire the individual imagination. Involvement strategies do not decorate communication, like frosting a cake, by adding something to the exchange of information. Rather, they constitute communication: They are the ingredients that make the cake. It is in large part through the creation of a shared world of images that ideas are communicated and understanding is achieved.

Before launching this chapter, I present, without comment, a story-within-a-story from Hymes (1973:14–15), the full excerpt cited by Rosen (1988:69–70) of which I cited the last lines only in the preceding chapter. I beg readers' indulgence, for I am breaking the rules of academic (but not literary) discourse by presenting a text without revealing (yet) my reason for doing so.

(1)   Let me mention here Mrs. Blanche Tohet, who in the summer of 1951 had David and Kay French and myself wait for a story until she had finished fixing eels. A tub of them had been caught the night before near Oregon City. Each had to be slit, the white cord within removed, and the spread skin cut in each of its four corners, held apart by sticks. The lot were then strung up on a line between poles, like so many shrunken infants' overalls, to dry. Mrs. Tohet stepped back, hands on hips, looking at the line of eels, and said: "Ain't that beautiful!" (The sentence in its setting has been a touchstone for aesthetic theory for me ever since.) All then went in, and she told the story of Skunk, when his musk sac was stolen and carried down river, how he travelled down river in search of his "golden thing," asking each shrub, plant and tree in turn, and being answered civilly or curtly; how down the river he found boys playing shinny-ball with his sac, entered the game, got to the "ball," popped it back in, and headed back up river; how, returning, he rewarded and punished, appointing those that had been nice to a useful role for the people who were soon to come into the land, denying usefulness to those who had been rude. All this in detail, with voices for different actors, gestures for the actions, and always, animation.

I will comment on this text later.

Details in conversation

Before presenting transcribed conversational examples, I will discuss three examples of details used to create images in conversation that I observed but did not tape record.

A Finnish colleague was telling me about his mother's experience as a member of a tourist group in the Soviet Union. Ageing and having little use for tact, she publicly challenged an Intourist guide on the official story of the Russo-Finnish war. Upon returning to Finland, she was held up at the border by a prolonged search of her belongings. My colleague dramatized the extremity of the search by telling the detail that the Soviet border guards squeezed the paste out of her tube of toothpaste.[3]

A woman was telling me how inappropriately prepared her elderly mother was when she arrived by plane for a winter-long visit. That the mother did not bring sufficient clothing was dramatized by the detail that she had with her only the single brassiere she was wearing. That the items she did bring were inappropriate was dramatized by the detail that her hand-held luggage was heavy because it was full of potatoes and onions which she did not want to throw out when she left home.

A friend was describing his meeting with a married couple, both artists, in an art museum: "She was standing in front of some Francis Bacons, exclaiming, 'That's painting!' He was in another part of the museum, looking intently at some obscure German expressionists." By referring to a specific painter (Bacon) and style of painting ("obscure German expressionists"), by using a graphic verb ("exclaiming") and adverb ("looking intently") to depict their actions, and by animating her dialogue which contrasts with his silence, the speaker created two contrasting scenes and, through these scenes, instant summaries of their contrasting personalities: hers, expansive and expressive; his, intense and brooding. Had he described their personalities in evaluative statements, his evaluation would have remained abstract and might even have been questioned. By creating images of the scenes in which he encountered them, he led the hearers (I was one) to draw conclusions about the artists' personalities, as if from direct observation.

The images of the artists in the museum, the old woman traveling by plane with potatoes and onions in her hand luggage, and the Russian border guards squeezing out toothpaste have remained with me, though the images I have constructed and kept must necessarily differ from those in the minds of the speakers who created them. Images, I am suggesting, are more convincing and more memorable than abstract propositions.

Put another way, images provide internal evaluation: They lead
hearers and readers to draw the conclusion favored by the speaker
or writer. I hope, with these and the following examples, to demonstrate why internal evaluation is more persuasive than external
evaluation, as Labov (1972) noted it is when he introduced the concept. My claim is that this is so because internal evaluation is more
involving. Hearers and readers who provide interpretations of
events based on such story-internal evidence as dialogue and images
are convinced by their own interpretations (for example, "all the
other patients are like, 'Uзh. Ugh.' They're bleeding everywhere
yknow"). In contrast, external evaluation seeks to convince hearers
or readers by providing interpretations in the storyteller's voice,
from outside the story (hypothetically, "This is the best part – the
other patients were disgusted by the sight of the boy's blood"). In
the former case, the meaning is dramatized, and the hearer does the
work of supplying it. In the latter, the meaning is stated, and
handed to the hearer ready-made.

Images and details in narrative

What are details doing in stories?

Amost any conversational narrative provides examples of details
and images that create scenes and hence involvement. The conversational stories told by Greek women about having been molested
by men yield innumerable instances. For example, a woman
describes the American who came to her rescue when a strange man
attacked her in Paris:

(2)   kai ekeini tin ora
       bainei,
       bainei san apo michanis theos,
       enas Amerikanos
       yiro sta evdhominda,
       dhen tha xechaso pote
       ena, forouse ena me megala karro poukamiso

(2)   and at that time,
       (there) enters
       enters like an act of God,

an <u>American</u>
about <u>seventy years old</u>,
I'll never forget
a, he was wearing <u>a shirt with large checks</u>

If communication were only a matter of conveying information, then the visual pattern on the American's shirt would not add materially to the story. Indeed, the fact that he was American might be deemed irrelevant. And yet these details do contribute to the story; they *make* the story.

In terms of Chafe's (1985:116) three types of involvement (self-involvement of the speaker, interpersonal involvement between speaker and hearer, and involvement of the speaker with what is being talked about), the pattern on the American's shirt is a sign of the speaker's involvement with her memory. Furthermore, in keeping with Chafe's (1987) discussion of what details are remembered over time, the checkered shirt may have been memorable to the Greek woman because it was unusual in Paris: a typically American fashion. But the detail of the checkered shirt also works to create interpersonal involvement: the rapport that is being created between the speaker and her audience by means of this story. In addition to involving me, an American listener, describing the shirt the man wore (and his age) helps all the hearers to imagine a man, a particular man dressed in a particular way. Finally, emphasizing that she remembers what he wore – indeed, that she will never forget what he wore – reinforces the hearer's sense of the vividness of the memory, and therefore its reportability and authenticity.

Throughout their stories, the Greek women I recorded told details of where they were going and what they were doing when they were molested. Some of these details include:

– The speaker was making a telephone call from a public phone; she tells whom she was calling and why

– The speaker was visiting a famous writer; she names him, tells what she was delivering, and for whom

– The speaker was on her way to bookstores in the Latin Quarter

– The speaker had seen the man who molested her, shortly before the time of telling, at a particular event which she names

- The speaker's niece, whom she was sponsoring at seamstress school, was staying with her at the time when she was receiving sexually harassing telephone calls at home

- The speaker was about to meet friends that night; she names the friends

- The speaker had gone to Piraeus, the port city near Athens, to accompany a friend who was seeing someone off; she names her friend, and tells where his friend was going and why

These are just a few examples taken from the Greek women's stories. They show that the details create images that serve multiple purposes. First, they set a scene during which the recounted events took place. Second, they provide a sense of authenticity, both by testifying that the speaker recalls them and by naming recognizable people, places, and activities. Further, they contribute to the point of the story and play a role in the speaker's presentation of self. The preceding examples show that many of the speakers, in telling about being molested, establish their own innocence and seriousness of purpose at the same time that they give relevant background information leading up to the molestation event. Thus Chafe's three types of involvement, along with others, are intertwined in context, each entailing the others to a degree.

Where do details appear in stories?

Narrative is a genre particularly given to the use of details since it is by definition devoted to describing events that take place in scenes. Within narrative, details are especially frequent in what Labov (1972) calls the orientation sections of conversational narratives: the part that provides background information. Such common orientational material as names, dates, and names of places are details. In conversation, speakers often make an observable effort to get these details right. For example, in beginning the story about having fainted on the New York subway excerpted early in chapter 3, the speaker said:

(3)   It was back in ... what. '66? '67?

In a way, such mental scavenging seems to be more for the speaker's satisfaction than for the hearer's. It is unlikely to make a difference to the hearer whether the event took place in 1966 or

1967. Yet retrieving the correct year, or feeling that one has retrieved it, seems to give satisfaction to a speaker. However, such evidence of struggle to retrieve correct details is not only a matter of the speaker's self-involvement: It also gives an impression of verisimilitude to a hearer. In addition to the verisimilitude of the recognizable details, the process of searching one's memory to fix a name or date or place is in itself a familiar, recognizable process which gives a listener a sense that true details about true events are being retrieved.[4]

Sometimes details cluster at the climax of a story, contributing to its main point. For example, in the conversational narrative from which Example (12) in chapter 4 was taken, about the experience of an American tourist in a Japanese bath, the main action is brought into focus partly by the marked use of details. In other words, the detailed level of description functions as a sort of internal evaluation signalling, "This is the important action right here" without explicitly stating so:

(4)   Anyway, what was I say-
       Oh we were at the Japanese bath
       and um they didn't tell us,
       first of all,
       that we were going into the bath,
       so we were standing in the room,
       and they said "Okay, take your clothes off."
       We're like "What?!"
       and um
       [listener: It's prison]
       they gave us these kimono
       and we put the kimono on,
       they brought us to this other room,
       and they said, "Okay take the kimono off."
       And we're like "What are you talking about?"
       So then the the teacher left.
       We were kind of wandering around,
       we saw the bath,
       so we figure out the deal,
       so we went down,
       got in the bath,
       and sitting there,
       this 74 year old man
       who was in our group
       from Austria

> jumped over our heads,
> into a three foot bath,
> splashed all over the place
> and started doing the back- backstroke
> in the tub.
> So the teacher's back at this time
> and he's going "Oyogenai de kudasai."
> "Don't swim!"

The key action in the story, highlighted in the transcript by under-lining, is described and made vivid by details. The age of the man (74), the country he was from (Austria), the graphic verbs "jumped" and "splashed" as well as the depiction of his actions ("jumped over our heads" and "splashed all over the place"), the measurement of the bath ("three foot"), the name of the stroke he was swimming ("backstroke") – all create an image of a scene that stands out in the otherwise relatively Spartan narration.[5]

Another part of narrative that is highly likely to be marked by detail is description. Descriptive detail can be directly representa-tional or metaphoric. There is often an association between detail and metaphor. In 1985, when Halley's Comet was expected, I was intrigued by an issue of a small magazine called *Guideposts* (40:9, November 1985) that I found in a motel room. In it, Joseph Hufham, 83, identified as "the local storyteller" of Delco, North Carolina and a columnist for a Whiteville, North Carolina newspaper, presented his own and others' accounts of the previ-ous appearance of Halley's Comet in 1910. The accounts of the other townspeople who are old enough to remember events in 1910 are vague about what the comet looked like. One man, who was 7 when he saw it, is quoted as saying, "It looked like a big old star, real bright, with a tail behind" (7). Hufham himself was only a year older at the time, but his description is rich with detail and simile:

The comet was yellow like the moon and it bulged like an onion. The tail on it looked like an old dollar sweep broom, not much longer than the body; I could just see it swooping down and scrubbing on mountains. (4)

Furthermore, Hufham set the description of the comet in a scene ("I remember standing on the big broad porch of Papa's store and looking up"), and the scene is set within a story about the events of the day. Hufham's account, in contrast to the snippets of interviews with others, seemed to demonstrate the skills and strategies that made him a storyteller and a writer.

Listing and naming

Thus stories are composed of scenes which are composed of images that are suggested by details. Details are associated not only with particular structural parts of narratives, such as orientation and climax, or particular functional parts, such as description or action, but also with particular strategies such as listing and naming. Chatwin (1987) writes of an Aboriginal view of the Australian landscape as a series of events "on one or other of the Songlines: The land itself may be read as a musical score" (47). Depicting a fictionalized conversation with a Russian companion he names Arkady and four elderly Aboriginals, Chatwin has Arkady ask one of them, " 'So what's the story of this place, old man?' " The old Aboriginal responds with a story about Lizard and his wife. His storytelling is a performance, including mime and song, in which the teller becomes each of the characters. After the Aboriginals have gone to sleep, Arkady tells the fictionalized Chatwin that the Aboriginals must have liked him, since they offered him the song. If they had been performing the song for their own people, however, it "would have named each waterhole the Lizard Man drank from, each tree he cut a spear from, each cave he slept in, covering the whole long distance of the way" (47).[6]

Nonnarrative or quasinarrative conversational discourse

Details and images are pervasive in nonnarrative or quasinarrative as well as narrative conversational discourse, since all conversation is intended, to some degree, to be persuasive, that is, to be understood in the way that the speaker intends it.

Like struggling to recall specific names, dates, and places, speakers are often specific about other details that might seem irrelevant to hearers if only information counted. For example, in the following excerpt from the Thanksgiving dinner conversation, Peter recites a childhood address. At this point in the interchange, as already seen in Example 18 in chapter 3, it has emerged that

Steve and Peter (who are brothers) had lived in quonset huts as children after the Second World War. As a participant in the conversation, I was intrigued to learn that friends I had known for years had actually lived in what for me had been exotic and strange clusters of buildings viewed from the highway on childhood excursions. I asked how long they had lived in them. Peter answered, "Three years." Then:

(5)   DEBORAH   It's a LONG TIME.
      STEVE   Yeah. From the time Í was ONE ...
                to the time Í was four and a half.
      DEBORAH   Did you go to s
                didn't you all have to go to school?
      PETER   Yeah I went to kindergarten and first grade.
      DEBORAH   Wow! ... So it was a whole community with other
                people living in them too.
      PETER   It was great!
      STEVE   It was a really close community
                cause everybody ⌈was
      DEBORAH   ⌊Would've been nice
      STEVE   /?/
      PETER   We all moved in at the same time,
                and j- just had to remember your address.
      →   Ours was ... 1418 F.

How is the audience helped by knowing the specific address of the quonset hut in which Peter and Steve lived? In an information-focused way, not at all. And yet, as suggested earlier in connection with narrative detail, one recognizes the urge, in telling of a past time, to recall and utter a precise address or telephone number or name. Because of the familiarity of the urge to remind oneself of addresses, telephone numbers, and names of people and places, specifying the address contributes something to the hearer's involvement with the speaker and with the recalled image. It also lends a sense of authenticity, of vivid recall. Furthermore, by reciting his childhood address, Peter demonstrates that he had memorized it. Moreover, hearing "1418 F," one gets an image of a large number of identical buildings, each differing from the others only by letter and number designation, whereas previously one had only the idea of multiple dwellings.

Similarly, Steve's addition of his precise ages at the time he lived in the quonset huts ("From the time Í was ONE ... to the time Í was

four and a half."), like Peter's naming of the grades he was in ("I
went to kindergarten and first grade"), does not contribute anything substantive to the answer that they lived in a quonset hut for
three years. And yet it contributes to the communication. It creates
a picture of a child of one to four and a half, of Steve as a child
of one to four and a half.

Another example from the Thanksgiving conversation is found
in the discussion of cartoons from which Examples 6, 14, and 20
in chapter 3 were taken: the conversation about cartoons in which
three men maintained that they had enjoyed cartoons as children,
whereas the two women recalled having been disturbed by the violence in cartoons. Steve claimed that the women, as children,
responded as they did because "You took them literally," whereas
his own response was sanguine because he knew that cartoons
weren't real. He explained,

It wasn't like there were hearts and liver.

This example illustrates my argument both in its form and in its
meaning. Steve is claiming that he didn't have an emotional
response to cartoon characters getting hurt because the cartoons
didn't show the detailed images of body parts that would have
made the characters seem real. At the same time, he makes his point
in the conversation by naming the specific body parts, "hearts and
liver," rather than by making an abstract statement like, "It wasn't
like they had human body parts."

Listing

In a casual brunch conversation among four adult friends (two
couples), the conversation turned to languages, since one of the
party is a graduate student in linguistics.[7] This speaker told of
having overheard a conversation in a foreign language that she tried
to identify:

(6)   And on top of sounding nasal
      it's a <u>Northern European language</u>
      it's obviously <u>Germanic</u> based,
      okay, that much I KNOW.
      But THEN ... is it ... uh <u>Flemish</u>?
      You know, is it- is it a <u>Dutch</u> derivative?

Is it Belgian?
And then I said "No
maybe it's /?/ Deutsch
cause it
it sounds like German but it's NOT High German
so what is it.
It's obvious-
it's got to be something like that in it."
I said "What could it be, Norwegian?"
I'm hearing the Tyrolean "ja" [yaw].
I'm hearing the rolling accent
of what sounds like Swedish.
Yeah and you know
the little hippity-hoppity sing-songy-
But that's also uh
Bavarian German has a lot of that too,
and Swiss-Deutsch has that so
uh . . . maybe it's Afrikaans,
I haven't heard it in so long,
you know, maybe it's something like that.

The pleasure this speaker seemed to be deriving from listing Germanic languages is reminiscent of a segment of the Thanksgiving dinner conversation in which I named the titles of books by Erving Goffman:

(7) CHAD: I read his books . . . a book . . . Asylums.
First but that's all because]
DEBORAH: [I didn't
read Asylums
but I know it's one of the brilliant ones.
CHAD: And I just . . . [read another one
DEBORAH: [Did you read Stigma?
CHAD: No but I've got]
DEBORAH: [It's wonderful.
CHAD: I've got . . . three or four other ones
that are like that.
DEBORAH: [Presentation of Self in Everyday Life
CHAD: [Presentation of
Self in Everyday Life, u:m
DEBORAH: a:nd uh Relations in Public,
. . . and Interactional Ritual,
CHAD: Right, Interactional Ritual.
DEBORAH: I never read that one.

This interchange also exemplifies the power/solidarity paradox:

The symbols that display power (differing status) and solidarity (equal status) are often the same, so every utterance is potentially ambiguous as to whether it is establishing power or solidarity. (In reality, I believe, every utterance displays both, in varying proportions.) Chad told me afterwards, during playback, that he was intimidated by my display of knowledge: how well I knew Goffman's work. From his point of view I was exercising power, making myself look good. I also said, however, in the course of listing the book titles, that I had not *read* most of these books; I simply knew *of* them. (As a matter of fact, I got the name of one title, *Interaction Ritual*, slightly wrong.) So from my point of view, I was not making myself look good, a point of view that was shared by Goffman who, after reading my dissertation, admonished me to read his books. I hope (and believe) it is not merely self-serving to claim that my intention in listing the names of Goffman's books was not to impress or overwhelm Chad. I simply got carried away with the aesthetic pleasure of listing book titles and felt driven to include as many as possible, for a certain aesthetic satisfaction. Operating on the assumption of solidarity, I saw myself as matching and feeding, not topping, Chad's interest in Goffman. (For his part, Chad seems to be experiencing the pleasure of repetition when he repeats many of the book titles I name). A similar inherent ambiguity applies to the graduate student listing names of Germanic languages. She could be seen as trying to show off, to impress her husband and friends with her expertise (and with her worldly experience, since she speaks as if she had heard all these language varieties). But my instinctive interpretation is in terms of what I myself had done: she was primarily carried away by the delight of naming related languages. The effect of such a listing strategy, like that of any conversational strategy, will depend upon the personal and cultural styles of co-conversationalists. They might enjoy such a list too, or be intimidated or bored. The result of such a strategy can be either enhanced or threatened rapport, depending on the interaction of the styles of participants.

"I had a little ham, I had a little cheese": Rapport through telling details

As discussed earlier, repetition and dialogue are highly valued in literary analysis but devalued in conventional wisdom applied to conversation. Similarly, the use of details is most frequently considered a conversational liability, as in "Let's skip the details and get down to business." "Tell me all the gory details" is heard as a marked request. A *New Yorker* article that gives a portrait of a middle American quotes him as preferring to read *U.S. News & World Report* because he "had found its articles admirably 'short and to the point.'" In negative contrast, "he had tried *Newsweek* but had found its articles too long and detailed" (58).[8] Here "detailed" is assumed to be "boring."

The assumption that details are boring seems also at the heart of an instance of private language reported to me by a woman whose family refers to Grandmother as "I had a little ham, I had a little cheese." This cryptic representation of her conversation captured, for them, the boring way that Grandmother reports insignificant details such as what she had for lunch. They wish she gave fewer details, or did not report her lunch at all, since they regard the topic as not worth telling about.

My Great-Aunt had a love affair when she was in her 70's. Obese, balding, her hands and legs misshapen by arthritis, she did not fit the stereotype of a woman romantically loved. But she was – by a man, also in his seventies, who lived in a nursing home but occasionally spent weekends with her in her apartment. In trying to tell me what this relationship meant to her, my aunt told of a conversation. One evening she had had dinner at the home of friends. When she returned to her home that evening, her man friend called. In the course of their conversation, he asked her, "What did you wear?" When she told me this, she began to cry: "Do you know how many years it's been since anyone asked me what I wore?"

In a book concerned with everyday conversations (Tannen 1986a), I observe that women are more inclined than men to report details of daily events and conversations to friends and intimates. When talking about conversational style in groups of women and men as well as on radio talk shows, I find that this observation sparks strong recognition and agreement. For example, after reading this book, a colleague wrote, "My wife and I could relate especially to my inability to relate in sufficient detail (for her) the conversations of others. It's been a topic of our conversations for our whole marriage."[9] This remark is interesting too in that it suggests dialogue can be a kind of detail.

That women are more inclined than men to value the telling of details about their daily lives and about other people (but also that not all men are not) is supported by novelist Marge Piercy. In *Fly away home*, a divorced woman is amazed to learn that her new partner, Tom, is different in this respect from her former husband, Ross:

(8) It surprised her what he knew about the people around him. Ross would never have known that Gretta disliked her son's teacher, or that Fay had just given walking papers to her boyfriend because he drank too much in front of her boys. For a man, Tom had an uncommon interest in the details of people's lives. Gossip, Ross would call it, but she thought it was just being interested in people. (218)

In depicting Tom's interest in the details of people's lives, Piercy recounts some of those details – specifically, with names: that "Gretta disliked her son's teacher, or that Fay had just given walking papers to her boyfriend because he drank too much in front of her boys." These details convey not just the idea of Tom's conversation but a brief experience of it.

Piercy's character Ross is not alone in disparaging an interest in the details of people's lives as "gossip." This was the attitude of Eudora Welty's mother, who wanted to keep the young Eudora from hearing the stories about people that the child loved, the very stories she credits with inspiring her to become a writer. The parallel between gossip and literature has been observed by many, including James Britton (1982).[10]

The intimacy of details

When my Great-Aunt told me it had been years since anyone had asked her what she wore, she was saying that it had been years since anyone had cared deeply about her. The exchange of relatively insignificant details about daily life is valued for its metamessage of rapport, of caring. It can also be a sign of romantic involvement, of sexual interest or intimacy. In the novel *Household words* (see Appendix I), when Rhoda is attracted to a man, her attraction is made evident in attention to the details of his body:

(9)   Eddie Lederbach's <u>hands were long and graceful, with soft, sparse</u>
      <u>hairs growing tenderly about the knuckles.</u> She was not prepared
      for a complexity of emotions ... <u>His lips moved wetly</u> in nervous
      speech. (101)

The other man that is remembered in such physical detail is
Rhoda's dead husband, and it is the recollection of details about
him that makes his memory painful. Furthermore, it is through details of description that the author leads the reader to experience a
sense of Rhoda's feelings of loss at her husband's death. Waking up
after having fallen asleep in her clothes following the funeral,

(10) She thought ... of <u>his body's outline, the particular barrel-shape</u>
      <u>of his ribs, and the chest, bifurcated and hard under the coating</u>
      <u>of light brown hairs.</u> The absence of his form <u>under the covers</u>
      <u>of the bed next to her</u> engendered in her a sudden rage, as
      though she'd been robbed in the night. His bed was undisturbed,
      <u>the chenille spread tucked properly around the pillow.</u> She felt
      panicked and afraid – <u>an actual physical shudder came over her,</u>
      and then she had a dreadful urge to <u>beat at the covers of his</u>
      <u>bed,</u> to make him come out. (85–6)

To say that "His bed was undisturbed" conveys the idea of her husband's absence. But the detailed description: "the chenille spread
tucked properly around the pillow," conveys the image of the bed,
not just the idea of it. "She felt panicked and afraid" tells what
Rhoda felt, but that "an actual physical shudder came over her"
and that she had an "urge to beat at the covers of his bed" convey
images that prompt the reader to imagine how she felt. For Rhoda,
and for readers, specific details trigger memories that trigger
emotions.

Spoken literary discourse

I give one final example of spoken discourse to illustrate how it
makes use of details to create an emotional response and understanding of the speaker's point. It is conversational, but not exactly
conversation. The following excerpt comes from a relatively formal
conversational genre: a radio talk show.[11] The guest, Vic Sussman, a writer who had left Washington DC to homestead in rural
Vermont, had recently resumed residence in Washington. In
answer to a question by the show's host, Diane Rehm, he explained

how he reached the decision to move back to the city. His explanation depicts what James Joyce called an epiphany: a moment of sudden insight which Joyce saw as the basis for the fictional short story. Sussman leads listeners to understand his epiphany, an internal intellectual and emotional experience, by providing details which depict an image of the scene that sparked and situated the epiphany. The emotional impact of the image created (together with the musical qualities of his oral delivery) is attested by the host's spontaneous response.

Immediately prior to the following excerpt, Sussman explained that he reached his decision to move back to Washington during a Thanksgiving visit to the city. He had delivered a piece of writing to *The Washington Post*, which is located in the midst of downtown DC. (Implicit in his discourse is the information that he had recently separated from his wife).

(11)   1 And I remember stepping out,
        2 I think this was November,
        3 and I stepped out onto
        4 somewhere around 18th and M,
        5 or 18th and L,
        6 at lunchtime,
        7 and it was one of those warm, clear days in November.
        8 And there was a lunchtime press of people,
        9 tremendous crowds, ...
       10 and I stood there,
       11 and for the first time
       12 I stood there,
       13 not as a member of uh of A marriage.
       14 I stood there alone.
       15 And, ... the traffic was there,
       16 the noise was there,
       17 the swirl of people, ...
       18 and I suddenly looked at it,
       19 for the first time,
       20 through MY eyes. ...
       21 And I loved it.⌉
               Host: ⌊Hm.

       22 And I've always had a dichotomous feeling
       23 about the city.
       24 I grew up in New York,
       25 and moved to Washington in the 50's,
       26 but THAT was the first time I stood there,

27 And I had HAD the experiences
28 that I had set out to have,
29 IN the country.
30 I didn't need to do it anymore.
31 And very few people,
32 I mean I'm very fortunate.
33 Very few people get to really live their fantasies.
34 It was over.
35 I- I wrote a piece for N P R,
36 in which I- I used the line,
37 I said,
38 (This actually happened.)
39 I said, "<u>An elegant woman brushed past me,</u>
40 <u>and the smell, the aroma of her perfume</u>
41 <u>mingled with the musk of asphalt.</u>"
42 And I just felt like,
43 ⌐"This is where I belong."
Host: ⌐[chuckle] hmmmmmmmm

The transcription of the host's responses ("hm," "[chuckle] hmmmmmmmmm" following lines 21 and 42) are inadequate to capture their vocal quality: They are moans of appreciation having the character of what Goffman (1981) called "response cries," spontaneous expressions of sudden feeling.

There are many poetic aspects of Sussman's account that contribute to the emotional impact of his discourse: repetition and variation (for example, "I stood there" in lines 10, 12, and 14, and "for the first time" in lines 11 and 19); a compelling rhythm, created in part by the repetitions and also strategic pauses (note, for example, the building of suspense by delaying introducing the key image by uttering lines 37–9: "I said, (This actually happened.) I said,"; words with literary connotations ("press" and "swirl of people" in lines 8 and 17, "aroma" – important enough to be self-corrected from "smell" – in line 40, and "mingled" in line 41). Moreover, Sussman's voice takes on a breathy, emotionally tinged quality beginning in line 17 with "the swirl of people" and building to the climax to which the host responds with her first "hm" following line 21. In addition to these and other poetic qualities, Sussman uses details, as highlighted by underlining. As observed in earlier examples, many of these details cluster in the opening orientation section. He tells the specific street corner he was on: lines 4–5 "somewhere around <u>18th and M</u>, or <u>18th and L</u>" (as was seen earlier with respect to dates, the difference between L and M Streets is insignificant but the display of effort to recall provides a sense of verisimilitude); the time: line 6 "at lunchtime"; the season and weather: line 7 "one of those warm, clear days in November"; and the scene: line 8 "a lunchtime press of people, tremendous crowds."

The final image that evokes a strong response from the host is especially interesting because it is identified as a quotation from a "commentary" Sussman wrote for delivery on National Public Radio (line 35 "a piece for NPR"). Thus it is an oral repetition of a text previously performed orally but originally written for oral delivery.[12] In these lines (39–41), the words are carefully chosen to capture the moment of epiphany in a combination of visual impressions ("an elegant woman," "the asphalt") and olfactory impressions ("the aroma of her perfume," "the musk of asphalt") which combine two seemingly incompatible worlds: one beautiful (the woman) and one ugly (the city street with its "traffic," "noise," and "asphalt"). The result is that the ugly city became infused with beauty and drew him to it. The host's response is overlapped with the verbal coda to the guest's story ("and I just felt 'This is where I belong,'"), evidence that her response is to the immediately preceding image rather than the evaluative coda.[13]

Written discourse

The preceding examples from *Household words* demonstrate strategic use of detail in fiction. Book reviewers frequently comment on writers' use of details (indeed, I have yet to read an issue of *The New York Times Book Review* that does not contain numerous remarks on use of details). In some cases, the authors' use of details is the basis for praise, in others for criticism. In both types of cases, the evaluations reveal the assumption that management of detail is a crucial part of writing. They also reveal specific ways that the critics believe details work.

One reviewer (Shapiro 1987) praises the use of details in a novel by saying the author "doesn't skimp, and she uses details of food and clothing to refine a scene rather than sum it up." Another reviewer (Humphreys 1985) refers to the use of detail in criticizing a novel written in the voice of a character named Cam, who is writing her first novel about another character named Jane:

(12) Jane was full of life, extraordinary, glamorous, innocent. But Jane
      isn't shown with the sort of detail that enlivens.
         Cam thought that in writing a novel she would be free from the
      struggle with detail. But a novel should be one long struggle with
      detail, not of dates and facts but of difficult scenes, of character
      caught off guard. Words like "passionate" and "glamorous" are the
      opposite of detail. They become in a novel almost useless, the
      vocabulary of eulogy.

Both these excerpts show that the critics regard details as elements
used in the creation of characters moving in scenes, and scenes involving characters in relation to each other as the basic material of
fiction.

   Reviewers commenting on works of nonfiction rather than
fiction also frequently cite the handling of details. A negative view
of details is found in a review (Geiger 1987) of a book about the
AIDS epidemic by Randy Shilts (1987).

(13) The reader drowns in detail. The book jacket says that Mr. Shilts –
      in addition to his years of daily coverage of the epidemic – con-
      ducted more than 900 interviews in 12 nations and dug out thou-
      sands of pages of Government documents. He seems to have used
      every one of them.

It is interesting to note that the reviewer gives specific numbers:
"900 interviews," "12 nations," "thousands of pages of Government documents." By being thus specific, he creates a sense of the
voluminousness of the detail in Shilts's book, but not the nature of
it. He did not give many specific examples of the details that he felt
drowned readers. (Perhaps he wished to avoid the affective fallacy
of convincing readers the book is boring by boring them in the
review.) I found more affecting, and more memorable, than
Geiger's review a shorter one by Miller (1987) which conveyed one
of the main points of Shilts's book by recounting a specific instance
of government negligence in dealing with AIDS.

   In writing this section, I had to decide whether to end my discussion with the preceding paragraph, having stated my perception of
the difference between the two reviews of Shilts's book, or whether
to provide a specific example of detail from Miller's review. I
decided to provide it:

(14) As so often in Shilts's book, one small incident is used to drive his
      point home. On July 27, 1982, officials convened in Washington,

D.C., to debate screening all blood donors in an effort to stem the
spread of the virus through the nation's blood supply. Despite urgent
pleas from researchers at the Centers for Disease Control, other
officials were skeptical. Underfunded and open, as always, to the
special pleading of special interests, the FDA deferred any decision
on imposing a potentially expensive blood-screening test. This bit of
waffling pleased both gay militants worried about discrimination
and cost-conscious blood bankers. But delaying testing, Shilts
argues, contributed, by the estimates of doctors at the CDC, to
thousands of needless deaths.   (91)

I invite readers to consider whether they had a more emotional
response to this specific illustration than to the general reference to
the government's negligence in the preceding paragraph, and, eventually, if they remember my reference to the book about AIDS and,
if so, what they remember about it.

Reviewers differ, then, in finding the details in particular books
effective or not. But they agree that managing details, finding the
right ones and the right amount, is a crucial part of writing. It was
seen earlier that at least one family finds it boring when Grandmother tells what she ate for lunch. Yet works of fiction frequently
report what people eat, if they report that they eat at all. Why, for
example, is it moving to be told what Rhoda ate for lunch in
Household words?

(15)   She sat in the kitchen eating her usual lunch, <u>a mound of cottage</u>
       <u>cheese piled over lettuce</u> (no eating from the container: like a
       colonist in an outpost, she was strict about keeping proprieties even
       when no one was looking).

The effectiveness of this passage comes from many linguistic strategies, including the simile that associates Rhoda with a colonist at
an outpost: an association that aptly suggests her feelings of isolation and abandonment on being suddenly widowed. But this simile
is enhanced, indeed triggered, by the image of Rhoda sitting down
to a frugal (by some standards), solitary, yet properly laid out lunch
of cottage cheese on lettuce.

Similarly, why does the narrator of a short story (Lipsky
1985:46) report, "I unload the rest of the groceries. There is a box
of spaghetti, Tropicana orange juice, brown rice, pita bread, a few
plain Dannon yogurts"? The brand names will trigger in the minds
of those familiar with these brands images of the packages.

Furthermore, the specific items and the adjectives describing them suggest a kind of frugality ("*plain* Dannon yogurt," "spaghetti"), a concern with health (*brown* rice), and even perhaps an alternative life style represented by "alternative" food (*pita* bread).

There is a cinematic analogue to verbal mention in fiction. The camera in the film *Hannah and her sisters* shows Woody Allen, newly (and temporarily) converted to Catholicism, unloading a grocery bag. The audience in attendance when I saw this film laughed when the camera focused on Allen withdrawing from the bag a loaf of Wonder Bread and a jar of Hellman's mayonnaise. I have asked numerous people why they laughed at these details, and have received a wide range of answers. Some familiar with Jewish custom and other Woody Allen movies think it suggests a scene Allen used humorously in *Manhattan* and elsewhere: a Christian orders a corned beef or pastrami sandwich (typical Jewish food) and asks to have it with mayonnaise on white bread. This is a violation of Jewish dietary law and Jewish tastes which prescribe that corned beef be eaten on rye bread with mustard. I found the scene funny partly because whereas Jews would never eat Wonder Bread, Hellman's is the brand of mayonnaise preferred by New York Jews. (I discovered that this was a cultural rather than a personal preference by reading as much in an amusing essay by Nora Ephron). Thus, though the character played by Allen has converted his religion and attempted to change his eating habits, he cannot help but remain fundamentally a New York Jew. Still others, the majority of Americans no doubt, must have laughed for other reasons. Although individuals may have different responses to the specific details of what Allen bought, it is the depiction of details that makes possible varied meaningful responses.

Listing

Woody Allen's unloading of items from a grocery bag can be seen as a visual list. *Household words* includes lists of details as well. For example, when guests flock to Rhoda's house following her husband's funeral, they

(16)   arrived with boxes of candy in their hands. Chocolates mostly: dark 'n' light assortments, cherries with cordial centers, butter creams. (83)

Not only does this detailed list of types of chocolate give a sense
of verisimilitude (all details and images do this), but they also contribute to the impression that a great many different people came
bearing chocolates. This helps the reader understand why Rhoda
feels overwhelmed by the crush of people in the house and their irrelevant gifts.

Feeling thus overwhelmed, Rhoda excuses herself and goes upstairs to her room where she lies down on her bed and falls asleep.
She awakes to an empty house, the feeling of which is conveyed in
a scene depicted by a list of the foods the guests left behind:

(17)   Food remained, piled on the dining room and cocktail tables – a
       catered turkey half picked over, platters of cold cuts, and an
       untouched steamship basket of fruit in cellophane. (85)

The "half picked over" turkey suggests the forlornness Rhoda feels.
The "untouched steamship basket of fruit in cellophane" suggests
the unlikely frivolity of the fruit's packaging and its irrelevance.
The list structure implies that there are more foods "piled" around
than are named.

As time passes, Rhoda's father spends increasing amounts of
time in her house, filling in the slot left empty by her husband's
death. His presence is both comforting and irritating, as conveyed
by the depiction of his typical conversation in a list:

(18)   Her father liked to tell her things from the newspaper – Marines
       returning from Korea with bizarre injuries remedied by miraculous
       prostheses, mothers throwing their children from burning buildings,
       flood victims finding their family heirlooms floating intact down-
       river. (89–90)

The specific list of her father's unrelated topics of conversation conveys the irrelevance of his presence.

A final example of a list comes from an informal written genre,
a personal letter. A Greek mother accompanied her daughter to the
United States and helped her get set up to begin graduate studies.
Upon returning to Greece alone, the mother began her correspondence with her daughter while still on the airplane headed for
Athens. At two points, her letter includes lists of the foods she ate
on the plane:

(19)   Ora 10 1/2. Molis efaga ryzi, souvlaki, mia bira, salata kai garidhes
       mikres, glyko kafe.

It's 10:30. I have just eaten rice, beef, a beer, salad with small shrimps, sweet coffee.

Alla i ora einai 4 to proï. ... Molis fagame to proino, kafe, gala, marmeladha, voutyro, tyri, psomi, portokaladha kai krouasan.

But it's 4 o'clock in the morning. ... We have just eaten breakfast, coffee, milk, marmalade, butter, cheese, bread, orange juice and croissant.

By providing her daughter with a detailed account of her trip, the mother gives her a sense of being present with her, softening the pain of their separation (and, in a way, heightening it, by giving a poignant and pointed impression of where she is and what she is doing).

All but one of the lists I have cited are of food: food eaten, offered as gifts, bought at the store. Perhaps this is simply because eating is a mundane, daily, but universal and personal activity. If eating together is a sign of intimacy, perhaps telling about eating is a way of signalling intimacy between people who are not co-present to eat together.

A detail may refer to a level of perception rather than a description. For example, the following observation is made in a novel by Celia Fremlin (1985:16–17).[14] A woman has sent her husband, Geoffrey, next door to extend a generous dinner invitation to a neighbor who has moved in that day. Geoffrey returns full of excitement, bubbling with admiration for and details about the new neighbor. He announces, starry-eyed, that the neighbor has invited *them* to dinner in her not-yet furnished home, and he asks his wife if she has a red ribbon for Shang Low, the neighbor's Pekinese. The wife responds with irony, but Geoffrey is slow to join in her ironic denigration of the neighbor's airs in ribboning her dog:

(20)   She giggled in terrible solitude for a fraction of a second; and then Geoffrey joined in, a tiny bit too late and a tiny bit too loud. And the joke did not lead to another joke. Murmuring something about "having promised...", Geoffrey hurried away out of the kitchen and out of the house, without any red ribbon. And this piece of red ribbon, which they didn't look for, didn't find, and probably hadn't got, became the very first of the objects which couldn't ever again be mentioned between them.

There are innumerable linguistic strategies at work in this passage

which beg for analysis, including, of course, repetition and dialogue. But I wish to draw attention only to the detailed level of perception of the delicate balance of irony and shared laughter,
precisely timed, that would establish solidarity between the narrator and her husband, in alliance against the outside world in the
form of another person. By failing to perform his part in expected
sequence, timing, and manner, Geoffrey launches a betrayal of his
wife: He is beginning to align himself instead with the attractive
new neighbor. Fremlin leads the reader to understand the wife's
jealousy by representing the fleeting betrayal, and the wife's experience of it, in slow-motion detail. Moreover, the husband's
romantic interest in the new neighbor leaks in his enthusiastic, un-
critical recounting of details about her, such as the name and breed
of her dog.[15]

Attention to details associated with a person can be (and is in
this novel) a sign of romantic interest.[16] That the red ribbon
became an object "which couldn't ever again be mentioned between
them" illustrates the way that feelings become associated with objects (or images, or details). Mentioning the ribbon would remind
both husband and wife of the moment in which it had figured and
hence of the beginning of his betrayal.

High-involvement writing

The following example is from a written genre but also one that
cannot easily be categorized as literary or nonliterary. Rather than
identifying the source at the outset, I would like to invite readers
to ask themselves what kind of text the following opening sentences
come from.

(21) Charles and Jeanne Atchison live near the Cowboy City dance bar
      on a gravel street in a peeling white and gold mobile home. Weeds
      sway in the breeze out front. It's a street with a melancholy down-
      on-one's-luck feel about it. The town is Azle, Tex., a tiny speck on
      the periphery of Fort Worth.
          A few years ago, the picture was a far prettier one. Charles
      (Chuck) Atchison was all set. He made good money – more than
      $1000 a week – enough to pay for a cozy house, new cars, fanciful
      trips. But all that is gone. He's six months behind on rent for his
      land, and don't even ask about the legal bills.
          "It's sort of like I was barreling along and I suddenly shifted into

reverse," Mr. Atchison said with a rueful smile. "Well, welcome to whistle blower country."

Chuck Atchison is 44, with a stony face and a sparse mustache. (Kleinfield 1986:1)

These lines are not from a short story or magazine article. The excerpt is from the front page of the Business section of *The New York Times* – that soberest section of the soberest of American newspapers.

The article begun by these lines, about a man whose career was ruined because he "blew the whistle" (made public his employer's improper activities) contains all the literary strategies I have been investigating. Note the use of dialogue ("'It's sort of like I was barreling along and I suddenly shifted into reverse,' Mr. Atchison said with a rueful smile. 'Well, welcome to whistle blower country.'") and figures of speech ("Mr. Atchison wound up out of a job and spinning in debt. He's working again, in another industry, slowly trying to patch the leaks in his life"). But most striking, I think, is the reporting of details of scene and character that are not just literary-like encasements for information but have no informational value at all. How can a journalist writing for the business section of the American "newspaper of record" justify "reporting" the name of the dance bar near which the subject lives, the colors of his mobile home, that his face was "stony" and his mustache "sparse"? When did journalism begin to sound like literary writing?

According to columnist Bob Greene, journalists turned their attention to everyday details in 1963, when Jimmy Breslin wrote a column entitled "A death in Emergency Room One" detailing the last moments of John Kennedy's life. According to Greene, Breslin's column "literally took his readers into the corridors and operating rooms of Parkland Hospital on that day." Greene calls it "the most vivid piece of writing to come out of the assassination of John F. Kennedy." Even the concern with "vivid" writing (rather than accurate, clear, or informative writing) seems out of place in reference to journalism. It is reminiscent of what Jakobson (1960) called the "poetic function" of language: "the set toward the message," that is, use of language in which it is the language itself that counts most.[17]

Greene observes, "Journalists today are trained to get those telling details quickly." He suggests that this style of reporting satisfies the public's curiosity. But why is the public curious about such details? I believe the key is to be found in Greene's observation that Breslin "literally [i.e. figuratively] took his readers into the . . . rooms." What purpose is served by feeling one had been in the rooms where an event occurred, if not the pleasurable sense of involvement?

When details don't work or work for ill

All of the examples I have adduced are illustrative of the effective use of details. But like any linguistic phenomenon (or nonlinguistic one), what can be used effectively can also be used ineffectively or effectively for ill. One can fabricate details to make a false story sound true, or pile on details about irrelevant topics to de-fuse, diffuse, or avoid a relevant topic. Lakoff and Tannen (1984) show that this strategy is used by the wife, Marianne, to avoid confronting the breakdown of her marriage in Ingmar Bergman's screenplay, *Scenes from a marriage*. Whereas hyperattention to the details associated with a person or subject can be positive, for example in love relationships or doing an important job or developing a skill or art, such attention is considered inappropriate, even obsessive, when the object of attention is deemed unworthy. It is perhaps for this reason that love is frequently considered an obsession, and has frequently been so depicted in art.

The effectiveness of attention to details can be manipulated, for example by pretending attention to the details of a person's appearance or discourse for purposes of seduction. I observed a benign, probably common fabrication of details when I overheard someone saying, "Yesterday I got five messages from him. I'm not exaggerating. I counted them." I happened to know that the speaker had gotten one message the day before from the person in question. Perhaps she had gotten more on another day. But what counts, I think, is that the speaker knew that being specific about a large number of messages would make her point more graphically than would a general or abstract statement.

The inappropriate use of details can be the basis for humor. For example, a list that is too detailed for its context can be comic, as in a cartoon showing a priest delivering a eulogy: "He was a man of simple tastes – baked macaroni, steamed cabbage, wax beans, boiled onions, and corn fritters." The cartoon is funny because the level of detail is inappropriate to the occasion (and also because of the banality of the items in the list).

If specific details spark an emotional response, the response they spark can be negative as well as positive. A painter was asked by an acquaintance to paint four small pictures of the city in which he lived. He did so, and mailed them to her. When they talked on the phone, she said that she and her husband liked three of the paintings but not the fourth. Had she stopped there, everything would have been fine. The painter was not insulted and did not mind her returning one painting. But she went on to explain what they didn't like about it: "It's cold. The blue is cold. And it's naive." These specific points of criticism engaged the painter emotionally; they made him feel rejected, defensive, and hurt. It was the specific details of criticism that were hurtful whereas the general fact of it was not.

If attention to detail is a sign of intimacy, as has been shown, then its appearance will be unpleasant if intimacy is not appropriate or not wanted. In a passage from *Household words*, for example, which was cited in another context at the beginning of chapter 4, a prospective buyer of Rhoda's husband's pharmacy tries to convince her that he can only afford a low price:

(22)   In Southern California he had run a thriving drug and stationery center in a shopping mall, but his wife had left him for a blond beach bum with a tattoo, and he had come east to make a new start. He had a lovely new wife, a baby on the way, and he could go no higher in price.
          Rhoda was not pleased to hear the sordid minutiae of his personal history ...   (93)

The "drug and stationery center" is made imageable by being set "in a shopping mall," and the "blond beach bum" is made imageable by the addition of "a tattoo," as well as the suggestion of dialogue in such phrases as "beach bum," "lovely new wife," and "baby on the way." For Rhoda, however, the details of the man's "personal history" are unwanted because she does not want intimacy with him.

Rhoda similarly resists intimacy invoked by details in another scene, this time uttered by a man who is a different sort of prospect: Friends have invited him to dinner along with Rhoda as a prospective love interest. The man, Eddie Lederbach, whose "long and graceful" hands were seen in (9), talks incessantly of his unfair blacklisting during the McCarthy era:

(23) "When I get up in the morning now, the first thing I think of is, *it's not fair*. Sometimes I wake up shouting it in my sleep."
     There was an awkward silence. Nobody wanted to know what he did in his sleep. (101)

Everyone has had the experience of being the recipient of unwanted details – details that seem pointless or excessive or demanding more or longer or more intimate attention than one wants to give. Many of the examples I have collected of people piling on details in conversation involve old people. I can think of many possible explanations for this. It may be that old people often want more involvement with young people than young people want with them, or that old people frequently cannot hear well and exercise the option of telling detailed stories to maintain interaction, or simply that old people are more inclined to reminisce about the past, consequently telling stories that are likely to include details.

It is a tenet of contemporary American psychology that mental health requires psychological separation from one's parents. One way of resisting overinvolvement, for some people at least, is resisting telling details. A middle-aged woman who is a psychotherapist was telling me that her sister is overly involved with their mother. As evidence of this overinvolvement, she said, "It's amazing, the details of Jane's life my mother knows." Later in the same conversation, she was explaining that she herself resists her mother's attempts to get overly involved in her life. As evidence of the mother's attempts to draw her into unhealthy involvement, the woman commented, "She's hungry for details." To give me an example of the obviously inappropriate questions her mother asks, she said, "If I tell her I went somewhere, she asks, 'What did you wear?'" I was struck because this was the same question that brought my Great-Aunt such happiness. The difference is that my Great-Aunt was seeking involvement with the man who asked her what she wore; this psychotherapist was resisting what she perceived as the excessive involvement her mother sought with her.

Presumably, however, when the speaker's sister talks to their mother, she does not feel that her asking "What did you wear?" is inappropriate. Perhaps, like my Great-Aunt, she values the show of caring and resulting involvement. Individuals differ with respect to the proportions of independence and involvement that seem appropriate, as well as what manifestations of those values – what ways of honoring independence and involvement – seem appropriate. Hence, individuals differ with respect to how many and which details seem appropriate to request or offer in a given context (where context is broadly defined to include the setting, the speech activity being engaged in, the interlocutors, and the relationship among them, perceived or sought).

In addition to individual differences, there are also, of course, cultural differences. Is it, perhaps, not by chance that the letter from the mother in (19) telling exactly what she ate on the airplane was written by a Greek mother? Would an American of Anglo-Saxon background be as likely to offer that level of detail in correspondence? (I am not saying the answer is no, only that the question is worth asking.) A review of a Japanese comic book translated into English notes, "It is . . . a Japanese convention to devote more attention to illustrative detail than clever dialogue" (Haberman 1988). Watanabe (in preparation) found, in a comparative study of small group discussions among Japanese, on the one hand, and Americans, on the other, that, in discussing topics set by the experimenter, the Japanese speakers tended to give more detailed accounts of reasons for making decisions. These disparate kinds of evidence support the frequently-made observation that Japanese culture pays more attention to detail than do Western cultures.

Similar differences obtain for literature. Literatures of different cultures and different genres differ with respect to how many and what details are included. And readers, like critics, differ in whether or not they find the level of details provided to be effective or not. Some love the exorbitant details of *New Yorker* articles; others lose patience with them. When one feels that a written work of art or persuasion is demanding too much involvement – trying to "pull" at one's "heart strings" – one resists (like the daughter who does not want her mother to be too involved in her life) and labels that work manipulative or sentimental (just as a daughter who resists involvement may label her mother with such contemporary psychological terms as manipulative, enmeshed, or neurotic).

Conclusion

I return now to the story-within-a-story from Hymes (1973) that I
quoted at the outset. I would like to ask readers to ask themselves
whether they recall Hymes's narrative as a story about Skunk, or
a story about eels. I am intrigued by this text because after having
read it a number of times in the process of editing the article by
Rosen (1988) in which it is cited, I had ample opportunity to observe that it is a story about collecting from a native American in-
formant a tale about Skunk. And yet I cannot stop thinking of it
as Hymes's story about eels. Indeed, at the point at which I began
composing this paragraph, I had to flip back to the text to remind
myself which animal the tale is about. But the image of Mrs. Tohet
cleaning and spreading the eels, and of the eels hanging up to dry
"like so many shrunken infants' overalls," is with me forever. The
reason, I suggest, is that that part of the story comes alive as a scene
because of the specific concrete details of Mrs. Tohet's actions, a
simile, and resultant images ("the white cord within removed, and
the spread skin cut in each of its four corners, held apart by sticks,"
the eels "strung up on a line between poles, like so many shrunken
infants' overalls"). Significant too is the detailed description of
action introducing her dialogue, which heightens the drama of the
dialogue by delaying its appearance ("Mrs. Tohet stepped back,
hands on hips, looking at the line of eels, and said: 'Ain't that beautiful!'"). In contrast, the story of Skunk remains fuzzy for me because it is presented in paraphrase and summary.[18]

A woman is raped and tortured in John Barth's novel *Sabbatical*.
When the woman's sister tells a man the details of what was done
to her, the man tells her to stop, saying, "The details are just dread-
fulness, even between ourselves" (65). But the sister disagrees,
saying, "Rape and Torture and Terror are just words; the details
are what's real." She is right, if what is real is what is experienced
and felt. Reading or hearing that a woman was raped and tortured
is distressing, and ultimately forgettable; reading or hearing a
detailed description of what was done to her (I will not recount here
the detailed account provided in this novel, even though it would
forcefully dramatize its emotional impact) is harrowing, nauseat-
ing, nightmare-making, and often unforgettable: a little closer to
the experience.

Hymes (1981:314) notes that his examination of an American Indian (Clackamas) narrative, applying "a dialectic method proposed by Lévi-Strauss showed further pattern, not of cognitive categories, but of sensory imagery and expressive detail. . ." Hymes advocates a view of discourse as simultaneously cognitive and aesthetic: communicating ideas and feelings at the same time, not only by the meanings of words but also by their form and the pattern they establish of constants and contrasts.

Returning to the terms of Friedrich, images work through the individual imagination to create involvement. The invoking of details – specific, concrete, familiar – makes it possible for an individual to recall and a hearer to recreate a scene in which people are in relation to each other and to objects in the world. In this way, and by a kind of paradox, the individual imagination is a key to interpersonal involvement, and interpersonal involvement is a key to understanding language.

6

Involvement strategies in consort:
literary nonfiction and political oratory

Each of the preceding three chapters focuses on a single involvement strategy. In this chapter, I show how the three strategies examined: repetition, constructed dialogue, and details and imagery,
work together with each other and with other strategies to create
involvement. Furthermore, there has been a movement, within
each chapter and across the chapters, from conversation to more
deliberately composed genres, both written and spoken discourse
types that combine involvement strategies in a variety of ways. This
chapter is concerned exclusively with nonconversational genres. It
analyzes, first, an example of academic writing that uses involvement strategies more commonly found in fiction, and then examines in detail a formal spoken genre: a political speech modeled
on the African-American sermon. Throughout, I emphasize again
the inseparability of emotion and thought.

Thinking with feeling

In her memoir of her parents, Margaret Mead and Gregory Bateson, Mary Catherine Bateson (1984) returns repeatedly to the inseparability of emotion and cognition. She notes that Gregory
Bateson "genuinely rejected the notion of a separation between
thought and feeling" (173). Similarly, Mead's "prose echoes with
the lines of memorized poetry" and with gospel (for example, "with
references to women 'great with child' rather than pregnant").
Mead used such "evocative language," Bateson observes, "to make
it possible for readers to respond emotionally as well as intellectually" (200–1).

The conviction that no discourse could, or should try to, be emotion-free became crucial to Mary Catherine Bateson when she confronted the task of communicating ideas that evolved in scholarly interaction. Appointed rapporteur for a conference her father organized on cybernetics, she "reached the conclusion that my book would be true to the event only if it followed some of the conventions of fiction" because the "conventions of academic reporting ... would mean editing out emotions that seemed to me essential to the process" (180).

Bateson contrasts her approach with the more usual one taken by Arthur Koestler, who organized a conference at Alpbach on a similar topic at the same time. According to Bateson, Koestler tried to separate ideas and emotions and produced two books, a conventional conference proceedings and a novel: "The emotion was edited out of the formal proceedings of the Alpbach Symposium, which came out dry and academic, and resurfaced in the novel as rage." In contrast, Bateson continues:

> There is a sense in which the emotion was edited into [my] book, for I used my own introspective responses of dismay or illumination to bring the reader into the room, and worked with the tape-recorded discussion so that the emotionally pivotal comments would be brought out rather than buried in verbiage.

Bringing "the reader into the room" is reminiscent of Jimmy Breslin's column taking readers into the hospital where John Kennedy died, as discussed in chapter 5. It is a way of achieving understanding through involvement.

The successful result of Bateson's effort is a book entitled *Our own metaphor* (1972) which uses involvement strategies to convey ideas as they evolved at the conference. Prominent among these strategies are repetition, dialogue, and imagery.

Literary nonfiction

To see how Bateson used involvement strategies to convey in writing a sense of discourse that took place in interaction, I examine an excerpt from *Our own metaphor* that begins in the middle of a presentation by a participant named Tolly:

(1)   "I'll begin with an extremely simple picture, by way of introduction, and then elaborate it. This will be like those initial minutes

in the movies when you see the introductory pictures which give you an idea of the kind of movie it's going to be while telling you who the main characters are, and so on.

"Let's imagine a pendulum swinging back and forth." Tolly hunted around for chalk and then he drew this picture. "This means that for some interval of time the pendulum swings to the right, shown by the arrow labeled R. Here's an occurrence, shown by a point, and then the pendulum swings to the left for some other interval, shown by the arrow labeled L. The occurrence is the end of the swing. You can think of the same picture as representing a billiard ball rolling back and forth on a frictionless table between two reflecting boundaries. Left, right, left, right, and the occurrences are the bounces."

↑ R
↑ L
↑ R
↑ L

Horst did a double-take. "You mean the *point* indicates the moment it changes from right to left?"

Tolly nodded gleefully. "Yeah. That's right. Unconventional." Once Horst had called my attention to it, I realized that this was indeed unconventional. The minute I stopped thinking that the arrow indicated the direction of the pendulum (which it did not, because the diagram of a light changing from red to green to red would have looked exactly the same), I realized that Tolly was doing the strange thing of using an *arrow* to represent something stable (an "interval of condition-holding" he called it) and a *point* to represent change, the occurrence that initiates new conditions. This was the exact opposite of the convention Barry had used in his diagram, where arrows had represented the transition from, say, organic to non-organic nitrogen compounds, or Fred, who had used arrows to represent causation. It was not yet clear whether these conventions were simply freakish and arbitrary, or whether this choice of symbols was a first step toward new kinds of meanings.   (166–7)

This excerpt is dialogic in far more ways than simply casting Tolly's ideas as first person speech rather than impersonal exposition. Calling the conference participants by first names (Tolly, Horst, Barry, Fred) brings them closer to readers than they would be if referred to by last names only (for example, Holt) or title-last-name (for example, Dr. Mittelstaedt or Professor Commoner). Moreover, Bateson uses words, phrases, and collocations that suggest a speaker's voice, such as colloquial interjections and diction ("say," "Yeah"), contractions ("I'll," "it's," "let's"), fragmented syntax ("Unconventional."), and italics for key words that would have been emphasized in speech ("*point*," "*arrow*"). These strategies bring readers closer to the participants and their ideas by creating a sense of immediacy and intimacy. At the same time, the strategies serve to evaluate the ideas: They provide a point of view on them, highlight parts, and show relationships among parts.

Another dialogic aspect of the exposition is that projected responses of readers are represented, prefigured, and created by the dramatized responses of the listening participants, including Bateson herself. Tolly's "unconventional" use of arrows and points, which could easily elude and confuse readers if it were presented without comment, is repeated and elaborated to highlight and discuss its significance. That it is surprising for Tolly to use "an *arrow* to represent something stable" is first portrayed in the reaction of a participant ("Horst did a double-take"). Moreover, Horst's response is presented, still dialogically but not verbally, as an image of nonverbal behavior. This requires readers to supply the meaning of a double-take much as they would if they observed one in face-to-face interaction.

By casting herself in the role of a naive listener, Bateson can verbalize the misinterpretations that readers are likely to make, and correct for them: "The minute I stopped thinking that the arrow indicated the direction of the pendulum (which it did not . . .)." In addition, many of the aspects of speech that let listeners know how speakers mean what they say, such as tone of voice, rhythm, intonation, laughter, facial expression, and kinesics, are suggested by adverbs ("Tolly nodded gleefully"). This simultaneously builds suspense.

Suspense is also created by scenically graphic description of behaviour such as, "Tolly hunted around for chalk and then drew this picture." How does it enhance an understanding of the ideas presented at the conference to report that the speaker hunted for chalk? To answer this question, contrast Bateson's version with the conventional academic-writing locution, "See Figure 1." Readers then see only the figure. Bateson shows not only the figure (or, rather, the "picture"), but also the human interaction that gave rise to it. The description of Tolly's movement also constitutes a delay in exposition that gives readers time to prepare to focus attention on the figure/picture, much as the conference participants prepared to focus on an illustration when Tolly displayed, by hunting for chalk, that he was about to draw something on the board.

Clarifications and discussions presented as participants' reactions to Tolly's presentation are repetitions and elaborations. With paraphrase more often than exact repetition, Bateson underscores the significance of Tolly's ideas by repeating them. Tolly's introduction is repeated when his statement of intention to "begin ... by way of introduction" is immediately followed by a simile explaining what his introduction is going to do. Repetition is also key in the presentation of Tolly's example (representing a pendulum's swing by arrows and points), embedded in the discourse:

1   "Let's imagine a pendulum swinging back and forth."
    . . .
2   the pendulum swings to the right,
3   shown by the arrow labeled R.
    . . .
4   and then the pendulum swings to the left
    . . .
5   shown by the arrow labeled L.
    . . .
6   Left, right, left, right,

The first mention, line 1 of the lines excerpted, states the idea that a pendulum is swinging. In standard academic prose the writer might then move on, having stated this premise. But Bateson repeats with variation: Lines 2–5 illustrate the pendulum's swing with a parallel construction highlighting the movement from right to left by slotting these words, with their corresponding representations "R" and "L," into otherwise identical constructions. Finally, the pendulum's swing is represented iconically by the repetition of just these words in line 6 ("Left, right, left, right"), which by now are a condensation of the preceding description.

In the final paragraph, Bateson "reports" her own developing thoughts to repeat once more the principle underlying Tolly's representation of the pendulum's swing and to elaborate on it. Finally, to encourage readers to compare Tolly's approach with those of other participants, Bateson repeats, in brief summary, the representational conventions used by Barry and Fred.

By using linguistic strategies common in fiction to convey the ideas that emerged at the cybernetics conference, Bateson artfully elaborated involvement strategies I have shown to be basic to conversation. She recreated in writing a sense of the conversations in which the ideas developed, simultaneously evaluating those ideas: that is, showing their relative importance and showing relationships among them and among participants. She presented ideas as dialogue, provided visual images, and dramatized participants' responses to the ideas and to each other, so readers could grasp the proceedings of the conference by imagining a scene in which ideas evolved in interaction.

Speaking and writing with involvement

The recursiveness of Bateson's approach illuminates the relationship between conversational and literary discourse: To convey ideas that evolved in conversation, she needed strategies common in fiction precisely because these strategies are drawn from the language of conversation.

Bleich (1988) observes that when purely cognitive approaches to language give way to an approach that recognizes meaning as an interactional achievement, dialogue and affect become central. The inseparability of emotion and cognition as well as the centrality of dialogue are also implied in Shirley Brice Heath's discussion of the acquisition of literacy. Heath (1985) explains that learning to read is not merely a matter of acquiring decoding skills. Children learn to read when written materials are integrated in their lives, when they know they will find themselves in situations requiring them to talk about what they have read. Similarly, to be motivated to read, children need models of literate adults with whom they feel intimate. It is the human intimacy, or involvement, that gives motivation and meaning to the acquisition of literacy, as to any other culturally significant activity.

Understanding written discourse is always a matter of interpretation and interaction. This is dramatized in the following excerpt from an essay about Lubavitcher Hasidim, an orthodox Jewish sect. In this excerpt, the author, Lis Harris (1985), constructs (I shall not, for now-obvious reasons, say that she "reports") a conversation with a Hasidic man:

(2)   "Thanks," I said. "By the way, are there any books about Hasidism that you think might be helpful?"
        "There are no books."

"No books? Why, what do you mean? You must know that hundreds of books have been written about Hasidism."

"Books about Hasidic matters always misrepresent things. They twist and change the truth in casual ways. I trust Lubavitcher books, like the 'Tanya' [a work written by the movement's founder] and the collections of the rebbes' discourses, because our rebbe got the information in them from the rebbe before him, and so on, in an unbroken chain. I trust scholars I can talk to, face to face."

The effectiveness of presenting this interchange of ideas as a dialogue is now evident. Harris presents herself as naive to the point of rudeness ("You must know . . ."), so that the Hasid can be shown to explain his view in detail. His explanation, furthermore, dramatizes the intertwining of speaking and writing in the passing down of a written text – the Tanya – by the great religious leaders (rebbes) who are also great scholars – interpreters as well as receivers of that text. The text, in other words, is meaningless apart from its interpretation, which is inseparable from people ("scholars I can talk to, face to face").[1]

Heath (1986) quotes the poet William Carlos Williams and cites classical and medieval rhetoricians and grammarians to the effect that "literate knowledge depended ultimately on oral reformulations of that knowledge" (282). Elsewhere (Heath 1985) she notes that early American schools emphasized opportunities for talk and for extended debate about interpretation of written materials. This predilection is still alive at meetings, conferences, lectures, and institutes: People want to see peers and experts face to face rather than encountering them only through their writing; they want to interact with them.

The Hasid's view of books and Harris's presentation of it, like Mary Catherine Bateson's depiction of the cybernetics conference and her discussion of how she depicted it, highlight the centrality of dialogue and its relation to other aspects of language that create involvement in speaking and writing. Like images, dialogue provides particulars by which listeners and speakers collaborate in imagining and participating in similar worlds.

Involvement in political oratory

The preceding section examines strategies in written discourse that

seeks to reflect meaning as it evolved in spoken discourse. I turn
now to a spoken genre, but a highly elaborated rather than a conversational one, and one based partly on a written text: political
oratory.

At the 1988 Democratic National Convention, the Reverend
Jesse Jackson delivered a speech that was widely regarded to be an
emotional peak of the convention. (Far more viewers watched the
convention on television the night Jackson spoke than on any other
night.) One journalist (Shales 1988) described the effect of Jackson's speech under the headline, "The Jackson triumph":

As few speakers have ever been able to do, Jackson makes florid oratory
work brilliantly on the intimate stage of television.
    "Thunder and lightning from Jesse Jackson," said Dan Rather of CBS
News. "He shook the hall in his own way just as he has shaken up the
Democratic Party."
    ... most seemed awestruck, as if witness to a spiritual vision.
    One could disagree strongly with some of Jackson's policies and still be
swept up and swept away with the passionate musicality of the rhetoric
and the eager participation of the crowd.
    ... those reaction shots on all three networks of teary-eyed onlookers
contributed to the overall impression that this speech was not merely the
proverbial raising of the roof, it was a stirring moment in American political history.

Another journalist (Ifill 1988), under the front page headline "Jackson evokes smiles, tears," quoted a delegate who cried on hearing
Jackson's speech: "It's a feeling you get when you go to church. You
must know the man is telling the truth."

Reactions to Jackson's speech were not universally laudatory.
Drew (1988:75–6) observed that his 1988 convention address "was
not nearly as electrifying as the one he gave in 1984." She explains,

Jackson came over forcefully on television, but in the hall it seemed that
he was out of gas – intellectually, emotionally, physically. He is so talented
a speaker, and has worked up so much material over the years, and he
knows so well how to speak from and to the soul, that he could still put
together a strong speech that captured many people. But he seemed spent
(as well as distracted by a failed teleprompter), strayed far from his text,
and pieced together a speech composed of a hodgepodge of his greatest hits
from the campaign trail. ... He spoke, as he often did in the campaign,
about his own early life, making it sound more wretched than it apparently
was .... Jackson, as he often is, was part poetry and part demagoguery.

If Drew is correct and Jackson delivered a moving speech under adverse conditions, it is all the more interesting to investigate the linguistic strategies that account for the emotional impact of his speech – an impact that was created, at least in part, by the strategies I have been discussing. The ensuing analysis demonstrates the interplay of these and other involvement strategies in Jackson's 1988 convention address. Analyzing them, moreover, sheds light on the relationship between poetry and oratorical power insofar as it lies in their use of involvement strategies.

Repetition

In Example 27 of chapter 3, I cite examples of parallel constructions and repetitions of familiar phrases in Martin Luther King's "I Have a Dream" speech. Jackson began his address with a salute to King, a salute communicated by both the meaning and the form of his words. While talking about King explicitly, Jackson paid homage to him implicitly by repeating, with variation, words from King's speech.[2] First I present again King's lines:

I have a dream that one day
on the red hills of Georgia
the sons of former slaves
and the sons of former slave-owners
will be able to sit down together
at the table of brotherhood.

Jackson used a parallel construction that echoed King's seemingly prophetic prediction of events in Georgia, the site of the convention at which Jackson was speaking:[3]

(3) Dr. Martin Luther King, Jr.,
       lies only a few miles from us tonight,
       Tonight he must feel good,
       as he looks down upon us,
       We sit here together.
       A rainbow,
       a coalition,
       the sons and daughters of slave masters,
       and the sons and daughters of slaves,
       sitting together
       around a common table,
       to decide the direction
       of our party and our country.

Jackson echoed King's metaphoric image but also updated it: He included "daughters" as well as "sons" and substituted his signature term "common" for the gender-exclusive term "brotherhood" to yield "common table" in place of "table of brotherhood." He also included his signature phrase "a rainbow coalition," reframing and highlighting it not only by placing it in the context of King's metaphor but also by rechunking it into two separate intonational contours.

Another strategy used by both Jackson and King is substituting one word for another in a similar paradigm that is phonologically and syntactically similar but semantically different or even opposite. King's use of this strategy was seen in Example 28, chapter 3, in which "content of character" was substituted for "color of skin" in King's dream. Jackson echoed King in also repeating and elaborating the idea of dreaming about a better world, suggested by verbal reversals:[4]

(4)   Dream.
      Of teachers
      who teach for life and not for a living.
      Dream.
      Of doctors who are concerned more about public health
      than private wealth.
      Dream.
      Of lawyers
      more concerned about justice than a judgeship.
      Dream.
      Of preachers
      who are concerned more about prophecy than profiteering.

Common ground

The theme of Jackson's speech was unity: unity among supporters of different primary contenders (including Jackson) to ensure that the Democratic party win the presidential election. The term "common" was a recurrent verbal representation of this theme. Jackson first introduced it in a parallel construction that, like other phrases and images he used, was a repetition and variation of parts of his 1984 convention address. In 1984, Jackson used a parallel construction that employed a paradigmatic substitution within the same syntactic frame:

(5) We must leave <u>the racial battle ground</u>
     and come <u>to the economic common ground</u>
     and <u>moral higher ground.</u>

The parallelism, with its repetition and reframing of the word
"ground," transforms something negative ("racial battle ground")
into something positive ("economic common ground") and then
into something exalted ("moral higher ground"). Jackson used the
same triple parallelism as the basis for a slightly elaborated and altered figure in 1988:

(6) Tonight there is a sense of celebration.
     Because we are moved.
     Fundamentally moved,
     <u>from racial battle grounds</u> by law,
     <u>to economic common ground.</u>
     Tomorrow we'll challenge to move,
     <u>to higher ground.</u>
     <u>Common ground.</u>

In this speech, the medial term, "common ground," was key, so this
is the one the parallelism focused on. Jackson repeated it immediately and then raised it to the level of a formula. As noted in chapter
3, Davis (1985) finds, "The most important characteristics of the
African-American sermonic formula are the groups of irrhythmic
lines shaped around a core idea." Thus "common ground" is the
core idea, a repeated phrase that captured Jackson's theme and
punctuated the points he made throughout his address. This can be
seen in (7). (The irrhythmicity of lines can be seen here as well but
will be discussed in a later section.)

(7) <u>Common ground.</u>
     Ea::sier said than done.
     Where do you FIND
     <u>common ground,</u>
     at the point of challenge.
     . . .
     <u>We find common ground</u> at the plant gate
     that closes on workers without notice,
     <u>We find common ground,</u>
     at the farm auction,
     where a good farmer,
     loses his or her land
     to bad loans,
     or diminishing markets,

Common ground.
At the schoolyard,
where teachers cannot get adequate pay,
and students cannot get a scholarship,
and can't make a loan,
Common ground.
At the hospital admitting room ...

In all, there were nineteen occurrences of the phrase "common
ground," in addition to "common grave," "common table,"
"common thread," "common good," "common direction,"
"common sense" (itself part of a repeated formula), and "one thing
in common."

Jackson frequently used a repetitive strategy that derives impact
from a surprising reversal. For example, there are metatheses of
phonemes:

(8)   No matter how tired or how tried,

of morphemes:

(9)   With so many guided missiles,
      and so much misguided leadership,

and of lexical items, frequently resulting in the figure of speech,
chiasmus:

(10)   I was born in the slum,
       but the slum was not born in me.

Repetitions of words and phrases are seen throughout the address
and throughout this analysis, dovetailing with other involvement
strategies.

Dialogue

At five points Jackson used dialogue to anticipate and animate
others' points of view. Four instances of dialogue came toward the
end of the speech, gradually shifting focus to Jackson's personal
life, as his address culminated in his "life story," scenes from his
childhood. By successive uses of dialogue, he gradually brought
listeners closer, preparing them to hear his life story. (At the same
time, the television producers made the performance dialogic for
viewers by interspersing shots of the speaker with "reaction shots"
of the audience.)

The first instance of dialogue was the longest and different in function from the other four. Here Jackson spoke in the voice of young drug addicts, "the children in Watts" to whom he says he listened "all night long":

(11)   They said, "Jesse Jackson,
          as you challenge us to say no to drugs,
          you're right.
          And to not sell them,
          you're right.
          And to not use these guns,
          you're right,
          . . .
          We have neither jobs,
          nor houses,
          nor services,
          nor training,
          no way out, . . ."

By framing these and other details of their situation in the voice of young drug addicts, Jackson lent authority to his claim that their situation is hopeless, and the government bears responsibility for allowing the availability of guns and drugs:

(12)   "We can go and buy the drugs,
          by the boxes,
          at the port.
          If we can buy the drugs at the port,
          don't you believe the federal government
          can stop it if they want to?"
          They say,
          "We don't have Saturday night specials any more."
          They say,
          "We buy AK-47s and Uzis,
          the latest lethal weapons.
          We buy them ACROSS the COUNTER
          on LONG BEACH BOULEVARD."

In this, as in all the other instances of dialogue, Jackson animated others addressing him by name. In this first extended use of constructed dialogue, he animated a voice addressing him by his full name; later he brought the audience closer by animating voices addressing him by first name only.

In the second instance of dialogue, like the others that followed, Jackson animated projected objections to his political positions:

(13) I'm often asked,
→   "Jesse, why do you take on these
→   tough issues.
→   They're not very political.
→   We can't win THAT way."

Jackson used this projected objection as the frame in which to
answer the objection. In (14), he went on to align himself, through
parallel constructions, with others who took stands that were un-
popular but "morally right." In the first four lines, he used chiasmus
to reverse the order of phrases "be political" and "be right". The
passage culminated in yet another instance of constructed dialogue.
(A number of repeated words and phrases are underlined.)

(14) If an issue is morally right,
       it will eventually be political,
       It may be political,
       and never be right,
       Fannie Lou Hamer didn't have the most votes
       in Atlantic City,
       but her principles have out-lasted
       every delegate who voted to lock her out,
       Rosa Parks
       did not have the most votes,
       but she was morally right,
       Dr. King didn't have the most votes
       about the Vietnam War,
       but he was morally right,
       If we're PRINCIPLED FIRST,
       our politics will fall into place.
→   "Jesse, why did you take these big bold initiatives."

The dialogue in the last line of (14) is a paraphrase of the line of
dialogue seen in (13), restating the question he is speaking to at this
point in his address, and reinforcing the closeness he is constructing
with the audience by casting himself in dialogue.

   Jackson moved from this section of his speech to a section in
which he addressed the audience directly, telling them (repeatedly)
to "Dream," "Go forward," "Never surrender," and 'Don't give
up." He then animated dialogue in which the audience addressed
him directly:

(15) Why can I challenge you this way.
→   "Jesse Jackson, <u>you don't understand my situation.</u>
→   You be on television. [laughter]
→   <u>You don't understand,</u>
→   I see you with the big people.
→   <u>You don't understand my situation.</u>"

The audience laughed, amused perhaps by Jackson's verbalization
of a thought some of them had, perhaps by his animation of vernacular Black English. Their laughter contributed to the effect of
the dialogue: Engaging the audience in dialogue with him provided
a kind of iconic analogue to inviting them to pull up a chair and
listen to his life story which ended and capped his speech.

"Understand," the key word and concept, was picked up from
the animated dialogue in (15) to form a phrase that was repeated
over and over as the story unfolded, driving home its point. This
begins in the introduction to the story:

(16) I <u>understand</u>,
        You're seeing me on TV
        but you don't know the <u>me</u>
        that <u>makes me me</u>,
→   They wonder "Why
        does Jesse <u>run</u>",
        Because they see <u>me running</u> for the White <u>House</u>,
        they don't see the <u>house</u> I'm <u>running</u> from,
        I have a story,

Here Jackson used dialogue to express the projected thoughts of
others ("Why does Jesse run?") while echoing the title of the novel
What makes Sammy run? He used parallel construction to reinter-
pret the meaning of the word "run" and to juxtapose the elegance
of the White House with the impoverishment of the house he grew
up in. Phonologically, the repeated /i/ sound created end-rhymes
in "TV" and "me," and the "ru /r ∧/ of "run" was repeated in
"from" (/fr ∧ m/), creating another end-rhyme.

"I understand" occurred fourteen times as Jackson described his
childhood. I present only a short excerpt, from the beginning:

(17) You see,
        I was born to a teenage mother,
        who was born to a teenage mother.
        <u>I understand.</u>
        I know abandonment,

and people being mean to you,
and saying you're nothing and nobody,
and can never be anything,
<u>I understand.</u>
Jesse Jackson,
is my THIRD <u>name</u>.
I'm adopted.
When I had no <u>name</u>,
my grandmother gave me her <u>name</u>,
My <u>name</u> was Jesse Burns,
'til I was twelve.
So I wouldn't have a blank space,
she gave me a <u>name</u>.
To hold me over.
<u>I understand</u>,
when nobody knows your <u>name</u>.
I understand when you have <u>no NAME</u>.
<u>I understand.</u>

In addition to the repetition of the phrase, "I understand," (17) shows an incremental repetition of the word "name" which finally blends into a variation of the title of a book by the Black writer James Baldwin, *Nobody knows my name*.

Details and images

In describing his childhood, Jackson used details to create images that would let listeners imagine what he must have felt:

(18)   I wasn't born
       in the hospital.
       Mama didn't have insurance.
→   I was born in the bed,
→   at house.
       I really do understand.
→   Born in a three room house,
→   bathroom in the back yard,
→   slop jar by the bed,
→   no hot and cold running water,
       I understand.
       Wallpaper used for decoration?
       No.
       For a windbreaker.
       I understand,

Jackson dramatized the poverty of his childhood by depicting specific details that allow hearers to imagine a scene they could elaborate in their minds with other images and associations.

Using specific details, Jackson also described a scene in which his family celebrated Thanksgiving:

(19) I understand.
         At three o'clock on
      Thanksgiving day,
      we couldn't eat turkey.
      Because Mama was preparing somebody else's turkey
      at three o'clock.
      We had to play football to entertain ourselves.
      And then around six o'clock,
      she would get off the /Alta Vista/ bus,
      and we would bring up the leftovers
      and eat our turkey,
      leftovers:
      the carcass,
      the cranberries,
      around eight o'clock at night.
      I really do understand.

The tolling of the clock from a repeated three o'clock, when the family should have been eating Thanksgiving dinner, to six o'clock, when the mother returned home, to eight o'clock, when they finally ate, provided an iconic analogue to the delaying of the children's Thanksgiving dinner. The specific naming of the hours, naming the game the children played while waiting for their mother, the name of the bus she rode, specifying the leftovers: "turkey carcass" and "cranberries," created the images from which listeners could construct a scene and imagine what they might have felt in that scene.

Jackson's description of his childhood was the last major section of his address. By involving the audience in his personal life, especially his vulnerability as a suffering child, he climaxed the process, begun by dialogue, of bringing the audience gradually closer to him. This climax in figurative movement is analogous to the emotional climax that Jackson created: The audience was moved by the rhythms of his speech which involved them in musical ensemble, and by participating in sensemaking as they constructed in their minds scenes of his childhood, based on the details and images he depicted. It was during this segment that the "reaction shots" shown on the television screen displayed weeping faces, evidence of the emotional impact of the speech.

Figures of speech

Many of the repetitive strategies I have illustrated are figures of speech – what Levin (1982) calls "style figures of speech," arraying words in identifiable syntagmatic patterns. Levin identifies another type of figure as "thought figures of speech," figures that Friedrich (1986) and Sapir (1977) call "tropes." These are figures that play primarily on meaning. Among them are similes and metaphors. Many of Jackson's similes and metaphors arose in connection with his personal life story, contributing to the climactic impact of that part of his speech.

The "common ground" theme is itself figurative. This metaphor was developed most elaborately in the section excerpted as (7). Several other metaphors were elaborated at other points in the address. Jackson's use of metaphor played a significant role in the emotional impact of his address: Each of these elaborations sparked a crescendo of audience applause at the time of delivery.

I discuss the following three metaphorical elaborations: (1) lions and lambs, (2) boats and ships, and (3) the patchwork quilt. All of these metaphors were woven back into the "common ground" theme.

Lions and lambs

Jackson echoed and then elaborated the conventional metaphor for peace of the lion lying down with the lamb. The metaphor is a repetition from popular culture and from the Bible, its original source:

(20)   1 The Bible teaches that when lions
        2 and lambs
        3 lie down together,
        4 none will be afraid
        5 and there will be peace in the valley.
        6 It sounds impossible.
        7 Lions eat lambs.
        8 Lambs flee from lions,
        9 Yet even lions and lambs find common ground. Why?
           [pause]

    10 Because neither lions,
    11 nor lambs want the forest to catch on fire.
    12 Neither lions nor lambs
    13 want acid rain to fall,
    14 Neither lions nor lambs can survive nuclear war,
    15 If lions and lambs can find common ground,
    16 surely we can as well,
    17 as civilized people.

Readers will have noted numerous repetitions in the elaboration of
this metaphor, including repetition of the words "lion(s)" and
"lamb(s)," and of several syntactic paradigms in which they are
reframed, such as chiasmus:

    7 <u>Lions</u> eat <u>lambs.</u>
    8 <u>Lambs</u> flee from <u>lions,</u>

Jackson used repetition to press the old lion-and-lamb metaphor
into service as a frame into which he fit the contemporary issues of
acid rain and nuclear war:

    10 neither lions, nor lambs want the forest to catch on fire.
    12 Neither lions nor lambs want acid rain to fall,
    14 Neither lions nor lambs can survive nuclear war,

Finally, he merged the lion-and-lamb metaphor with the one he had
previously established and elaborated, common ground.

    9 Yet even lions and lambs find common ground.
      . . .
    15 If lions and lambs can find common ground,
    16 surely we can as well,

Thus Jackson used a conventional metaphor as the basis of novel
elaboration and ultimate integration into his theme of party unity.

Ships

Fairly early in his address, Jackson praised Michael Dukakis, the
man everyone knew would be nominated to run for president.
Then he compared Dukakis to himself in a series of parallelisms
contrasting the circumstances in which they grew up. Having thus
emphasized their differences, he used a metaphor to express the
bond between them:

(21)   His foreparents came to America
        on immigrant ships.
        My foreparents came to America
        on slave ships.
        But whatever the original ships,
        we're in the same boat tonight.

The audience cheered when Jackson reframed the literal ships on
which his and Dukakis's foreparents came to America in terms of
the conventional metaphoric expression, "We're in the same boat."
The aesthetic pleasure of the reframing contributed to highlighting
the theme of unity.

Jackson then elaborated a slightly different boat metaphor,
depicting himself and Dukakis as navigating ships:

(22)   Our ships,
            could pass in the night,
            if we have a false sense of independence,
            or they could collide and crash,
            We would lose our passengers,
            But we can seek a higher reality,
            and a greater good.
        Apart,
            we can drift on the broken pieces of Reaganomics,
            satisfy our baser instincts,
            and exploit the fears of our people.
        At our highest,
            we can call upon noble instincts,
            and navigate this vessel,
            to safety.
        The greater good,
            is the common good.

Here, too, the boat metaphor, like the lion and lamb, reinforced
the theme of party unity: Bad things happen if boats navigating the
same waters do not coordinate their movements; good things
happen if they do.[5]

The boat metaphor resurfaced later, in answer to the question
Jackson posed in the form of dialogue which was seen in (14):
"Jesse, why did you take these big bold initiatives?" In answering
this projected question, Jackson cited "a poem by an unknown
author":

(23)   As for Jesse Jackson,
        "I'm tired of sailing my little boat,

far inside the harbor bar,
I want to go out where the big ships float.
Out in the deep,
where the great ones are,
And should my frail craft,
prove too slight,
the waves that sweep those /?/ o'er,
I'd rather go down in a stirring fight.
Than drown to death
in the sheltered shore."
We've got to go out my friends
where the big boats are.

In this second elaboration, the boat became a metaphor for Jackson's life: He would rather risk failure in a dramatic effort than find his end in safety and obscurity. This metaphor provided a transition to the climax of Jackson's address. He moved from it to challenging the audience to "Dream" and "Never surrender" (in other words, like him, to move out from a small familiar harbor) and then to his life story.

The patchwork quilt

Another extended metaphor compared America to a patchwork quilt. The metaphor grew out of an image from Jackson's childhood:

(24)   Common ground.
       America's not
       a blanket
       woven from one thread,
       one color, one cloth.
       When I was a child growing up
       in Greenville, South Carolina
       and Grandmother could not afford,
       a blanket,
       she didn't complain and we did not freeze.
       Instead she took pieces of old cloth.
       Patches,
       wool, silk, gabardine, /crockersack/,
       only patches,
       barely good enough to wipe off your shoes with.
       But they didn't stay that way very long.
       With sturdy hands,

and a strong cord,
she sewed them together.
Into a quilt.
A thing of beauty
and power
and culture.

Jackson transformed his grandmother's quilt into a metaphor for
the Democratic party and used it as the basis for a repetitive
strategy listing groups to whom the Democrats might appeal. Each
group and its demands were underlined and punctuated by reference to the patchwork metaphor. (In the first line below, rather
than using "sew" or another verb appropriate to quilting, he invited
party members to "build" a quilt – a verb that is assonant with
"quilt" and has more forceful connotations.)

(25)   Now, Democrats, we must build such a quilt.
       Farmers,
       you seek fair prices
       and <u>you are right</u>,
       but you cannot stand alone.
       <u>Your patch is not big enough.</u>
       Workers,
       you fight for fair wages,
       <u>You are right,</u>
       <u>But your patch labor</u>
       <u>is not big enough.</u>
       Women,
       you seek comparable worth and pay equity.
       <u>You are right.</u>
       <u>But your patch</u>
       <u>is not big enough.</u>
       Women,
       mothers,
       who seek head start,
       and day care,
       and pre-natal care,
       on the front side of life,
       rather than jail care and welfare
       on the back side of life,
       <u>You're RIGHT,</u>
       <u>but your patch</u>
       <u>is not big enough.</u>
       Students,
       you seek scholarships.

> You're right,
> but your patch is not big enough.
> Blacks and Hispanics, when we fight
> for civil rights,
> we are right,
> but our patch is not big enough.
> Gays and lesbians,
> when you fight
> against discrimination,
> and a cure for AIDS,
> you are right,
> But your patch
> is not big enough.
> Conservatives and progressives,
> when you fight for what you believe,
> right-wing,
> left-wing,
> hawk,
> dove,
> you are right,
> from your point of view,
> but your point of view is not enough.
> But don't despair,
> Be as wise as my Grandmama.
> Pool the patches,
> and the pieces together,
> bound by a common thread,
> When we form a great quilt
> of unity,
> and common ground,
> we'll have the power
> to bring about health care
> and housing
> and jobs
> and education
> and hope to our nation.

Here again, the metaphor was elaborated with repetitive strategies and sound play (for example, "patches and pieces," "right-wing, left-wing").[6] And here again Jackson brought the audience closer by shifting from "Grandmother" to "Grandmama," figuratively bringing them into his family.

Other metaphors

In addition to these extended metaphors, there were many fleeting ones:

(26)   Whether you're a hawk or a dove,
       you're just a bird,
       living in the same environment,
       the same world,

Phonological and metric repetition set this bird metaphor into a
poem-like frame. Sound repetition creates a near rhyme between
"bird" and "world," while the beats per line result in a 3-2-3-2
pattern:

       Whéther you're a háwk or a dóve,
       you're júst a bírd,
       líving in the sáme envíronment,
       the sáme wórld,

   In (27), Jackson describes the drug addicts whose voice he animated in (11) and (12) in terms of a grape/raisin metaphor.

(27)   1 I met
       2 the children in Watts,
       3 who are unfortunate
       4 in their despair.
       5 Their grapes of hope have become raisins of despair.

The impact of the grape/raisin metaphor was also intensified by
rhythm. There is an unexpected break in prosody between subject
and object ("I met/ the children in Watts") that makes lines 1–4
rhythmically fragmented and choppy. This contrasts with the unexpected length of line 5, the clause containing the metaphor. Furthermore, the raisins of despair echo the poem, "A dream
deferred," by the Black poet Langston Hughes, and the play about
Black experience which borrowed an image from that poem for its
title, *A raisin in the sun*.

Surprising prosody

Jackson's delivery was characterized by what Davis (1985:50) calls
"irrhythmic semantic sensibility." The first word of a syntactic sentence was often rhythmically linked to the preceding one and
bounded by a pause and sentence-final falling intonation. This prosodic contour characterized the repetition of the word "dream" in
(4), so that sentence-final intonation and pause followed the word
"Dream," even though it was syntactically linked to the phrase that

followed. In other words, each prosodic unit began with the word
"Of" and ended with the word "Dream." This highlighted the word
"dream" as well as the various images the audience was told to
dream of. This prosodic contour also characterized the repetition
of "common ground" in (7) and in (28):

(28)   We find common ground
       at the farm auction
       where a good farmer
       loses his or her land
       to bad loans
→   or diminishing markets. Common ground.
       [pause]
       At the schoolyard
       where teachers cannot get adequate pay,
       and students cannot get a scholarship
→   and can't make a loan, Common ground.
       [pause]
       At the hospital admitting room ...

Similar prosody marked the repeated use of the word "leadership":

(29)
→   Leadership.
       Must meet the moral challenge of its day.
       . . .
→   Leadership.
       What difference will we make?
→   Leadership.
       Cannot just go along to get along.
       We must do more than change
       presidents,
       We must change direction,
→   Leadership,
       must face the moral challenge of our day,
       The nuclear war,
       build-up,
       is irrational,
→   Strong leadership,
       cannot desire to look tough,
       and let that stand in the way of the pursuit of peace,
→   Leadership.
       Must reverse,
       the arms race.

The effect of this prosody was to highlight the repeated word and
also to highlight, by isolating, the points that were punctuated by it.

Recursive formulas

Just as a word can be lifted from a phrase or extended figure to become a punctuating formula, so too a word that has been pounded home by repetition can blend back into the flow of discourse and give way to another formula. Thus the "leadership" theme merged into a brief figure built around the phrase "real world" and then into a series of parallel constructions in which the word "support" became the punctuation, each instance interspersed with a supporting backup phrase:

(30)   This generation,
          must offer <u>leadership</u> to the real world.
          We're losing ground in Latin America,
          the Middle East,
          South Africa,
          because we're not focusing on the REAL WORLD,
          that REAL WORLD.
          We must use BASIC PRINCIPLES.
          <u>Support</u>
          international law.
          We stand the most to gain from it.
          <u>Support</u>
          human rights.
          We believe in that.
          <u>Support</u>
          self-determination.
          You know it's right.

By being prosodically separated from its grammatical object, the word "support" became part of a three-part repetition. The last phrase, "You know it's right," also echoed a number of repetitions of the formula "You're right" which were seen in (25).

   Immediately before he began his life story, Jackson intensified his voice and also intensified repetition and variation of the phrase "Don't surrender":

(31)   <u>Do not surrender</u> to drugs.
          The best drug policy is a no first use.
          <u>Don't surrender</u> with needles and cynicism,
          Let's have no first use
          on the one hand,
          our clinics on the other.
          <u>Never surrender</u>,
          young America.

Go forward.
America must <u>never surrender</u> to malnutrition.
We can feed the hungry and clothe
the naked,
<u>We must never surrender,</u>
We must go forward,
<u>We must never surrender</u> to illiteracy.
Invest in our children,
<u>Never surrender,</u>
and go forward,
<u>We must never surrender</u> to inequality,
. . .
<u>Don't surrender</u>, my friends.
Those who have AIDS tonight,
you deserve our compassion.
Even with AIDS
<u>you must not surrender</u> in your wheelchairs.
. . .
But even in your wheelchairs,
<u>don't you give up.</u>
. . .
<u>Don't you surrender and don't you give up.</u>
<u>Don't you surrender and don't you give up.</u>

Interspersed with the "don't surrender" formula were repetitions of
"go forward" and other repetitive strategies. In this section, Jackson's voice became strong and loud. The last repetitions of "Don't
you surrender and don't you give up" punctuated loud applause
from the audience (a far more active and interactive way to manage
audience response than simply waiting for it to die down). It was
immediately after this section that Jackson turned to the telling of
his life story that climaxed his performance.

   Following the section in which he told his life story, Jackson
reiterated the phrases, "You can make it," and "Don't surrender."
In these he incorporated a parallel construction that he also used
in his 1984 convention speech, one marked by anadiplosis, beginning an utterance with the same unit that ended the preceding utterance. In both addresses he said, near the end of each speech:[7]

(32) Don't you surrender.
  →   Suffering breeds character,
  →   Character breeds faith,
  →   In the end,
        faith will NOT disappoint.
        You must not surrender.

The 1988 speech then ended with a short play of a number of repeated phrases culminating with four repetitions of "Keep hope alive!," the phrase that was the rallying cry of his campaign.

Conclusion

In this speech, Jackson used repetition, dialogue, and details, along with other involvement strategies such as storytelling and tropes, to communicate his ideas and move his audience toward acceptance of them and of him.

   Considering the emotional impact of Jackson's oratory as seen in audience reactions and journalists' reports, and recalling the emotion I felt when I first heard and saw his speech on television, and felt again each time I watched the videotape to check transcription for this study, I returned in my mind to the response expressed by the delegate who said, "It's a feeling you get when you go to church. You must know the man is telling the truth." This response suggested to me that Jackson's performance provides a contemporary analogue to the classical poetic performance discussed by Havelock (1963).

   Like Reverend King's "I Have a Dream" speech, Reverend Jackson's political oratory is modeled on what Davis (1985) calls "the performed African-American sermon." It is performed in a way comparable to what Lord (1960) documented for contemporary Yugoslavian oral bards and what Havelock described for ancient ones: The poet spontaneously creates a discourse in performance by repeating and elaborating previously used formulas in new ways. This oral composition strategy is what Drew described when she said Jackson "strayed far from his text, and pieced together a speech composed of a hodgepodge of his greatest hits from the campaign trail." Although she may well have been correct in observing weaknesses in Jackson's performance, her negative view of straying from a written text and recycling formulas from previous speeches is influenced by a different oratorical tradition.

   Havelock's interest in oral formulaic performance, as discussed in chapter 2, grew out of his attempt to explain why Plato would have banned poets from political processes in the Republic. He noted that classical poets were orators who moved audiences emotionally. This is the way he describes the effect of their performances:

the audience listened, repeated, and recalled and so absorbed it. . . . [The performer] sank his personality in his performance. His audience in turn would remember only as they entered effectively and sympathetically into what he was saying and this in turn meant that they became his servants and submitted to his spell. . . . Psychologically it is an act of personal commitment, of total engagement and of emotional identification. (159–60)

"Total engagement and emotional identification" seem to describe the response of the delegate who *felt* Jackson must be "telling the truth." This emotional source of persuasion, Havelock suggests, is the reason for Plato's distrust of oratorical power.

My interest has been to identify the linguistic strategies that account for oratorical power by creating the "emotional identification" Havelock describes. I suggest, based on the foregoing analysis, that the persuasive power of oratory lies in the artful elaboration of involvement strategies – the same linguistic strategies that create involvement and make understanding possible in everyday conversation.

Readers, like journalists, will differ in their evaluations of Jackson's speech, but there is no doubt that many found it moving. That the Reverend Jesse Jackson has become a major force in American politics makes clear that involvement strategies play a formidable role in the public life of the nation as well as in the private lives of conversationalists, as I have tried to show in this book.

Afterword
Toward a humanistic linguistics

In 1985 I directed a summer Institute entitled "Humanistic approaches to linguistic analysis," with support from the National Endowment for the Humanities. In a lecture delivered at that Institute, Becker (1988:31) explains,

> The problem many of us have with science is that it does not touch the personal and particular. ... By adopting scientific constraints on the statements we make, we move away from the very thing we want to study. This seems to me to be one of the major points of Wittgenstein's *Philosophical Investigations*.

This accurately reflects the kinds of constraints most see as required by science, but there is no reason that scientific, in the sense of rigorous, disciplined, and systematic, investigation must exclude the personal and the particular. Just as the scientific study of whales or elephants or chimpanzees must include painstaking observation and description of particular, individual creatures interacting with each other in their natural environments, so the scientific study of language must include the close analysis of particular instances of discourse as they naturally occur in human and linguistic context.

A similar perspective is expressed by Sacks (1987:41), who shows that modern medicine, in contrast with earlier naturalistic medical studies, has resulted in "a real gain of knowledge coupled with a real loss in general understanding." Pleading for a reintegration of what has been split into a "soulless neurology" and a "bodiless psychiatry," Sacks calls for a "personal or Proustian physiology," a "personalistic neurology" (1986:3).

Science can embrace not only the personal and the particular but the aesthetic as well. In introducing the papers on discourse delivered at the 1981 Georgetown University Round Table on

Languages and Linguistics, I confronted the question of whether linguistics should be counted among the humanities or the sciences or even the arts. I cited Judson's (1980) claim that science is an art and his quotation of Nobel laureate physicist Paul Dirac who said, "It is more important to have beauty in one's equations than to have them fit experiment" (11). Linguistics too can be scientific, humanistic, and aesthetic. It must be, as we are engaged in examining the eternal tension between fixity and novelty, creativity within constraints.

I suggested at the outset that discourse analysis is an inclusionary multidiscipline. The inclusion of a humanistic approach to linguistic analysis is not intended to expel any other type. Becker (1988:20) said that he spoke "not in opposition to another kind of linguistics, but rather to identify a kind of work which needs doing." Analysis of involvement strategies in conversation, and how other genres (particularly literary discourse) take up and elaborate these strategies, seems to me a kind of work which needs doing. It is in this spirit that I offer this book.

Appendix I
Sources of examples

Following is a list of major sources of examples and background information about their collection and choice.

Thanksgiving dinner conversation

The largest number of examples is taken from transcripts of tape-recorded conversation. The largest number of these are from two and a half hours of dinner table conversation that I recorded on Thanksgiving day 1978. This conversation comprised the material for my book *Conversational style* (1984), as well as a number of other papers I have written. With a few exceptions, the examples used here are being used for the first time. Participants in the conversation were six middle-class white professionals between the ages of 29 and 35. The dinner was at the home of Steve (33). Guests included his brother Peter (35) and his best friend Deborah (33), who is also the author. (Names other than mine are pseudonymous.) Steve, Peter, and I are natives of New York City of East European Jewish background. In the course of the study that led to the aforementioned book, I discovered that these three speakers used many similar discourse strategies which together constitute a conversational style that I characterized as "high-involvement": When faced with a choice between observing positive face by showing involvement vs. observing negative face by refraining from imposing, they were more likely to choose to show involvement and risk imposing. Of the other guests, David (29), Steve's friend of four years, and Chad (30), David's friend since college but a new acquaintance of everyone else, are from Southern California. David's background is English/Irish; Chad's is English and Italian; both were raised Catholic. In a number of ways David's and Chad's conversational styles are similar to each other (though in other ways they are not); I characterized their style as "high-considerateness": When faced with a choice between positive and negative face, they were more likely to choose not to impose and risk offense by insufficient display of involvement. (I would not characterize their styles as "low-involvement" because "involvement" is always the happy result when styles are shared.) The sixth guest, Sally (29), a native of London,

England, and daughter of an American mother and British father of East European Jewish background, had previously lived with Steve for six years and thus knew Deborah and David well. Her style was the most divergent from the others', as she grew up in a different country.

Participants knew they were being taped. However, as sociolinguists have repeatedly observed and argued, the length of the interaction and the social relationships among participants ensured that they shortly became swept up in the interaction and forgot the presence of the taperecorder. This then raises an ethical question: If they have forgotten about the tape recorder, is their informed consent not thereby canceled? To correct for this, each participant later listened to the sections I analyzed, approved their use, and further commented on the interaction from their own perspectives. (Further details and discussion of the participants, their relationships to each other, the situation, and issues related to the use of "natural" conversation as data are to be found in Tannen 1984.)

Other conversational discourse

Some examples are taken from conversational discourse recorded by students in my classes at Georgetown University. These were collected in either of two ways. Students in the course entitled "Discourse Analysis: Conversation " are instructed to record casual conversation in which they happen to take part. From the tapes they record, they choose and transcribe a short segment that focuses on a coherent topic and has an identifiable beginning and end. Students typically record conversations among their friends or family or a combination of both. Students in the course entitled "Discourse Analysis: Narrative" begin in a similar way, but they choose and transcribe a segment in which a speaker tells a story. Most have little or no difficulty locating a story that arose "naturally" in conversation. A few each semester do and consequently resort to eliciting a story by asking someone to tell them one. Most of these conversations and narratives occurred face-to-face; a few occurred on the telephone.

Elicited stories

In addition to the stories recorded by my students which were found in interaction among friends and family, I collected a corpus of narratives that I elicited from speakers while I was associated with the NIMH-supported "pear project" under the direction of Wallace Chafe at the University of California, Berkeley (see Chafe 1980 for a collection of papers from that project). My first intention, inspired by the previously described study in which I compared New York and California conversational styles, was to collect comparable stories in California and New York. At the suggestion of Charlotte Linde, I took advantage of the recent opening of a subway in San Francisco to record "subway stories." The results were other than what

I had sought. In San Francisco and Berkeley, I was unable to elicit narratives about experiences people had had on the subway. What I got instead were evaluations of the new subway system. In New York City, my question, "Have you had any interesting experiences on the subway?" did easily elicit subway stories, but it turned out that the vast majority of those stories were told by women about having been molested on the subway by men. Therefore, when I sought a comparable collection of stories in Athens while living there in 1975, I asked not about subway experiences but rather, "Have you ever been molested?" Every woman I asked responded in the affirmative, and willingly offered accounts for my audition and taping. In this as in all other instances in which I have taped modern Greek discourse, I found everyone eager to fulfill my request with minimal or no questions asked. The stories analyzed in this book include not only those told by Americans about having been molested but other "subway stories" as well. Most of these stories, in English and Greek, were elicited in small groups, sometimes made up of women I had not previously known. In most cases I began by telling my own. In a few cases I elicited the stories in dyadic conversation with someone I knew well.

Literary discourse

The main focus of this book is conversational discourse. However, the larger project of which it is a part is concerned with the relationship between conversational and literary discourse, and my interest in the strategies analyzed here was sparked by observations about this relationship. Some examples, therefore, are taken from literary discourse. My primary source for this type of discourse is a novel, *Household words*, by Joan Silber, which won the Hemingway Award for first novels. I chose this novel for a number of reasons. My main motivation was that my original research design called for comparing a writer's fiction with the same writer's conversation. I had comparable samples in modern Greek because I had written a book about a modern Greek novelist, *Lilika Nakos*, and I had tapes of her in conversation with me and with other Greeks. I was not fully satisfied with my plan to use talk show interviews with American writers as a source of their conversation, because, as noted in chapter 5, such talk is more formal than casual conversation. By chance, I came across a reference to the writer Joan Silber in *The New York Times Book Review* and recognized the name as belonging to someone who had been my best friend when we were teenagers. I looked her up; we met; and by recording our conversation, I was able to obtain the kind of language sample I needed. Based on my own reading of Silber's novel as well as the external evidence of the award she had won (she was subsequently awarded a Guggenheim as well), I was convinced that hers was an effective novel, and, equally important for my purposes, a lyrical (rather than minimalist) one. *Household words* is about a woman, Rhoda, whose husband dies: It recounts her marriage, her widowhood, her raising her children alone, and her death.

Drama

In addition to my desire to compare speaking and writing by the same person, I was interested in comparing discourse of different genres about the same subject. Here too I had an unusual opportunity. A playwright, Glen Merzer, came across an article I had written for *New York Magazine* about New York conversational style. He wrote to me and asked to see the complete Thanksgiving transcript as well as my dissertation, which eventually became the book *Conversational style*. He was sufficiently intrigued to write a play about a graduate student in linguistics from New York, living in California, who tape records a Thanksgiving dinner among her friends in order to write her dissertation based on it. That play, *Taking comfort*, received Equity productions in Lansing, Michigan and Los Angeles, California, as well as a number of other productions and readings. Its characters, though clearly different from the Thanksgiving participants I taped, are also clearly inspired by them. This play provides another source of literary discourse in another genre, drama, that I discuss in relation to the Thanksgiving transcript.

Appendix II
Transcription conventions

Examples are presented in poetic lines rather than prosaic blocks. I believe that this better captures their rhythm and makes the text easier to read. Lines represent intonation units, to capture in print the natural chunking achieved in speaking by a combination of intonation, prosody, pausing, and verbal particles such as discourse and hesitation markers. (See Chafe 1986 for a discussion of the multidisciplinary research that documents the universality of such chunking in oral discourse.) In transcription, punctuation represents intonation, not grammatical conventions. In most cases I depart from my previous practice, and, I believe, the most common practice, of representing selected expressions in reduced form, such as "gonna" for "going to," "hadda" for "had to," "woulda" for "would have," because I have been convinced by Preston (1982) that such nonstandard spelling is always inconsistently applied and has the effect of giving readers a negative impression of the speaker, an impression that does not follow from the casual pronunciation in speech. Preston (1985) found that readers consistently rate the social class of speakers lower if their conversation is transcribed using such nonstandard spellings. Because such reduced phonological realizations are standard in casual speech, representing them by a nonstandard spelling misrepresents them.

Transcription conventions

The following transcription conventions are used.

.	indicates sentence final falling intonation
,	indicates clause-final intonation ("more to come")
?!	indicates exclamatory intonation
. . .	three dots in transcripts indicate pause of ½ second or more
..	two dots indicate perceptible pause of less than ½ second
. . .	three dots show ellipsis, parts omitted in quotations from other sources
´	accent indicates primary stress
CAPS	indicate emphatic stress
Í	accent on words already in CAPS shows emphatic stress

⌈ Brackets (with or without top flap) show overlap.
⌊ Two voices going at once. ⌞ Simultaneously.
    Brackets with top flap reversed show
    latching.⌉
            ⌊ No perceptible inter-turn pause

:   colon following vowel indicates elongated vowel sound
::   extra colon indicates longer elongation
-         hyphen indicates glottal stop: sound abruptly cut off
" "   quotation marks highlight dialogue
          Underlining highlights key words and phrases
→   Left arrows highlight key lines
          arrow at right of line indicates →
          speaker's turn continues without interruption →
          so look for continuation on succeeding line
A   upper case "A" indicates pronunciation of the indefinite arti-
          cle ("a") as the diphthong /ey/. (Note that distinguishing
          between the unstressed form of the article "a" and the hesi-
          tation marker "uh" is always an interpretation, as they both
          have the same phonetic realization (/ʌ/).
/words/ in slashes show uncertain transcription
/?/   indicates inaudible utterance
( )   Parentheses indicate "parenthetical" intonation: lower ampli-
          tude and pitch plus flattened intonation contour

Greek transliteration

Transliteration from Greek is based on the system developed by Peter Bien and Julia Loomis for the Modern Greek Studies Association, with a few minor changes. This system has weaknesses and inconsistencies that will be particularly apparent to those with linguistic training, but I use it because more linguistically sophisticated transliteration systems confuse readers who are not linguistically trained. A few conventions that may benefit from explanation:

    dh = /ð/, the Greek letter delta (δ), a voiced interdental fricative as in English "then."

    th = /θ/, the Greek letter theta (θ), a voiceless interdental fricative as in English "thick."

    ch = /x/, the Greek letter chi (χ), a voiceless velar fricative not found in English; rather like "h" with more constriction in one's throat.

    x = /ks/, the Greek letter (ξ), pronounced like the English letter "x" as in "ax."

    ou = /u/, the Greek letters omicron upsilon (ου) spelled in English as in Greek, and pronounced like the "ou" in the English word "you."

    ai = /ε/, the Greek letters alpha iota (αι), pronounced like the vowel in English "met."

i = /i/, pronounced like the vowel in "see," is used to represent the Greek letters iota (ι) and eta (η). These are two of five Greek orthographic variants for this vowel sound. The three others follow.

y = /i/, the Greek letter upsilon (υ). (Note it can be pronounced this way in English too, e.g. softly.)

ei = /i/, the Greek letters epsilon iota (ει). (Note these letters have this pronunciation in the English word "weird.")

oi = /i/, the Greek letters omicron iota (οι).

Notes

1 Introduction

1 The crucial role of similarity relations as a key to meaning in language motivated Jakobson's frequently reiterated interest in parallelism, inspired by his reading of Peirce, as Waugh and Neufield (in press) explain. They note, for example, that the simplest type of icon in Peirce's system is the image, which is physically similar to, or imitative of, the meaning it represents.

2 Mary Catherine Bateson (1984:107) reports that she became interested in the field of linguistics upon reading Sapir's *Language*. After receiving her doctorate in linguistics in 1970, however, she redefined herself as an anthropologist, because "the balance of professional interest in linguistics had shifted from the diversity of human patterns of communication to highly formalistic studies." It seemed to her then impossible "to combine and sustain my interests in some coherent pattern" within the discipline of linguistics. The rise of discourse analysis should preclude the expulsion of linguists and potential linguists with interests in "the diversity of human patterns of communication" from the field.

2 Involvement in discourse

1 Moreover, I characterize the styles of three of the participants in this conversation as "high-involvement." By this I mean that they put more emphasis on serving the need for positive face, that is, honoring others' need for involvement. This is in contrast to the styles of the other speakers, which I characterize as "high-considerateness," because they put more emphasis on serving the need for negative face, that is, honoring others' need not to be imposed on, or, put positively, their need for independence.

2 In their introduction, the translators of Voloshinov ([1929] 1986) explain that the widely held belief that this work and others published under the names of Bakhtin's friends Voloshinov and Medvedev are actually the work of Bakhtin is not firmly established.

3 In responding to a draft of that early study, Susan Philips reminded me

that the general significance of my particular insight about the short
story was the importance of genre. This is comparable to Goffman's
([1964] 1972) reminder of the importance of the situation in interaction, or, in the terms of his later work (Goffman 1974), of the frame:
what individuals think they are doing when they produce discourse.

4 For an example of a repeated discourse structure taken from examples
   analyzed here see note 15 chapter 3.

5 Levin (1982:112) notes, "The matter of elocution was divided in the
   ancient handbooks into three major categories: figures of speech,
   figures of thought, and tropes." In this schema, figures of speech played
   on form, figures of thought played on meaning, and "a trope involved
   the use of a word or phrase in an unaccustomed meaning" (121). I use
   the word trope, following Friedrich (1986) and Sapir (1977), in the
   sense that Levin suggests the ancient rhetoricians used the term "figures
   of thought": those figures that play on meaning rather than form.

6 In the Greek spoken narratives, dialogue was introduced with forms of
   "say" 71% of the time, in the Greek novel 69%. In the American
   English narratives, the percentage was 43% for spoken, 49% for written. But when instances of "tell" were added (in Greek there is only a
   single unmarked verb of saying), the percentages rose to 47% for the
   conversational stories and 52% for the novel.

7 For example, a reviewer criticizes an author for not accurately
   representing speech:

   Only in the chapters that attempt to render the sensibility of the native characters in their own words and idioms does the author falter; in his failure to capture the poetic subtlety and integrity of the patois, he too often suggests broken
   English and a limited intelligence. (Michael Thelwell, review of *Sting of the
   bee* by Seth Rolbein, *The New York Times Book Review*, October 4, 1987, p.
   28)

   This captures as well the danger of creating negative impressions of
   speakers through attempts to represent speech in writing, also a danger
   in the scholarly transcription of speech, as Preston (1982, 1985)
   demonstrates.

8 One must bear in mind, however, that when language is signed, then
   dialogue is also visual. In his current research, Sacks is investigating the
   implications of this and other factors involving the language of the
   deaf.

9 It is difficult to paraphrase Sacks's remarkable writing, so I will present
   a rather long passage, from a footnote as it happens, which captures
   this seemingly magical power of music to restore movement to otherwise paralyzed people:

   This power of music to integrate and cure, to liberate the Parkinsonian and give
   him freedom while it lasts ('You are the music/while the music lasts', T. S.
   Eliot), is quite fundamental, and seen in every patient. This was shown beauti-
   fully, and discussed with great insight, by Edith T., a former music teacher. She
   said that she had become 'graceless' with the onset of Parkinsonism, that her

movements had become 'wooden, mechanical – like a robot or doll', that she had lost her former 'naturalness' and 'musicalness' of movement, that – in a word – she had been 'unmusicked'. Fortunately, she added, the disease was 'accompanied by its own cure'. We raised an eyebrow: 'Music,' she said, 'as I am unmusicked, I must be remusicked.' Often, she said, she would find herself 'frozen', utterly motionless, deprived of the power, the impulse, the *thought*, of any motion; she felt at such times 'like a still photo, a frozen frame' – a mere optical flat, without substance or life. In this state, this statelessness, this timeless irreality, she would remain, motionless-helpless, *until music came*: 'Songs, tunes I knew from years ago, catchy tunes, rhythmic tunes, the sort I loved to dance to.'

With this sudden imagining of music, this coming of spontaneous inner music, the power of motion, action, would suddenly return, and the sense of substance and restored personality and reality; now, as she put it, she could 'dance out of the frame', the flat frozen visualness in which she was trapped, and move freely and gracefully: 'It was like suddenly remembering myself, my own living tune.' But then, just as suddenly, the inner music would cease, and with this all motion and actuality would vanish, and she would fall instantly, once again, into a Parkinsonian abyss. (294–5)

Sacks goes on, but this excerpt suggests the way he conveys, here and elsewhere, that music is an essential element in human movement and human life.

10 It might be thought that the discourse type which is distinguished from both conversational and literary discourse is expository prose, a genre which purports to convince by means of logical persuasion. In reality, however, all discourse operates on the coherence constraints which I describe. McCloskey (1985) demonstrates that economic theories which come to predominate are no more accurate than others in predicting economic developments; rather, the ones that win out among professional economists are those that exhibit rhetorical elegance.

3 **Repetition in conversation: toward a poetics of talk**
Earlier versions of parts of this chapter appear in: "Repetition in Conversation: Toward a Poetics of Talk," *Language* 63 (1987): 3.574–605; "Repetition in conversation as spontaneous formulaicity," *Text* 7 (1987): 3.215–43; and "Ordinary conversation and literary discourse: coherence and the poetics of repetition," *The uses of linguistics*, edited by Edward Bendix (Annals of the New York Academy of Sciences, in press).

1 I have borrowed this quotation from Law (1985:26). It was Becker (1988) who called my attention to Gertrude Stein's use of repetition. According to Walker (1984:43), "The final version of *The making of Americans* was shaped by [Stein's] increasingly radical commitment to presenting repetition as the 'reality' that informs human history."

2 Note however that the intonation shifted from stressing "could" in "couldn't care less" to "I" and "less" in "I could care LESS." If the new form is uttered with stress on "could" ("I could care less") it seems to emphasize the change in meaning rather than mask it.

3 The fact that I used the same expression in speaking about this topic with different people on different occasions is an example of individual diachronic repetition. It seems that when we tell about the same thing repeatedly, we often make use of phrasings we have previously devised and found effective.

4 My thanks to Diane Tong for reporting this fused formula and to Carolyn Adger for reporting "pipe in." Jane Frank reported a conversation including the expression "humble crow" without having noticed that the formula was fused, evidence that such fusions are perfectly acceptable and often unnoticed in conversation.

5 Heidegger's sense of "fore-having" is also rendered "fore-sight" and "fore-conception."

6 The work of Gumperz (1982) elaborately demonstrates that people often fail to recognize the extent to which this is true. Not realizing that interlocutors of differing cultural or subcultural backgrounds are talking in a way that is routinized and commonplace in their speech community, many cross-cultural conversationalists draw unwarranted (often negative but possibly positive) conclusions about the others' personalities, abilities, and intentions. See also the Introduction and papers included in Tannen (1986c).

7 Except of course as it is being used and preserved here. And this use is in itself a repetition of another: Paul Hopper (1988b), having read my discussion of this example in a draft of a paper, made reference to it in a paper of his, unbeknownst to me. Unbeknownst to him, I subsequently deleted this section from the paper he cited, leaving his citation as an echo, a trace, a quotation of a source that had since ceased to exist. It is partly to re-enter that charmed circle of reference that I reinstate the example here.

8 The review of research on repetition referred to earlier (Tannen 1987a) includes many studies of child discourse.

9 On the original pear story project, we collected narratives from both women and men, but we used only the women's narratives in order to avoid having to double our data to take into account gender differences. However, two of my students, Jane Patrick and Susan Dodge, compared the American narratives told by men to those told by women. They found that the men used more linking repetition as transitions, where the women used more hesitations and fillers. (The Greek example presented here exhibits both linking repetition and hesitations.) The result was that the men's narratives, on the whole, appeared more "fluent."

10 Here and elsewhere, I focus on the positive functions of repetition, because they are less commonly acknowledged, and because it is my natural predilection. I realize, however, that for every positive use there is a negative one. Repetition can be used to challenge, question, mock, ridicule, and trivialize. For example, Gilligan (1982) describes an experimental interview designed to test children's moral develop-

ment. The interviewer, finding a girl's responses to be inadequate because they do not fit the standard model that was developed based on boys' responses, repeats the questions in an effort to encourage the expected response:

> But as the interviewer conveys through the repetition of questions that the answers she gave were not heard or not right, Amy's confidence begins to diminish, and her replies become more constrained and unsure. (28–9)

Thus, if repeating another's words shows ratification of them, repeating one's questions shows dissatisfaction with the other's responses. Moreover, for every effective use, there can be an ineffective one. And what is effective for one speaker may seem ineffective to another. For example, I was told by a colleague whom I complimented on his effective use of repetition in lecturing that his wife thinks he repeats too much. Two possible sources of this difference in valuation are his wife's different cultural background and a phenomenon I call (Tannen 1986a) "intimate criticism": the inclination to evaluate negatively habits and mannerisms of those one is closest to.

11 My thanks to Victoria Krauss for recording and initially transcribing the conversation in which this and (2) occurred, and to Antonia Nicosia for (3).

12 The sense in which grammar can be iconic has been suggested to me by Maschler (1987) following Becker (ms.).

13 In composing this sentence, I paraphrased several lines from the transcript, telescoping action and eliminating repetition. This is how Terry worded her recommendation:

> I know!
> Go up to Key Bridge
> and stand in the middle of Key Bridge
> and watch the water go under the bridge.
> THAT's a good way to daydream.

That summarizing often entails eliminating repetition (and consequent musical rhythm) indicates a type of repetition that is characteristic of speaking and accounts in part for the poetic character of speech.

14 The repetition of "ice" in Chad's utterance raises the question of the status of self-repetitions which seem to be false starts. Ochs (1979) considers them lexical repetitions. I believe, however, that a repetition which is part of a false start and is therefore seemingly unintentional differs fundamentally from one which seems intentional. Norrick (1987) takes a similar view. Nonetheless, "ice" is repeated, and the repetition affects the texture of the text. Furthermore, false starts, hesitations, and other errors cannot be viewed solely from the perspective of cognitive processing. From the social perspective, they may be purposeful in terms of presentation of self: As Lakoff (1979) observes, a hesitant speaker may be more likable.

15 There is a striking similarity in structure and rhythm between this four-unit utterance and the one cited in note 13. Consider them together:

> Go up to <u>Key Bridge</u>
> and stand in the middle of <u>Key Bridge</u>
> and watch the water go under <u>the bridge</u>.
> THAT'S a good way to daydream.

> Yknow, and he'd set up <u>a room</u>,
> and he'd describe <u>the room</u>,
> and people in <u>the room</u>
> and where they were placed,

This illustrates the level of repetition I have been referring to as longer discourse sequences.

16 Playwright Glen Merzer found this three-line repetition amusing enough to reproduce it verbatim in his play, *Taking comfort* (see Appendix I for an explanation of the relation between this conversation and that play).

17 It is not only humor that is repeated for savoring. In the following example from a short story (Mattison 1988:31) both self- and allo-repetition show appreciation for the gutsiness of a statement. In the story, a high school freshman is being harassed in his gym class because he is the shortest boy in the class. He wants to put off taking gym for a year, until he has grown. His mother calls the school guidance counselor to enlist her aid. When she returns from the telephone call, she announces:

> "I said maybe we were making too much of it, but she just said, 'Well, I'll yank him out!' Just like that – 'I'll *yank* him out!'"

When the father returns home, he is told the story with the key phrase appreciatively repeated:

> "'I'll yank him out!'" Philip repeats with satisfaction.

18 Here breathy, loud voice quality signifies rhetorical disbelief, or appreciation. Such use of displayed disbelief as a sign of appreciation is not used or recognized by all Americans. Having read my account of Steve's use of this strategy in *Conversational style*, David commented that he finally understood a way in which his good friend Steve often inadvertently hurt his feelings. When Steve showed appreciation of something David said by a display of disbelief, David understood it not as a show of appreciation but as a literal lack of belief in his veracity: If it was so unbelievable, it must not have happened, so David must be mistaken or misrepresenting. Having previously commented on this phenomenon in print (Tannen 1986a), I have heard from others who report experiencing similar misunderstandings due to this difference in conversational style.

19 Later in this chapter I cite the Reverend Martin Luther King's "I Have a Dream" speech. A tape recording of the original performance of this speech reveals frequent response calls from members of the audience.

20 Cf. the two excerpts juxtaposed in note 15. This excerpt has a structure again reminiscent of the other two, in that the repeated word is
a stressed noun coming at the end of each subsequent line. In contrast,
this speaker uttered four such lines, whereas those cited in note 15
uttered three.

21 In addition to repetition, this excerpt also includes (as Paul Hopper
pointed out to me) an example of the figure of speech, chiasmus:
reversing the order of constituents in immediate juxtaposition:

American teachers and teachers from other lands
   X   Y   Y   X

22 The text is taken from Kywell (1974), where only the last segment of
the speech, its most ritualized and best known part, is reproduced. In
a coincidence that was quite uncanny, I happened to be revising this
section on the twenty-fifth anniversary of the March on Washington at
which this speech was delivered. In commemoration of that anniversary, National Public Radio aired excerpts from that march, including
a tape recording of King's speech. This provided the opportunity to
check the transcription and observe the paralinguistic effects that accompanied and reinforced the repetition and other poetic strategies
that characterized King's masterful performance. I have imposed line
breaks on this basis.

23 From Davis (1985:77):

> Previously, "formula" was defined as a "group of hemistich phrases shaped into
> an irrhythmic unit when spoken to express an aspect of a central theme." The
> irregularity of the sermonic line is made rhythmic, not uniformly rhythmical,
> through the techniques of melisma, dramatic pause, emphatic repetition, and a
> host of devices commonly associated with African-American music. The most
> important characteristic of the formula, however, is not the irrhythmic line. The
> most important characteristics of the African-American sermonic formula are
> the groups of irrhythmic lines shaped around a core idea.

Shortly thereafter, Davis refers to King's "I Have a Dream" speech as
an example of such a sermon.

24 My thanks to Ahmet Egriboz for calling my attention to this passage.

25 For example, in line 8, I offered "Columbus Circle" as a show of understanding of Steve's description. In line 9 Steve incorporated my offer
into his description: "Right on Columbus Circle." He then repeated it
again in line 10 ("Here's Columbus Circle,") linking his continuing exegesis to this anchor. (This is a conversational use of the previously
mentioned figure of speech, anadiplosis: beginning a new utterance
with the word or phrase that ended the previous one.)

26 Another neurological disease characterized by compulsive repetition is
OCD, Obsessive-Compulsive Disorder, a disease whose sufferers feel
compelled to repeat gestures, motions, and words. Formerly thought
to be primarily psychogenic, OCD has been shown to have a strong
biological component by Dr. Judith Rappaport (1989), who character-

izes it as "a mental hiccough" and has found that it too can be at least
partially controlled by the administration of a drug.

4 **"Oh talking voice that is so sweet": constructing dialogue in
conversation**
Earlier versions of some of the material in this chapter is in "Waiting
for the mouse: Constructed dialogue in conversation," *The dialogic
emergence of culture*, edited by Bruce Mannheim and Dennis Tedlock
(Philadelphia: University of Pennsylvania Press, in press); "Introducing
constructed dialogue in Greek and American conversational and literary narratives," *Direct and indirect speech*, edited by Florian Coulmas
(Berlin: Mouton, 1986, 311–22); "The orality of literature and the
literacy of conversation," *Language, literacy, and culture: Issues of
society and schooling*, edited by Judith Langer (Norwood, NJ: Ablex,
1987, 67–88), and "Hearing voices in conversation, fiction, and mixed
genres," *Linguistics in context: Connecting observation and understanding*, edited by Deborah Tannen (Norwood, NJ: Ablex, 1988,
89–113).
1 Even seemingly made-up words must be patterned on familiar phonological and morphological configurations to have meaning at all. For
example, the playful neologisms of Lewis Carroll's "Jabberwocky" are
traceable to familiar words and set in regular syntactic frames. "'Twas
brillig" suggests a scene-setting description of weather reminiscent of
"brilliant;" "slithy toves" suggests creatures ("toves," resembling
"toads"?) characterized by the adjective "slithy" which blends "sliding,"
"slimy," "blithe," and so on.
2 My thanks to Carolyn Kinney for calling this proverb to my attention
and Hayib Sosseh for translating it.
3 There is a burgeoning and overwhelming literature on the structure
and functions of narrative. Since this book is not primarily about narrative, I cannot adequately cover these sources. A few are mentioned
in chapter 2. Readers seeking an overview of linguistic work on narrative might consult the entry entitled "Narratives in conversation" by
Charlotte Linde in the forthcoming *Oxford International Encyclopedia
of Linguistics*. Work by Labov and Waletzky (1967) and Labov (1972)
are classic on narrative structure, as is Kirshenblatt-Gimblett (1974) on
narrative function. Schiffrin (1984) and Basso (1984) are major contributions to analysis of the function of storytelling in conversation; Johnstone (in preparation) explores regional narratives in interaction. In
addition to the body of work by linguists, sociolinguists, anthropologists, and discourse analysts, a recent book by Bruner (1987) is devoted
to the importance of narrative as a cognitive mode, and Oliver Sacks
(1986) has much to say on the subject, as seen in chapter 2.
4 Note too that the dialogue expresses the speaker's reaction in terms of
a simile: "like a bolt."

5 Dennis Tedlock pointed out this further recursiveness. Adams (1987) presents an intriguing discussion of "the two contexts and their relationship to each other" in quotation of sources in scholarly writing.

6 Yet again, I have separated the strategies I am investigating to give order to my analysis, but the texts continually confound me. This short excerpt depends crucially not only on dialogue but also on repetition of the word "listening," on the simile "like a mouse from its hole," and on the visual image of a scene created by the simile.

7 Unless one speaks of absent parties with the intention that one's remarks be repeated to them. I believe this is a manipulation of the more common situation in which one does not foresee one's remarks being repeated. Similarly, mistreatment of individuals who are members of groups seen as "other" is made possible by their not being seen as persons. I am told that the word for members of their own tribe, in some American Indian languages, is simply "human being." This seems an explicit expression of what underlies most people's world view: only those who are seen as fundamentally like one are deeply believed to be persons. Surely this accounts for much of the dreadful cruelty humans inflict on just some other humans.

8 The examples in this section come from discourse recorded and initially transcribed by students in my discourse analysis classes. I thank them for their permission to use them: Example (1) Faith Powell, (2) Deborah Lange, (3) Nancy Zelasko, (4) Jane White, (5) Karen Marcum, (6), which I taped and spoke, was originally transcribed by Tulinabo Mushingi, (7) L. H. Malsawma, (8) David Robinson, (10) and (17) Diane Hunter Bickers, (11) Mary Ann Pohl, (12) Wendy Zweben, (13) Susan Huss, (14) Gayle Berens, (18) Kimberly Murphy. Names in all transcripts are pseudonymous, except mine.

9 In a study of how dialogue is introduced in conversation and fiction, I found use of "be + like" to introduce dialogue to be fairly frequent in the conversational stories of college-age speakers (Tannen 1986b). That this locution strikes adult ears as marked is encapsulated by a colleague's remark that his teenaged daughter is "a native speaker of like English."

10 No system for transcribing intonation is satisfactory. I attempt to give a broad sense of intonational contour (but not, unfortunately, of voice quality) by using Bolinger's convention of arranging letters on the page in a way that reflects the rise and fall of pitch and amplitude. Elsewhere (Tannen 1988c) I use lines drawn over the printed words to indicate the intonation contours in the same lines that are presented here.

11 This is in keeping with Goffman's (1959) observation that doctors, when they function professionally, do not represent themselves as individuals but as representatives of a team, of doctors as a group.

12 No doubt the fact that the stories were being told in a group (as explained in Appendix I) enhanced their elaboration since the large audience created more of a performance atmosphere and each story

inspired the next. Many of the stories I collected from American women, however, also took place in a group, so this alone cannot account for the greater elaboration of the Greek stories.

13 The features typifying the Greek narratives that I identified (Tannen 1983a) as contributing to involvement are:

1 repetition
2 direct quotation in reported speech
   (a) dialogue exchanged
   (b) thoughts of speaker
   (c) thoughts of man
3 historical present verbs
4 ellipsis
   (a) deletion of verb of saying
   (b) deletion of copula
   (c) deletion of comment or proposition
5 sound-words
6 second person singular
7 minimal external evaluation

5 Imagining worlds: imagery and details in conversation and other genres

This chapter includes material that appears in "How is conversation like literary discourse?: The role of imagery and details in creating involvement," *Literacy and linguistics*, edited by Pamela Downing, Susan Lima, and Michael Noonan (Amsterdam and Philadelphia: John Benjamins, in press).

1 I am grateful to Paul Friedrich for bringing this quotation to my attention. It comes from Hughes and McCullough 1982:170.

2 The universality of the association of the meaning "small" with the sound /i/ is observed by Sapir (1929), Jespersen (1933), and Jakobson and Waugh (1979).

   For those who do not know, a sweet pea is a flower. In partial contradiction of my point about images, I was not entirely certain, when I first heard this utterance, whether sweet peas were flower or vegetable, and I certainly did not know (and still don't) what they look like. I did, however, get an image of a small thing growing – and all the other semantic and sonorous dynamics I describe were in play. Those who do know what sweet peas look like, and have personal memories involving them, will have different, richer associations, as Eleanor Berry reminded me.

3 When I checked this use of his story with my colleague, he responded in a letter clarifying, correcting, and elaborating the story. I reproduce here his repeat performance, an informally written account, partly because it is hard to resist the chance to compare spoken and written versions of the same story, but mostly because it points up a number of significant aspects of the use of details in narrative.

If my memory is right, what the customs man in Tallinn actually did was to try the screw in the bottom of my mother's lipstick, rather than to squeeze out her toothpaste (but I may be the guilty party here, because I sometimes like to improve a bit on reality). And in fact the story was – again if my memory is right – not so much on the Russo-Finnish war as on Estonian history, the achievements in Estonia between 1919 and 1940 (which the communist regime liked to belittle) and the way in which Estonia joined its Great Neighbor in 1940 (voluntarily and with delight, said the official version). My mother was then well over eighty and one of her old-age symptoms was an – even for her! – unusual absence of constraints. So if she thought a guide was talking rot she said so in no uncertain terms, in fact collecting her skirts and mounting the base of a patriotic statue to harangue the crowds from the same heights as the guide! And the guide was completely lost: she had enough respect for old age to find the situation difficult, and tried to joke it off, with little success as all the Finns in the group knew which version was historically correct.

In the matter of the toothpaste tube vs. the lipstick screw, my colleague is correct in suspecting his own embellishment. He definitely described to me a toothpaste tube, and for good reason: The image of toothpaste being squeezed out of a tube in a customs station creates a more amusing scene than the image of a screw being tested on a lipstick tube. In the matter of the Russo-Finnish war vs. Estonian history, I am sure that my constructive memory is at fault, as my knowledge of European history is weak enough for the point on which his mother differed with the Intourist guide to have become fuzzy. I am further intrigued by the graphic description now added of his octogenarian mother climbing on a statue to harangue the crowds from the same heights as the guide, a scene whose drama is heightened by the use of such words as "harangue" and "crowds," the account once more benefiting from the trope, hyperbole.

4 There is an irony here: The best storytellers (oral and literary) are adept not so much at retrieving such details accurately as at creating and using details that give the impression of verisimilitude. It is possible that there is an inverse relation between art and truth: the more truthful the detail sounds, the less likely it is to be literally accurate. In a similar way, as Lakoff and Tannen (1984) observe, transcripts of actual conversation strike the lay reader as incoherent, whereas the distilled dialogue of drama and fiction often strikes them as highly realistic. Writers frequently observe that they have to alter events to make them seem real.

5 This observation was made by Wendy Zweben, who recorded and transcribed the story.

6 The association of place names with stories that encapsulate cultural values is also found by Basso (1984) among the Western Apache.

7 My thanks to Jane Frank who had the conversation, recorded it, transcribed it, and identified the segment I am citing. Although other participants made occasional brief contributions during the speaker's discourse, I am omitting their contributions from this transcription because they are irrelevant to the point I am making here. About a year

after this conversation took place, I was amazed to find myself party to a conversation in which a remarkably similar list of languages was produced by a speaker (not I) in a similar context and spirit.

8 Jonathan Schell, "History in Sherman Park I," January 5, 1987, p. 58. Reading this, I wondered what this man would say about the level of detail that characterizes the magazine in which this article appears – indeed that characterizes this article – a highly marked level of detail for which *The New Yorker* is known and which, I believe, has something to do with its status as a highly literary magazine.

9 I am not suggesting that men do not tell details, just that they tell them about other topics, such as sports, politics, cars, fishing, machinery. This is supported by Friedrich (Friedrich and Attinasi in press), as well as much of the literature on gender and conversation.

10 Mary Catherine Bateson (1984:193) draws yet another parallel, between gossip and anthropology. She recalls that her mother, Margaret Mead, told her "you'll never be an anthropologist because you don't enjoy gossip, you're not really interested in the details of other people's lives."

11 The excerpt comes from a show aired on WAMU-FM, Washington DC, February 18, 1988. My thanks to host and guest for permission to use it. Strictly speaking, talk show (in England, chat show) talk is not conversation, but an interview. There is precedent in the sociolinguistic literature for using conversational interviews as conversational data, most notably the extended work of Schiffrin (for example, Schiffrin 1987). I will not tackle here the theoretical question of the status of such data but will note that it is a spoken genre intermediate between conversational and formal speaking, something more formal/planned than dinner-table conversation but less formal/planned than a lecture and far less formal/planned than an academic article.

12 Bawer (1988:421) reports a similar experience: In a radio talk show interview occasioned by his writing a newspaper op-ed piece (an opinion article that appears facing the editorial page) he notes, "when I'd spoken to the point most clearly and succinctly there had been no spontaneity on my part whatsoever. On the contrary, I'd been working from a script – reciting from memory, that is, the words of my op-ed piece."

13 Eleanor Berry pointed out that "elegant woman" is not specific; it leaves a lot to be imagined by the hearer. But it does, I submit, suggest a line of interpretation along which the hearer can imagine and therefore care about an image. Berry suggests, too, that such familiar themes for images are always in danger of slipping into cliche. This is so, I believe, because both effective art and cliche or stereotype operate on the familiarity or recognizability of pattern. Artists must seek a balance between fixity and novelty: using familiar patterns or altering them in order to comment on them or present them in a new light.

When I called Sussman to get his permission to use this excerpt, it emerged in our conversation that although the incident described in this striking image "really happened," it didn't actually happen at a single moment. In writing this memorable line, Sussman integrated impressions that he had experienced at different moments during the day. This is not prevarication but artistic creation: reworking experience to make it maximally evocative. The writer also provided further external evidence for the effectiveness of his image: It was upon reading this line in Sussman's NPR commentary that a *Washington Post* editor decided to consider hiring him for his current job. The editor remarked, "That's the best writing I've seen in weeks." (As a metacomment on the writing of this text, I now confess that I have just altered slightly Sussman's account, compressing two editors into one. As Sussman retold events to me, the general editor of the newspaper, on reading this image in the NPR commentary, made the remark cited above and referred Sussman to the editor of a new magazine section who offered him the job. It seemed to me, in composing this text, that detailing the participation of the two editors would lengthen the story without strengthening it. However, I used the verb "*consider* hiring him" rather than saying the editor offered him the job, because, this being a scholarly book, I wanted to be accurate as well as effective. Had I been writing a short story, I would simply have merged the two editors into one and portrayed him as reading the image and offering a job on the spot.)

14 My thanks to Steve Barish for bringing this excerpt, and the later one from John Barth's *Sabbatical*, to my attention.

15 If recalling a name is a sign of caring, failure to recall a name can be seen as a sign of lack of caring. I have heard complaints from people whose parents disapprove of their partners or friends and seem to display their disapproval subtly by habitually referring to them by the wrong names or failing to recall their names. In a positive manipulation of the same phenomenon, I have a friend who has remained in touch with my ex-husband because he is a friend of her husband. In an unnecessary but appreciated gesture of solidarity with me, she has persisted in referring to my ex-husband's second wife as "Whatshername." The metamessage, I believe, is intended (and taken) to be, "Even though I see her, I don't really care about her. You are the one who counts to me."

16 See Czikszentmihalyi (1978) for a discussion of the significance of attention.

17 In a letter to J. H. Reynolds dated February 3, 1818, Keats expressed just the opposite view: "Poetry should be great & unobtrusive, a thing which enters into one's soul, and does not startle it or amaze it with itself but with its subject." I would not want my citation of Jakobson's separation of the poetic function from others to be taken as an endorsement.

18 A possibility suggested by a member of an audience at which I talked about this is that the Skunk story, familiar to Native Americans, is

unfamiliar to me. Doubtless there is some truth to this, but I have
vividly recalled aspects of unfamiliar story types – just those aspects
which describe images. Such a one is "The war of the ghosts," an
Eskimo story used by Bartlett (1932) to demonstrate constructive
memory. (Bartlett showed that subjects who had heard the story of an
unfamiliar type tended to recast it in recall to make it conform more
closely to familiar story conventions, forgetting aspects that did not fit
into schemas meaningful to them.) For example I remember something
black coming out of a man's mouth when he dies, partly because it is
odd, and partly because it forms a graphic image in my mind.

6 **Involvement strategies in consort: literary nonfiction and political
oratory**
Parts of my analysis of Mary Catherine Bateson's book *Our own
metaphor* appear in "The orality of literature and the literacy of conversation," *Language, literacy, and culture: Issues of society and
schooling*, edited by Judith Langer (Norwood, NJ: Ablex, 1987, 67–
88) and "Hearing voices in conversation, fiction, and mixed genres" in
Linguistics in context: Connecting observation and understanding,
edited by Deborah Tannen (Norwood, NJ: Ablex, 1988, 89–113).
1 A similar image of Hasidic disdain for written materials disconnected
from people emerges in Myerhoff's (1978:271–2) account of a great
Hasidic rabbi who "ordered that all written records of his teachings be
destroyed. His words must be passed from mouth to mouth, learned
by and in heart."
2 Using a similar strategy in his address to the same convention, Senator
Edward Kennedy paid homage to his brother, the late John Kennedy,
by echoing his famous lines, "Ask not what your country can do for
you; ask what you can do for your country."
3 It is impossible to capture the rhythm, prosody, and voice quality of
this oral performance by transcribing its words. I began with a transcription purchased from the Federal News Service and refined the
transcription based on a videotape, supplying line breaks where Jackson paused or his intonation pattern marked the end of an intonation
unit. Many grammatical sentences ended with rising intonation, as I
have indicated by ending the transcribed sentence with a comma rather
than a period. If the following word nonetheless had the rhythmic
quality of a sentence beginning, I begin it with a capital letter. Jackson's voice was at times loud, insistent, and yelling; at times soft and
pleading; at times thick and cracking. Excerpts from Jackson's 1984
convention address are taken from *The New York Times*, July 18,
1984, p. A19.
4 It may have been the force of such morphological repetitions that triggered a speech error which was noted by a number of journalists:

> Dream of peace.
> Peace
> is rational and reasonable.
> War
> → is irrationable
> in this age,
> and unwinnable.

It seems that the "-able" from "reasonable" and "winnable" got stuck onto "rational" or "rational and reasonable" (a paraphrastic double), together with the addition of the prefix "ir-."

5 Yet another level of metaphoric play is what Lakoff and Johnson (1980) identify as an "up is good" metaphor that underlies many of our figures of speech: The ships' success would stem from "a higher reality" and "noble instincts" which emerge when we are "At our highest." In contrast, the ships will "drift" if we "satisfy our baser [i.e. lower] instincts."

6 So compelling was the rhythm of these repetitions reinforcing the quilt metaphor that it mattered not at all when Jackson omitted a word ("for"). When he told lesbians and gays, "when you fight against discrimination and a cure for AIDS," he did not mean that they fight "against" a cure for AIDS but rather that they fight *for* one. Furthermore, it is gay men, as a group, not lesbians, who are especially concerned with fighting for a cure for AIDS. But no matter. The message got through in the metamessage established by the list: that all the groups' and individuals' demands would be more likely met if they joined together.

7 *The New York Times* transcription of Jackson's 1984 speech omitted the word "end" in the phrase "in the end," yielding:

> Suffering breeds character.
> Character breeds faith,
> and in the faith will not disappoint.

My conjecture that this is a mistranscription is based in part on the form taken by the same construction in 1988.

References

Achebe, Chinua. 1958. *Things fall apart*. London: Heinemann.

Adams, Jon-K. 1987. Quotation and context. Paper presented at the Annual Meeting of International Pragmatics Association, Antwerp, Belgium.

Alberoni, Francesco. 1983. *Falling in love*. Trans. by Lawrence Venuti. New York: Random House.

Allen, Woody. 1982. *Four films of Woody Allen*. New York: Random House.

Auden, W. H. [1956]1986. Remarks on receiving award for "The shield of Achilles." "Three cheers for good marks": Writers on their prizes, 3, 46. *The New York Times Book Review*, November 16, 1986.

Bakhtin, M. M. [1975]1981. *The dialogic imagination*. Austin: The University of Texas Press.

    [1952–53]1986. The problem of speech genres. *Speech genres and other late essays*, ed. by Caryl Emerson and Michael Holquist, trans. by Vern W. McGee, 60–102. Austin: The University of Texas Press.

Barley, Nigel. 1972. A structural approach to the proverb and maxim with special reference to the Anglo-Saxon corpus. *Proverbium*, 20. 737–50.

Barry, Lynda. 1988. *The good times are killing me*. Seattle: The Real Comet Press.

Bartlett, Frederic C. 1932. *Remembering*. Cambridge: Cambridge University Press.

Basso, Keith H. 1984. "Stalking with stories": Names, places and moral narratives among the Western Apache. *Text, play, and story*, ed. by Edward M. Bruner, 19–55. Washington, DC: American Ethnological Society. Rpt: Prospect Heights, IL. Waveland Press 1988.

Bateson, Gregory. 1972. *Steps to an ecology of mind*. New York: Ballantine.

    1979. *Mind and nature*. New York: Ballantine.

Bateson, Mary Catherine. 1972. *Our own metaphor: A personal account of a conference on conscious purpose and human adaptation*. New York: Knopf. Rpt. Washington, DC: Smithsonian Institution Press, forthcoming.

1984. *With a daughter's eye: A memoir of Margaret Mead and Gregory Bateson*. New York: William Morrow.

Bawer, Bruce, 1988. Literary interviews. *The American Scholar*, Summer. 1988, 421–9.

Becker, A. L. 1979. Text-building, epistemology, and aesthetics in Javanese Shadow Theatre. *The imagination of reality*, ed. by A. L. Becker and Aram Yengoyan, 211–43. Norwood, NJ: Ablex.

1982. Beyond translation: Esthetics and language description. *Contemporary perceptions of language: Interdisciplinary dimensions. Georgetown University Round Table on Languages and Linguistics 1982*, ed. by Heidi Byrnes, 124–38. Washington, DC: Georgetown University Press.

1984a. Biography of a sentence: A Burmese proverb. *Text, play, and story: The construction and reconstruction of self and society*, ed. by Edward M. Bruner, 135–55. Washington, DC: American Ethnological Society. Rpt Prospect Heights, IL: Waveland Press 1988.

1984b. The linguistics of particularity: Interpreting superordination in a Javanese text. *Proceedings of the Tenth Annual Meeting of the Berkeley Linguistics Society*, 425–36. Berkeley, CA: University of California, Berkeley.

1984c. Goffman's animated language game: Review of *Forms of talk*, by Erving Goffman. *Raritan*, 3: 95–112.

1985. Review of Richard Bauman, *Let your words be few. Language*, 61.4: 916–18.

1988. Language in particular: A lecture. *Linguistics in context: Connecting observation and understanding*, ed. by Deborah Tannen, 17–35. Norwood, NJ: Ablex.

Ms. Correspondences: An essay on iconicity and philology.

In press. On the difficulty of writing: Silence. *Thinking about writing and writing about thinking*, ed. by Barbara Morris.

Bennett-Kastor, Tina L. 1978. Utterance repetition and social development: A case study of Genie and her caregiver. Ph.D. dissertation, University of Southern California.

1986. Cohesion and predication in child narrative. *Journal of Child Language*, 13: 353–70.

Besnier, Niko. In press. Reported speech and affect on Nukulaelae. *Responsibility and evidence in oral discourse*, ed. by Jane H. Hill and Judith Irvine. Cambridge: Cambridge University Press.

Biber, Douglas. 1988. *Variation across speech and writing*. Cambridge: Cambridge University Press.

Birdwhistell, Ray L. 1970. *Kinesics and context*. Philadelphia: University of Pennsylvania Press.

Bleich, David. 1988. *The double perspective*. New York and Oxford: Oxford University Press.

Bloodgood, Fred "Doc". 1982. The medicine and sideshow pitches. *Analyzing discourse: Text and talk. Georgetown University Round*

Table on Languages and Linguistics 1981, ed. by Deborah Tannen, 371–82. Washington, DC: Georgetown University Press.

Bolinger, Dwight. 1961. Syntactic blends and other matters. *Language,* 37.3: 366–81.

1976. Meaning and memory. *Forum Linguisticum,* 1.1: 1–14.

Britton, James. 1982. Spectator role and the beginnings of writing. *What writers know: The language, process, and structure of written discourse,* ed. by Martin Nystrand, 149–69. New York: Academic Press.

Brown, Penelope and Stephen Levinson. [1978]1987. *Politeness: Some universals in language usage.* Cambridge: Cambridge University Press.

Bruner, Jerome. 1986. *Actual minds, possible worlds.* Cambridge, MA: Harvard University Press.

Bugarski, Ranko. 1968. On the interrelatedness of grammar and lexis in the structure of English. *Lingua,* 19: 233–63.

Chafe, Wallace L. 1968. Idiomaticity as an anomaly in the Chomskyan paradigm. *Foundations of Language,* 4. 109–25.

(ed.) 1980. *The pear stories: Cognitive, cultural, and linguistic aspects of narrative production.* Norwood, NJ: Ablex.

1982. Integration and involvement in speaking, writing, and oral literature. *Spoken and written language: Exploring orality and literacy,* ed. by Deborah Tannen, 35–53. Norwood, NJ: Ablex.

1984. Integration and involvement in spoken and written language. *Semiotics unfolding,* ed. by Tasso Borbe, 1095–1102. Berlin: Mouton.

1985. Linguistic differences produced by differences between speaking and writing. *Literacy, language and learning: The nature and consequences of reading and writing,* ed. by David R. Olson, Nancy Torrance, and Angela Hildyard, 105–23. Cambridge: Cambridge University Press.

1986. How we know things about language: A plea for catholicism. *Languages and linguistics: The interdependence of theory, data, and application. Georgetown University Round Table on Languages and Linguistics 1985,* ed. by Deborah Tannen, 214–25. Washington, DC: Georgetown University Press.

1987. Repeated verbalizations as evidence for the organization of knowledge. Paper delivered at the XIV International Congress of Linguists, Berlin, GDR. August. To appear in proceedings, ed. by Werner Bahner.

Chatwin, Bruce. 1987. The lizard man. *The New York Review of Books,* August 13, 1987, 47–8.

Cheepen, Christine. 1988. *The predictability of informal conversation.* London: Pinter.

Condon, William S. 1963. Lexical-kinesic correlation. Ms. Pittsburgh: Western Psychiatric Institute.

Corsaro, William. 1979. "We're friends, right?": Children's use of access rituals in a nursery school. *Language in Society*, 8: 315–36.

Coulmas, Florian. 1986. *Conversational routine*. The Hague: Mouton.

1986. *Direct and indirect speech*. Berlin: Mouton.

Crews, Harry. 1988. Review of Mary McGarry Morris, *Vanished*, *The New York Times Book Review*, July 3, 1988, 5.

Crystal, David and Derek Davy. 1975. *Advanced conversational English*. London: Longman.

Czikszentmihalyi, Mihaly. 1978. Attention and the holistic approach to behavior. *The stream of consciousness: Scientific investigation into the flow of human experience*, ed. by Kenneth S. Pope and Jerome L. Singer. New York and London: Plenum.

Davis, Gerald L. 1985. *I got the word in me and I can sing it, you know: A study of the performed African-American sermon*. Philadelphia: University of Pennsylvania Press.

Dreifus, Claudia. 1987. *Albert Finney*. TWA Ambassador, May 1987, 54, 56, 65.

Drew, Elizabeth. 1988. Letter from Washington. *The New Yorker*, August 15, 1988, 65–78.

Duranti, Alessandro. 1986. The audience as co-author: An introduction. *The audience as co-author*, ed. by Alessandro Duranti and Donald Brenneis, special issue of *Text*, 6.3: 239–47.

Erickson, Frederick. 1982. Money tree, lasagna bush, salt and pepper: Social construction of topical cohesion in a conversation among Italian-Americans. *Analyzing discourse: Text and talk. Georgetown University Round Table on Languages and Linguistics 1981*, ed. by Deborah Tannen, 43–70. Washington, DC: Georgetown University Press.

1984. Rhetoric, anecdote, and rhapsody: Coherence strategies in a conversation among Black American adolescents. *Coherence in spoken and written discourse*, ed. by Deborah Tannen, 81–154. Norwood, NJ: Ablex.

1986. Listening and speaking. *Languages and linguistics: The interdependence of theory, data, and application. Georgetown University Round Table on Languages and Linguistics 1985*, ed. by Deborah Tannen and James E. Alatis, 294–319. Washington, DC: Georgetown University Press.

Erickson, Frederick and Jeffrey Shultz. 1982. *The counselor as gatekeeper: Social interaction in interviews*. New York: Academic Press.

Fanselow, John. 1983. Over and over and over again. *Applied linguistics and the preparation of second language teachers. Georgetown University Round Table on Languages and Linguistics 1983*, ed. by James E. Alatis, H. H. Stern, and Peter Strevens, 168–76. Washington, DC: Georgetown University Press.

Ferguson, Charles A. 1976. The structure and use of politeness formulas. *Language in Society*, 5: 137–51.

Fillmore, Charles J. 1976. The need for a frame semantics within linguistics. *Statistical methods in linguistics.* Stockholm: Skriptor, 5–29.

    1985. Frames and the semantics of understanding. *Quaderni di Semantica*, 6.2: 222–54.

Fillmore, Charles J., Paul Kay, and Mary Catherine O'Connor. 1988. Regularity and idiomaticity in grammatical constructions: The case of *let alone. Language*, 64.3: 501–38.

Fillmore, Lily Wong. 1979. Individual differences in second language acquisition. *Individual differences in language ability and language behavior*, ed. by Charles Fillmore, Daniel Kempler, and William S.-Y. Wang, 203–28. New York: Academic Press.

Finnegan, Ruth. 1977. *Oral poetry: Its nature, significance, and context.* Cambridge: Cambridge University Press.

Fremlin, Celia. 1985. *The jealous one.* Chicago: Academy.

Friedrich, Paul. 1986. *The language parallax: Linguistic relativism and poetic indeterminacy.* Austin, TX: University of Texas Press.

Friedrich, Paul and John Attinasi. In press. Dialogic breakthrough: Catalysis and synthesis in life-changing dialogue. *The dialogic emergence of culture*, ed. by Bruce Mannheim and Dennis Tedlock. Philadelphia: University of Pennsylvania Press.

Geiger, H. Jack. 1987. Review of Randy Shilts, *And the band played on. The New York Times Book Review*, November 8, 1987, 9.

Gibbs, Raymond W., Jr. 1980. Spilling the beans on understanding and memory for idioms in conversation. *Memory and Cognition*, 8.2: 149–56.

    1986. Skating on thin ice: Literal meaning and understanding idioms in conversation. *Discourse Processes*, 9.1: 17–30.

Gibbs, Raymond W., Jr., and Gayle P. Gonzales. 1985. Syntactic frozenness in processing and remembering idioms. *Cognition*, 20: 243–59.

Gilbert, N. Nigel and Michael Mulkay. 1984. *Opening Pandora's Box: A sociological analysis of scientists' discourse.* Cambridge: Cambridge University Press.

Gilligan, Carol. 1982. *In a different voice: Psychological theory and women's development.* Cambridge, MA: Harvard University Press.

Glockner-Ferrari, Deborah. 1986. Whale research. *Women and work: Photographs and personal writings*, text ed. by Maureen R. Michelson, photographs ed. by Michael R. Dressler and Maureen R. Michelson. Pasadena: NewSage Press.

Goffman, Erving. 1953. Communication and conduct in an island community. Ph.D. dissertation, University of Chicago.

    1959. *The presentation of self in everyday life.* New York: Doubleday.

    [1964]1972. The neglected situation. *Language and social context*, ed. by Pier Paolo Giglioli, 61–6. Harmondsworth and Baltimore: Penguin.

    1974. *Frame analysis.* New York: Harper & Row.

1981. Response cries. *Forms of talk*, 78–123. Philadelphia: University of Pennsylvania Press.

Goodwin, Charles. 1981. *Conversational organization: Interaction between speakers and hearers.* New York: Academic Press.

1986. Audience diversity, participation, and interpretation. *Text*, 6.3: 283–316.

Goodwin, Marjorie Harness and Charles Goodwin. 1987. Children's arguing. *Language, gender, and sex in comparative perspective*, ed. by Susan U. Philips, Susan Steele, and Christine Tanz, 200–48. Cambridge: Cambridge University Press.

Gould, Stephen J. 1987. Animals and us. *The New York Review of Books*, June 25, 1987, 20–25.

Gumperz, John J. 1982. *Discourse strategies.* Cambridge: Cambridge University Press.

Gumperz, John J., Hannah Kaltman, and Mary Catherine O'Connor. 1984. Cohesion in spoken and written discourse: Ethnic style and the transition to literacy. *Coherence in spoken and written discourse*, ed. by Deborah Tannen, 3–19. Norwood, NJ: Ablex.

Gumperz, John J. and Deborah Tannen. 1979. Individual and social differences in language use. *Individual differences in language ability and language behavior*, ed. by Charles Fillmore, Daniel Kempler, and William S.-Y. Wang, 305–24. New York: Academic Press.

Haberman, Clyde. 1988. Review of Shotaro Ishinomori, *Japan Inc.: An introduction to Japanese economics (The comic book). The New York Times Book Review*, July 3, 1988, 2.

Halliday, M. A. K. 1967. Notes on transitivity and theme in English. Part 2. *Journal of Linguistics*, 3: 199–244.

Halliday, M. A. K. and Ruqaiya Hasan. 1976. *Cohesion in English.* London: Longman.

Hansell, Mark and Cheryl Seabrook Ajirotutu. 1982. Negotiating interpretations in interethnic settings. *Language and social identity*, ed. by John J. Gumperz, 85–94. Cambridge: Cambridge University Press.

Harris, Lis. 1985. Lubavitcher Hasidim, Part I. *The New Yorker*, September 16, 1985, 41–101.

Havelock, Eric. 1963. *Preface to Plato.* Cambridge, MA: Harvard University Press.

Heath, Shirley Brice. 1983. *Ways with words.* Cambridge: Cambridge University Press.

1985. Being literate in America: A sociohistoric perspective. *Issues in Literacy: A Research Perspective. Thirty-Fourth Yearbook of the National Reading Conference*, ed. by J. A. Niles and R. V. Lalik, 1–18. Rochester, NY: The National Reading Conference Inc.

1986. Literacy and language change. *Languages and linguistics: The interdependence of theory, data, and application. Georgetown University Round Table on Languages and Linguistics 1985*, ed. by

Deborah Tannen and James E. Alatis, 282–93. Washington, DC: Georgetown University Press.

Heidegger, Martin. 1962. *Being and time.* New York: Harper & Row.

Herzfeld, Michael. 1985. *The poetics of manhood.* Austin, TX: University of Texas Press.

Hill, Jane H. and Judith Irvine (eds.) In press. *Responsibility and evidence in oral discourse.* Cambridge: Cambridge University Press.

Hopper, Paul J. 1988a. Emergent grammar and the a priori grammar postulate. *Linguistics in context: Connecting observation and understanding,* ed. by Deborah Tannen, 117–34. Norwood, NJ: Ablex.

    1988b. Discourse analysis: Grammar and critical theory in the 1980s. *Profession 88.* New York: Modern Language Association, 18–24.

Hughes, Ted and Frances McCullough (eds.) 1982. *The journals of Sylvia Plath.* New York: Ballantine.

Humphreys, Josephine. 1985. Review of May Sarton, *The magnificent spinster. The New York Times Book Review,* October 27, 1985, 26.

Hymes, Dell. 1973. Toward linguistic competence. *Sociolinguistic Working Paper #16.* Austin, TX: Southwest Educational Development Laboratory.

    1981. *"In vain I tried to tell you": Essays in Native American ethnopoetics.* Philadelphia: University of Pennsylvania Press.

Ifill, Gwen. 1988. Jackson evokes smiles, tears. *The Washington Post,* July 20, 1988, A19.

Jakobson, Roman. 1960. Closing statement: Linguistics and poetics. *Style in language,* ed. by Thomas A. Sebeok, 350–77. Cambridge, MA: MIT press.

    1966. Grammatical parallelism and its Russian facet. *Language,* 42: 398–429.

Jakobson, Roman and Krystyna Pomorska. 1983. *Dialogues.* Cambridge, MA: MIT press.

Jakobson, Roman and Linda R. Waugh. 1979. *The sound shape of language.* Bloomington: Indiana University Press.

Jefferson, Gail. 1972. Side sequences. *Studies in social interaction,* ed. by David Sudnow, 294–338. New York: The Free Press.

    1978. Sequential aspects of storytelling in conversation. *Studies in the organization of conversational interaction,* ed. by Jim Schenkein, 219–48. New York: Academic Press.

Jespersen, Otto. 1933. Symbolic value of the vowel i. *Linguistica: Selected papers in English, French, and German,* 283–303. Copenhagen: Levin & Munksgaard.

Johnstone, Barbara. 1987a. An introduction. *Perspectives on repetition,* ed. by Barbara Johnstone, special issue of *Text,* 7.3: 205–14.

    1987b. Parataxis in Arabic: Modification as a model for persuasion. *Studies in Language,* 11.1: 85–98.

    In preparation. *A city speaks: Narrative discourse, community, and place.*

Judson, Horace Freeland. 1980. *The search for solutions.* New York: Holt Rinehart Winston.

Kawin, Bruce F. 1972. *Telling it again and again: Repetition in literature and film.* Ithaca: Cornell University Press.

Kay, Paul. 1984. The *kind of/sort of* construction. *Proceedings of the Tenth Annual Meeting of the Berkeley Linguistics Society*, 157–71. Berkeley, CA: University of California, Berkeley.

Keenan, Elinor. 1977. Making it last: Repetition in children's discourse. *Child discourse*, ed. by Susan Ervin-Tripp and Claudia Mitchell-Kernan, 125–38. New York: Academic Press.

Kempton, Willet. 1980. The rhythmic basis of interactional microsynchrony. *The relationship of verbal and nonverbal communication*, ed. by Mary Ritchie Key, 67–75. The Hague: Mouton.

Kendon, Adam. 1981. *Nonverbal communication, interaction, and gesture.* The Hague: Mouton.

Kendon, Adam, Richard M. Harris, and Mary Ritchie Key, eds. 1975. *Organization of behavior in face-to-face interaction.* The Hague: Mouton.

Kiparsky, Paul. 1973. The role of linguistics in a theory of poetry. *Daedalus*, 102: 231–44.

Kirshenblatt-Gimblett, Barbara. 1974. The concept and varieties of narrative performance in East European Jewish Culture. *Explorations in the ethnography of speaking.* ed. by Richard Bauman and Joel Sherzer, 283–308. Cambridge: Cambridge University Press.

Kleinfield, N. R. 1986. The whistle blowers' morning after. *The New York Times*, November 9, 1986, Section 3, pp. 1, 10.

Koch, Barbara Johnstone. 1983a. Presentation as proof: The language of Arabic rhetoric. *Anthropological Linguistics*, 25.1: 47–60.

1983b. Arabic lexical couplets and the evolution of synonymy. *General Linguistics*, 23. 51–61.

1984. Repeating yourself: Discourse paraphrase and the generation of language. *Proceedings of the Eastern States Conference on Linguistics*, 1984, 250–9.

Kochman, Thomas. 1981. *Black and White styles in conflict.* Chicago: University of Chicago Press.

1986. Strategic ambiguity in Black speech genres: Cross-cultural interference in participant-observation research. *Text*, 6.2: 153–70.

Kristeva, Julia. 1974. *La révolution du langage poétique.* Paris: Seuil.

1986. Word, dialogue and novel, trans. by Alice Jardine, Thomas Gora and Leon S. Roudiez. *The Kristeva reader*, ed. by Toril Moi, 34–61. New York: Columbia University Press.

Kywell, Martin (chief compiler and editor). 1974. *Afro-American encyclopaedia*, 5: 1421–3. North Miami, FL: Educational Book Publishers.

Labov, William. 1972. The transformation of experience in narrative syntax. *Language in the inner city*, 354–96. Philadelphia: University of Pennsylvania Press.

Labov, William and David Fanshel. 1977. *Therapeutic discourse*. New York: Academic Press.

Labov, William and Joshua Waletzky. 1967. Narrative analysis: Oral versions of personal experience. *Essays on the verbal and visual arts*, ed. by June Helm, 12–44. Seattle: University of Washington Press.

Ladefoged, Peter. 1972. Phonetic prerequisites for a distinctive feature theory. *Papers in linguistics and phonetics in memory of Pierre Delattre*, ed. by Albert Valdman. The Hague: Mouton.

Lakoff, George and Mark Johnson. 1980. *Metaphors we live by*. Chicago: University of Chicago Press.

Lakoff, Robin. 1973. The logic of politeness, or minding your p's and q's. *Papers from the Ninth Regional Meeting of the Chicago Linguistics Society*, 292–305.

Lakoff, Robin Tolmach. 1979. Stylistic strategies within a grammar of style. *Language, sex, and gender*, ed. by Judith Orasanu, Mariam Slater, and Leonore Loeb Adler. *Annals of the New York Academy of Science*, 327: 53–78.

Lakoff, Robin Tolmach and Deborah Tannen. 1984. Conversational strategy and metastrategy in a pragmatic theory: The example of *Scenes from a marriage*. *Semiotica*, 49.3/4: 323–46.

Law, Barbara Lamberts. 1985. Repeating is in every one: An analysis of repetition in Gertrude Stein's *Three lives*. Ph.D. dissertation, Michigan State University.

Leech, Geoffrey. 1969. *A linguistic guide to English poetry*. London: Longmans.

Levin, Samuel R. 1973. *Linguistic structures in poetry*. The Hague: Mouton.

    1982. Are figures of thought figures of speech? *Contemporary perceptions of language: Interdisciplinary dimensions. Georgetown University Round Table on Languages and Linguistics 1982*, ed. by Heidi Byrnes, 112–23. Washington, DC: Georgetown University Press.

Lipsky, David. 1985. Three thousand dollars. *The New Yorker*, November 11, 1985, 43–50.

Lord, Albert B. 1960. *The singer of tales*. Cambridge, MA: Harvard University Press.

McCloskey, Donald. 1985. *The rhetoric of economics*. Madison: The University of Wisconsin Press.

McDermott, R. P. and Henry Tylbor. 1983. On the necessity of collusion in conversation. *Text*, 3.3: 277–97.

McQuown, Norman A., *et al*. 1971. The natural history of the interview. *Microfilm collection of manuscripts in cultural anthropology*. Series 15, numbers 95, 96, 97, and 98. University of Chicago Library.

Makkai, Adam. 1972. *Idiom structure in English*. The Hague: Mouton.

Maschler, Yael Leah. 1988. The language games bilinguals play: A discourse analysis of Hebrew–English bilingual conversation. Ph.D. dissertation, University of Michigan.

Matisoff, James A. 1979. *Blessings, curses, hopes, and fears: Psychoostensive expressions in Yiddish.* Philadelphia: Institute for Study of Human Issues.

Mattison, Alice. 1988. The flight of Andy Burns. *The New Yorker*, June 20, 1988, 28–32.

Merritt, Marilyn. 1976. On questions following questions (in service encounters). *Language in Society*, 5: 315–57.

  1982. Distributing and directing attention in primary classrooms. *Communicating in the classroom*, ed. by Louise Cherry-Wilkinson, 223–44. New York: Academic Press.

Mieder, Wolfgang. 1978. Proverbial slogans are the name of the game. *Kentucky Folklore Record*, 24: 49–53.

Miller, Jim. 1987. Review of Randy Shilts, *And the band played on. Newsweek*, October 19, 1987, 91, 93.

Mills, C. Wright. [1940]1967. Situated action and vocabularies of motive. *Symbolic interaction*, ed. by Jerome G. Manis and Bernard N. Meltzer, 355–66. Boston: Allyn & Bacon.

Moss, Cynthia. 1988. *Elephant memories: Thirteen years in the life of an elephant family.* New York: William Morrow.

Nietzsche, Friedrich. [1988]1968. *The will to power.* Trans. by Walter Kaufman. New York: Vintage.

Nordberg, Bengt. 1985. Om ungdomars samtalsstil. Några preliminära iakttagelser. *Nysvenska Studier*, 64 (1984): 5–27.

Norrick, Neal. 1985. *How proverbs mean: Semantic studies in English proverbs.* Berlin: Mouton.

  1987. Functions of repetition in conversation. *Text*, 7.3: 245–64.

Ochs, Elinor. 1979. Planned and unplanned discourse. *Discourse and syntax*, ed. by Talmy Givon, 51–80. New York: Academic Press.

Ohala, John J. 1984. An ethological perspective on common cross-language utilization of FO of voice. *Phonetica*, 41: 1–16.

Ortega y Gasset, José. 1957. What people say: Language. Toward a new linguistics. *Man and people*, trans. by Willard R. Trask. New York: Norton.

Ott, Mary Miglio Bensabat. 1983. Orality and literacy in Brazilian and American storytelling: A comparative study. Ms., Georgetown University.

Pawley, Andrew. 1986. Lexicalization. *Languages and linguistics: The interdependence of theory, data, and application. Georgetown University Round Table on Languages and Linguistics 1985*, ed. by Deborah Tannen and James E. Alatis, 98–120. Washington, DC: Georgetown University Press.

Pawley, Andrew and Frances Hodgetts Syder. 1983. Two puzzles for linguistic theory: Nativelike selection and nativelike fluency. *Language and communication*, ed. by Jack C. Richards and Richard W. Schmidt, 191–225. London and New York: Longman.

Piercy, Marge. 1984. *Fly away home*. New York: Fawcett.

Pinter, Harold. 1961. *The birthday party* and *The room*. New York: Grove Press.

Polanyi, Livia. 1985. *Telling the American story: A structural and cultural analysis of conversational storytelling*. Norwood, NJ: Ablex.

Prescott, Peter S. 1983. Review of *Pitch dark* by Renata Adler. *Newsweek*, December 19, 1983, 82.

Preston, Dennis R. 1982. 'Ritin Fowklower Daun 'Rong: Folklorists' failures in phonology. *Journal of American Folklore*, 95.377: 304–26.

1985. The Li'l Abner syndrome: Written representations of speech. *American Speech*, 60.4: 328–36.

Quinn, Arthur. 1982. *Figures of speech*. Salt Lake City: Gibbs M. Smith.

Rappaport, Judith. 1989. *The boy who couldn't stop washing*. New York: E. P. Dutton.

Reddy, Michael. 1979. The conduit metaphor: A case of frame conflict in our language about language. *Metaphor and thought*, ed. by Andrew Ortony, 284–324. Cambridge: Cambridge University Press.

Rosen, Harold. n.d. *Stories and meanings*. Kettering, Northamptonshire, UK: National Association for the Teaching of English.

1988. The autobiographical impulse. *Linguistics in context: Connecting observation and understanding*, ed. by Deborah Tannen, 69–88. Norwood, NJ: Ablex.

Ryave, Alan L. 1978. On the achievement of a series of stories. *Studies in the organization of conversational interaction*, ed. by Jim Schenkein, 113–32. New York: Academic.

Sacks, Harvey. 1971. Lecture notes, March 11, 1971.

1978. Some technical considerations of a dirty joke. *Studies in the organization of conversational interaction*, ed. by Jim Schenkein, 249–69. New York: Academic Press.

Sacks, Harvey and Emanuel Schegloff. 1974. Opening up closings. *Ethnomethodology*, ed. by Roy Turner, 233–64. Harmondsworth and Baltimore: Penguin.

Sacks, Oliver. [1973]1983. *Awakenings*. New York: E. P. Dutton.

1984. *A leg to stand on*. New York: Harper and Row.

1986. *The man who mistook his wife for a hat and other clinical tales*. New York: Simon and Schuster.

1987. Tics. *The New York Review of Books*, January 29, 1987, 37–41.

Sapir, Edward. 1929. A study in phonetic symbolism. *Journal of Experimental Psychology*, 12: 225–39.

Sapir, J. David. 1977. The anatomy of metaphor. *The social use of metaphor: Essays on the anthropology of rhetoric*. ed. by J. David Sapir and J. Christopher Crocker, 3–32. Philadelphia: The University of Pennsylvania Press.

Sapir, J. David and J. Christopher Crocker (eds.) 1977. *The social use of metaphor: Essays on the anthropology of rhetoric.* Philadelphia: The University of Pennsylvania Press.

Saussure, Ferdinand de. 1959. *Course in general linguistics*, ed. by C. Balley and A. Sechehaye, trans. by Wade Baskin. New York: Philosophical Library.

Scheflen, Albert E. 1972. *Body language and the social order.* Englewood Cliffs, NJ: Prentice-Hall.

Schegloff, Emanuel. [1968]1972. Sequencing in conversational openings. *Directions in sociolinguistics: The ethnography of communication*, ed. by John J. Gumperz and Dell Hymes, 346–80. New York: Holt, Rinehart, Winston. Rpt Oxford: Basil Blackwell.

1982. Discourse as an interactional achievement: Some uses of 'uhuh' and other things that come between sentences. *Analyzing discourse: Text and talk. Georgetown University Round Table on Languages and Linguistics 1981*, ed. by Deborah Tannen, 71–93. Washington, DC: Georgetown University Press.

1988. Discourse as an interactional achievement II: An exercise in conversation analysis. *Linguistics in context: Connecting observation and understanding*, ed. by Deborah Tannen, 135–58. Norwood, NJ: Ablex.

Schenkein, Jim. 1978. *Studies in the organization of conversational interaction.* New York: Academic Press.

Schieffelin, Bambi B. 1979. How Kaluli children learn what to say, what to do, and how to feel. Ph.D. dissertation, Columbia University.

Schiffrin, Deborah. 1981. Tense variation in narrative. *Language, 57.1:* 45–62.

1982. Cohesion in discourse: The role of non-adjacent paraphrase. *Working Papers in Sociolinguistics*, 97. Austin, TX: Southwest Educational Development Laboratory.

1984. Jewish argument as sociability. *Language in Society, 13.3:* 311–35.

Scollon, Ron. 1982. The rhythmic integration of ordinary talk. *Analyzing discourse: Text and talk. Georgetown University Round Table on Languages and Linguistics 1981*, ed. by Deborah Tannen, 335–49. Washington, DC: Georgetown University Press.

1985. The machine stops: Silence in the metaphor of malfunction. *Perspectives on silence*, ed. by Deborah Tannen and Muriel Saville-Troike, 21–30. Norwood, NJ: Ablex.

Scollon, Ron and Suzanne B. K. Scollon. 1981. *Narrative, literacy and face in interethnic communication.* Norwood, NJ: Ablex.

1984. Cooking it up and boiling it down: Abstracts in Athabaskan children's story retellings. *Coherence in spoken and written discourse*, ed. by Deborah Tannen, 173–97. Norwood, NJ: Ablex.

Seitel, Peter. 1969. Proverbs: A social use of metaphor. *Genre, 2:* 143–61.

Shales, Tom. The Jackson triumph. *The Washington Post*, July 20, 1988, pp. C1, C6.

Shapiro, Laura. 1987. Review of Mona Simpson, *Anywhere but here*. *Newsweek*, February 2, 1987, 69.

Shilts, Randy. 1987. *And the band played on: Politics, people, and the AIDS epidemic*. New York: St. Martin's Press.

Shuman, Amy. 1986. *Storytelling rights: The uses of oral and written texts by urban adolescents*. Cambridge: Cambridge University Press.

Silber, Joan. 1976. *Household words*. New York: Viking.

Smith, Barbara Herrnstein. 1978. *On the margins of discourse: The relation of literature to language*. Chicago: University of Chicago Press.

Smith, Stevie. [1936] 1982. *Novel on yellow paper*. New York: Pinnacle.

Stein, Gertrude. 1935. *The gradual making of 'The Making of Americans.'* *Lectures in America*. New York: Random House.

[1925]1966. *The making of Americans: Being a history of a family's progress*. New York: Something Else Press.

Sudnow, David. 1979a. *Ways of the hand*. New York: Bantam.

1979b. *Talk's body*. New York: Knopf.

Svartvik, Jan and Randolph Quirk. 1980. *A corpus of English conversation*. Lund: CWK Gleerup.

Tannen, Deborah. 1978. The effect of expectations on conversation. *Discourse Processes*, 1.2: 203–9.

1979. What's in a frame? Surface evidence for underlying expectations. *New directions in discourse processing*, ed. by Roy O. Freedle, 137–81. Norwood, NJ: Ablex.

1980a. A comparative analysis of oral narrative strategies. *The pear stories*, ed. by Wallace Chafe, 51–87. Norwood, NJ: Ablex.

1980b. Implications of the oral/literate continuum for cross-cultural communication. *Current issues in bilingualism. Georgetown University Round Table on Languages and Linguistics 1980*, ed. by James E. Alatis, 326–47. Washington, DC: Georgetown University Press.

1982. Oral and literate strategies in spoken and written narratives. *Language*, 58.1: 1–21.

1983a. "I take out the rock – dok!": How Greek women tell about being molested (and create involvement). *Anthropological linguistics*, Fall 1983, 359–74.

1983b. When is an overlap not an interruption?: One component of conversational style. *The First Delaware Symposium on Language Studies*, ed. by Robert J. Di Pietro, William Frawley, and Alfred Wedel, 119–29. Newark, Del.: University of Delaware Press.

1984. *Conversational style: Analyzing talk among friends*. Norwood, NJ: Ablex.

1985. Relative focus on involvement in oral and written discourse. *Literacy, language, and learning: The nature and consequences of reading and writing*, ed. by David R. Olson, Nancy Torrance, and Angela Hildyard, 124–47. Cambridge: Cambridge University Press.

1986a. *That's not what I meant!: How conversational style makes or breaks your relations with others.* New York: William Morrow, Ballantine.

1986b. Introducing constructed dialogue in Greek and American conversational and literary narrative. *Direct and indirect speech*, ed. by Florian Coulmas, 311–32. Berlin: Mouton.

(ed.) 1986c. *Discourse in cross-cultural communication.* Special issue of *Text*, 6:2.

1987a. Repetition in conversation: Toward a poetics of talk. *Language*, 63.3: 574–605.

1987b. Repetition in conversation as spontaneous formulaicity. *Text*, 7.3: 215–43.

(ed.) 1988a. *Linguistics in context: Connecting observation and understanding.* Norwood, NJ: Ablex.

1988b. The commingling of orality and literacy in giving a paper at a scholarly conference. *American Speech*, 63.1: 34–43.

1988c. Hearing voices in conversation, fiction, and mixed genres. *Linguistics in context: Connecting observation and understanding*, ed. by Deborah Tannen, 89–113. Norwood, NJ: Ablex.

In press. Ordinary conversation and literary discourse: Coherence and the poetics of repetition. *The uses of linguistics*, ed. by Edward H. Bendix. Annals of the New York Academy of Science.

Tannen, Deborah and Piyale Cömert Öztek. 1981. Health to our mouths: Formulaic expressions in Turkish and Greek. *Conversational routine*, ed. by Florian Coulmas, 37–54. The Hague: Mouton.

Tedlock, Dennis. 1972. *Finding the center: Narrative poetry of the Zuni Indians.* New York: Dial. [2nd edn: Lincoln: University of Nebraska Press, 1978.]

Tyler, Stephen. 1978. *The said and the unsaid.* New York: Academic Press.

van Dijk, Teun (ed.) 1985. *Handbook of discourse analysis*, 4 vols. London: Academic Press.

Van Lancker, Diana. 1987. Nonpropositional speech: Neurolinguistic studies. *Progress in the psychology of language*, vol. 3, ed. by Andrew W. Ellis, 49–117. Hillsdale, NJ: Erlbaum.

Varenne, Herve and R. P. McDermott. 1986. "Why" Sheila can read: Structure and indeterminacy in the reproduction of familial literacy. *The acquisition of literacy: Ethnographic perspectives*, ed. by Bambi B. Schieffelin and Perry Gilmore, 188–210. Norwood, NJ: Ablex.

Voloshinov, V. N. [1929]1986. *Marxism and the philosophy of language*, trans. by Ladislav Matejka and I. R. Titunik. Cambridge, MA: Harvard University Press.

Walker, Jayne L. 1984. *The making of a modernist: Gertrude Stein from 'Three lives' to 'Tender buttons'.* Amherst: University of Massachusetts Press.

Watanabe, Suwako. In preparation. Framing in American and Japanese group discussions. Ph.D. dissertation, Georgetown University.

Waugh, Linda R. and Monique Monville-Burston. In preparation. Roman Jakobson: His life, work and influence. *Jakobson on language*, ed. by Linda R. Waugh and Monique Monville-Burston. Cambridge, MA: Harvard University Press.

Waugh, Linda R. and Madeleine Newfield. In press. Iconicity and the morpheme: Toward a model of the lexicon. *Lingua*.

Welty, Eudora. 1984. *One writer's beginnings*. Cambridge, MA: Harvard University Press.

Whitaker, Harry. 1982. Automaticity. Paper presented at the Conference on Formulaicity. Linguistic Institute, University of Maryland, July 1982.

Widdowson, Henry. 1988. Poetry and pedagogy. *Linguistics in context: Connecting observation and understanding*, ed. by Deborah Tannen, 185–97. Norwood, NJ: Ablex.

Wittgenstein, Ludwig. 1958. *Philosophical investigations*. Trans. by G. E. M. Anscombe. New York: Macmillan.

Woodbury, Anthony C. 1985. The functions of rhetorical structure: A study of Central Alaskan Yupik Eskimo discourse. *Language in Society*, 14.2: 153–90.

Zimmer, Karl. 1958. Situational formulas. Ms., Linguistics Department, University of California, Berkeley.

Author index

Subject index

Printed in the United States
64036LVS00002B/52-78

9 780521 379007